Elementary Geometry for College

Charles W. Tryon

MOUNT SAN ANTONIO COLLEGE

Elementary Geometry
for College

 HARCOURT, BRACE & WORLD, INC.

NEW YORK   CHICAGO   SAN FRANCISCO   ATLANTA

Library of Congress Catalog Card Number: 69–19142

Printed in the United States of America

preface

Introductory geometry until recently stood apart from other major areas of mathematics, in that points in a Euclidean plane or space were not associated directly with numbers and hence not with algebraic methods of study. Modern mathematics has changed this; geometry uses algebra and the ideas of set theory to extend and improve its system of logic.

This text is intended for college students whose high school courses in geometry did not expose them to the broader possibilities of modern mathematics, or who, if exposed, will benefit from a concise course at the college level.

Chapters 1 and 2 describe the major changes in the presentation of Euclidean geometry. Postulates are stated and theorems are developed using the logic possible with point-number correspondence and the theory of coordinates. The traditional statements frequently are given as alternates.

The student should survey the first three chapters and begin to learn the meaning of words in the vocabulary before attempting to write proofs. When he has practiced the development of a proof, a review of Chapter 3 will help him understand the logic upon which a proof depends — the flow of concepts through a necessary series of steps. The direction taken by each step is controlled by the reason selected to validate the step; that reason must be based soundly on preceding steps.

All statements and propositions required in the course, including those of simple numerical relations, are expressed in the text. In proofs each reason is given as a condensed sentence rather than being referred to by a title, such as "Definition of a bisector." This helps the student understand not only the true meaning of each proposition, but also why one is correct above all others as the reason for each step in a proof. The condensations needed for all exercises are listed at the ends of chapters, and the Appendix contains all postulates and theorems in condensed form, the latter topically organized to bring out the relationships among them.

At the ends of most of the chapters are summary tests. The questions in each test are arranged in the order of presentation of topics in the text and provide both review and a means of increased understanding.

The author is indebted to the School Mathematics Study Group for the splendid development of modern geometry so functionally presented in their Units 47 and 48. Many of the concepts in that work have been employed in this book. The informal method of writing proofs is often used. The coordinate concept distinguishes between geometric figures and their numerical properties. A chapter on coordinates and vectors strengthens the traditional course in this important direction and helps prepare a student for physics.

The test of a textbook is its use in teaching. My deepest appreciation goes to the instructors at Mount San Antonio College who read the manuscript and then taught the course, continually finding ways of improving the material and generously considering all the small refinements which are so significant to success.

Charles W. Tryon

contents

symbols

$\in$	is an element of	$\perp$	perpendicular; is (are) perpendicular (to)
$\subseteq$	is a subset of		
$\subset$	is a proper subset of	⦜	right angle
$\varnothing$	the empty set	$\not\cong$	congruent segment
$\cap$	intersection	⊀	segment congruent to itself
$\cup$	union	⋨	congruent angle
$\overleftrightarrow{AB}$	line *AB*	⋨	angle congruent to itself
$\overline{CD}$	segment *CD*	$\parallel$	parallel
$\overrightarrow{EF}$	ray *EF*	$\uparrow\uparrow$	parallel lines
$\overset{\frown}{AB}$	arc *AB*	$\square$	parallelogram
CD	length of segment *CD*	$>$	is greater than; greater
m	slope of line in equation of line	$<$	is less than; lesser
$\angle$	angle; ⧩ angles	$\leq$	is equal to or less than
$\triangle$	triangle; ⧩ triangles	$\geq$	is equal to or greater than
$\odot$	circle; ⑤ circles	$\neq$	is not equal to; are unequal
$=$	equals; is (are) equal (to); as	$\sim$	similar; is similar to
$\cong$	congruent; is (are) congruent (to)	$:$	is to
		$10°$	10 degrees
$\leftrightarrow$	corresponds to	$8'$	8 minutes
$|a|$	the absolute value of *a*	$6''$	6 seconds

abbreviations

AA	angle, angle		prop	proportion, proportional(ly)
alt	alternate		quad	quadrilateral
ASA	angle, side, angle		R	reflexive
comp	complement(ary)		rect	rectangle
coord	coordinate		reg	regular
corresp	corresponding		rt	right
def	definition		S	symmetric
diag	diagonal		SAS	side, angle, side
diam	diameter		sec	secant
diff	difference		SSS	side, side, side
dist	distance, distant		st	straight
ext	exterior		sub	substituted
hyp	hypotenuse		supp	supplement(ary)
int	interior		T	transitive
m	measure		tan	tangent
opp	opposite		thm	theorem
post	postulate		trans	transversal
prod	product		trap	trapezoid

Elementary Geometry for College

chapter **1**

Geometry Past and Present

1.1 The Glorious Past

When we study geometry, we are sharing a very ancient and honored tradition. A manuscript of Egyptian geometry in the British Museum was copied from a still older one in about the sixteenth century B.C. The precision of buildings and of the Pyramids in Egypt testifies to the Egyptians' knowledge of and careful application of geometric principles to construction.

The story comes down to us that the early Egyptian farmers were allocated parcels of land along the Nile River. But often in the spring the river would overflow its banks and destroy the boundary marks of the plots. Surveyors measured out the plots again and put in new markers. These men carried ropes knotted with thirteen knots equally spaced. With one of these ropes stretched out on the ground they could make a triangle with sides of three lengths, four lengths, and five lengths, and therefore an accurate right angle.

Thales in the sixth century B.C. learned about geometry in Egypt and brought it to Greece. The word *geometry* comes from Greek words meaning "earth measure." Thales was the first Greek whom we can really call a mathematician. He proved several of the theorems of geometry which we still study. He developed deductive reasoning to a high degree of perfection. Tradition tells us that he found the height of a pyramid in Egypt by measuring its shadow.

Perhaps the greatest pupil of Thales was Pythagoras. He established a school, or brotherhood, of philosophers. They developed the theorem which still bears his name, and many other theorems included in geometry today.

The Greeks were interested in mathematics and science from a philosophical standpoint—in knowledge for its own sake, developed through study, whether or not it had any practical value. They used geometric proofs as exercises in logical reasoning. One of the greatest philosophers of all was Plato, who lived in the fourth century. He considered geometry so important as a tool of correct reasoning that he is said to have inscribed over the door of his school: "Let no one ignorant of geometry enter here." Eudoxus, a pupil of Plato's, developed the logic of contradiction which we use in our method of indirect proof.

Archimedes of Sicily in the third century was one of the greatest mathematicians of all times. He computed an early value of *pi*. As well as advancing knowledge of pure mathematics, he developed many practical applications of mathematics to physics.

Geometry as it has been passed down through the centuries bears most of all the stamp of Euclid. He was a professor of mathematics in Alexandria, Egypt. He gathered all the known material on the subject and compiled it into thirteen "books" about 300 B.C. Each proof in his work is a complete logical arrangement, based entirely on material which precedes it, and beginning with a few simple assumptions. The first six books deal with plane geometry, the rest with arithmetic and solid objects. This compilation, called the *Elements*, is considered to be the most important textbook of all time. Probably no book except the Bible has contributed more to the intellectual life of the world.

1.2   The Shape of Things to Come

The geometry of Euclid was considered complete until modern times, when mathematicians developed a chain of reasoning which led to some interesting results. The suppositions which we accept without proof in elementary geometry, men try to prove in more advanced work. One of these which Euclid accepted as obvious, later scholars tried to prove without success. It is named the *Parallel Postulate*. Paraphrased in

Held taut, a rope with thirteen equally spaced knots will measure twelve units of distance in a straight line. With the end knots held together, it can be pulled out into a triangle having sides of three, four, and five unit lengths; then one angle is a right angle. Ancient Egyptians used such a rope for laying out plots of ground. A modern picture from Egypt shows that the ground is still being divided into small plots. Irrigation ditches supply water. Photo by Tor Eigeland from Black Star.

English, it reads: "Through a point not of a line in one plane there is exactly one line parallel to the given line." It has been demonstrated by means of calculus that this cannot be proved conclusively.

Early in the nineteenth century, Gauss, whose name is associated with the study of electricity, recognized that it is possible to have a system of geometry which does not include this postulate. In the 1820's Bolyai, a Hungarian, and Lobachevski, a Russian, developed a system of geometry in which more than one line parallel to the given line can pass through a given point. Their study is called hyperbolic geometry. Riemann, a German, developed a geometry, called elliptic, in which there is no line parallel to the given line through the point. Each of these systems proceeds on its own set of assumptions, self-contained, logical, and complete. Each is a system of *non-Euclidean* geometry, and is useful in theoretical physics of relativity, atomic activity, or outer space.

We accept and use the Parallel Postulate; we could not have Euclidean geometry without it. This geometry is the basis for the building of structures and machines which make our mechanized world possible. In the late nineteenth century two Germans helped modernize Euclidean geometry. Klein emphasized the invariant parts of relationships — the properties which do not change within an individual situation. Hilbert reviewed all the *Elements* and reaffirmed the absolute necessity for postulating some basic statements, that is, adopting them because they are consistent with the whole subject whether or not they can ever be proved. He and Birkhoff, an American, developed the present system of postulates customarily used in modern geometry. Also they emphasized the use of coordinates and numerical measures, associating points with numbers.

> DEFINITION A basic initial assumption accepted without proof is a **postulate**.

Euclid's work, a bulwark of mathematical reasoning which had stood intact for so many centuries, has a few defects when judged by the rigorous standards of this scientific age. When we consider the fragmentary and scattered resources with which he had to work, and the great task of collecting and compiling them, it is a wonder that Euclid did as well as he did. His work is a masterpiece of organization and completeness. To this day we find it consistent, that is, without contradiction.

The recent changes in geometry come from an attempt to explain more precisely why certain relationships are true and to perfect the statements which are used in making proofs rigorous, or strictly accurate. The modern student who has studied some traditional geometry may be at a loss to realize where its weaknesses lay. For his benefit this outline of the improvements is presented. Euclid's work had four major defects, each of which will be summarized in terms of what modern mathematicians have done to strengthen the traditional material. Three of them follow in this chapter; the fourth is the subject of Chapter 2.

1.3   Undefined Terms

The first of the defects was that Euclid attempted to define every term. He evidently failed to see that a logical treatment of any branch of mathematics must start with undefined terms. From long usage, with agreement which is almost universal, we can converse about a *point*, a *line*, a *plane*, or a *direction* with real understanding. We here describe some of the characteristics of each of these ideas and some of its relationships with geometric objects, but will not attempt to give a definition of it. With these as a basis, we go on to define other objects.

Actually, *point* is an abstract idea. When we make a dot on a paper or chalkboard, we mark an area of considerable size. The point of which this is a representation is infinitesimal in size. We can think about such a point even if we cannot see one. This is what we mean by **point** in geometry. It locates a position; it has no size nor dimensions.

Likewise we can think of a line—thinner and straighter than any we can see, straighter than a thread stretched tight or hanging down with a weight on its end. When we use the word **line** in geometry, we mean such a straight line of whatever length we need for any geometric purpose. Our elementary geometry is limited to finite distances, that is, distances which are measurable with a definite number of units.

Also we think of a **plane** of adequate size for our purpose and perfectly flat. There is a piece of glass called an optical flat. If it lies on a flat surface, the distance between any corresponding points of the two is measured by a wavelength of light, about six hundred-millionths of a centimeter. A theoretical plane is flatter than that.

1.4   Definitions

Starting with a few undefined terms, we develop a vocabulary of words and symbols which are carefully defined. A definition is an agreed use of words or symbols, each expression having a single limited meaning which remains unvaried. We need to make certain that every word in a scientific discussion is used according to a dictionary meaning or is defined in the text before it is put to use.

In this text, if the definition is rather simple, the substitution of one word for another, the word we are adopting is in **boldface** type, as, for example, in "The number which coincides with the point is the **coordinate** of the point." Other definitions requiring more specific expressions of their meaning are set off and identified with the title DEFINITION; the defined words again are boldfaced.

A definition is a reversible statement. The term being defined can always be substituted for its definition, and vice versa. In this book the descriptive statement is usually stated first and the words being defined are last. Reversing the order of these two, with word changes to make the sense, produces the **converse** of the original.

An illustration of the dual expression of a definition follows. The subject of the first sentence contains the words *one line*, which are in the predicate of the converse. The predicate of the first contains *collinear points*, which becomes the subject of the converse.

> DEFINITION   The points of one line are **collinear points**.
>
> CONVERSE   Collinear points determine one line.

New words, such as *determine*, can be introduced to retain the meaning. A similar example follows:

> DEFINITION   The points of one plane are **coplanar points**.
>
> CONVERSE   Coplanar points determine one plane.

Each form of the statement has its distinct place. Often in this text, when both forms are frequently used, both are written out.

Several basic statements in this text will have corollaries. A second statement which is naturally inferred directly from a first is the **corollary** of the first. Corollaries of the above definitions are:

> COROLLARIES   All points not of one line are **noncollinear** points. All points not of one plane are **noncoplanar** points.

1.5   Foundation Stones for Proof

The second defect of Euclid is found in his system of postulates. He made general statements which he did not include among his postulates and which he could not prove from those he gave.

We can make hundreds of statements about geometric objects and their relations. Geometry requires that we have adequate bases for accepting each one, for verifying that it conforms to all the rest of the system. The proof of each is based solely on previously adopted statements. We are thus pushed back eventually to the first statements which we have proved and the definitions which we have determined. Just as the first definitions are based on undefined terms intuitively arrived at, so the first statements to be proved require foundation statements mutually agreed upon without proof. These primary ones are **postulates** and **properties**. (In traditional geometry the properties of numbers were the axioms.) Each postulate or property is a basic expression of a definite relation. We keep the number of these down to a minimum. Developed from these are the **theorems** which are accepted only after being thoroughly and carefully proved.

Most of the postulates seem like reasonable statements of fact, some of them so obvious that we wonder why they are included. They seem too simple to be given a place of importance. This may be why Euclid did not specifically express them. But postulates do not need to be self-evident truths, conforming to our observation of our objective world. These declarations about geometric objects are creations of man's mind, adopted because they fit into a total pattern of reasoning. The necessary consideration is that the whole system must be consistent, which means that no postulate may contradict another and that no theorem derived from them may contradict another theorem. We cannot postulate that "through a point not of a line there is exactly one line parallel to the given line," and then later prove that there are two lines through such a point parallel to the given line.

DEFINITION   Lines in one plane which do not intersect are **parallel lines**.

Some of the modern postulates are copied from Euclid, some are modifications of his, and some are new. They are all necessary as a foundation from which the theorems may be developed. The most basic are given first to establish the setting, the "launching pad" of points, lines, and planes for the other postulates which follow. This is the basis upon which the system can be built.

The first postulates are formal expressions of the answers to such questions as these:

How many lines can be drawn through a single dot on a piece of paper? How many can be drawn through two dots?

Over how many nails must a string be stretched to make it straight? Over how many to divide it up into two straight parts?

How many legs are required to hold up a table top? Assuming that the top ends of the legs are points, in the position which makes the top horizontal, can they support another plane which is not horizontal? If a fourth leg is introduced, can it support the top and allow the top to remain horizontal? Can the fourth leg lift the top to a new orientation not horizontal, with the first three legs still supporting it, or with one of the first three left behind?

If a straight string is glued across a flat card, can some of the string between the edges be away from and not touching the card. With the ends of the string at fixed points, in how many positions may the card be held?

Postulate 1   **For every two distinct points in space there is exactly one line containing them.**

Another useful wording of this postulate is:

Through two distinct points exactly one line can be drawn.

When the expression *exactly one* is used, it means *one and only one.* Two conditions are involved: there is *at least one*, and there is *at most one.* When exactly one point is required in a condition, it is also called a **unique** point. When it is necessary to prove exactly one, the proof usually is developed in two parts. The condition of at least one is **existence**, that of at most one is **uniqueness**. As will be shown in Chapter 5, the only possibilities available are *less than one*, *exactly one*, and *more than one.* Existence proves that less than one is eliminated and uniqueness proves that more than one is impossible. The only remaining option is **exactly one**.

Postulate 2   **Every line is a set of points and contains at least two distinct points.**

Postulate 3   **For every three noncollinear points there is exactly one plane containing them.**

Postulate 4   **Every plane is a set of points and contains at least three noncollinear points.**

Postulate 5   **A plane which contains two points of a line contains the entire line.**

Postulate 6   **Space is the set of all points and contains at least four noncoplanar points.**

Postulates 1 and 2 are converses of each other, as are postulates 3 and 4.

1.6 Superposition

The third defect of Euclid was his omission of a careful description of how to superimpose one angle upon another in order to prove that two triangles had exactly the same size and shape. He used a method of fitting corresponding parts of two triangles together so that all parts of one coincided with all parts of the other. This superposition is no longer considered adequate. We seek a theoretical rather than a physical means of making figures correspond. We can use a concept of numerically relating the sizes of parts and ascertaining the order in which the parts are arranged in relating the two figures. The theory of correspondence is a part of Chapter 2.

1.7 Summary Test

On answer sheet mark T or F for each number. If a statement is false, give a corresponding statement which is true.

1. The geometry of Euclid has been used over 3000 years.
2. The purpose of revising geometry in this century is to remove the inconsistencies of Euclid's work.
3. A geometric *point* is smaller than any visible point made on paper.
4. A dot on paper is a theoretical point.
5. Euclid's attempt to define a line is now thought to be inadequate.
6. A line may be extended in either direction indefinitely.
7. In this text the use of the word *line* includes both straight and curved lines.
8. A plane has no edges.
9. A definition, first accepted, is later proved.
10. Every definition in geometry has a true converse.
11. A line is a collinear set of points.
12. We may accept postulates which cannot be verified as true.
13. Three points of a line determine exactly one plane.
14. All the points of a line are coplanar.
15. If a plane contains one point of a line, it contains the whole line.
16. If one theorem contradicts another theorem, both are not proved from the same postulates and definitions.

chapter **2**

The Assistance
of Measure

2.1   Coordinates to the Rescue

The fourth defect of Euclid's work was a lack of precise notation by which to locate points, lines, and geometric figures relative to each other. He compared the lengths of lines and sizes of figures by writing that one was the same size as, or larger or smaller than, the other without a scale with which to give the comparison numerical values. He used a makeshift kind of calculation, and for a very good reason—the exact algebra which we use was developed by the Arabs after he lived. We take advantage of algebraic concepts to strengthen the traditional geometry.

The modern development is based on the concept of **order**. The numbers which we use in counting have a customary sequence from one upward; they are always accepted as coming in the same order. If we place these numbers along a line in succession with the distance between each two consecutive numbers constant, we have a linear **scale**. The negatives

```
  -2          -1    -½     0    ³⁄₈     1     1.5    2        3 π        4
```

of these numbers progress from negative one successively in the opposite direction. Between +1 and −1, spaced like all the others, is zero. These numbers are the integers. All fractional or decimal parts of a unit have their exact locations on the line between the integers. All the numerical quantities which can be located anywhere on this line are the **real numbers** of algebra. The numbers, whole integers and fractional or decimal parts, are always in the same order.

A number line is applied to two points in space, as a ruler is used for measuring. Coinciding with one point is a position on the scale, either at a mark or along a space between marks. Then exactly one position on the scale is available to coincide with the second point. The relation between points and numbers is an example of **one-to-one correspondence**. Another case is: if each student of a class sits in the same seat each day, there is a one-to-one correspondence between the occupied seats and the students present.

As we shall see more fully in Chapter 12, the number which coincides with a point is the **coordinate** of the point. The two-coordinate system, employed so successfully in the making of graphs, is built around two intersecting lines in a plane. Each of these lines is an **axis**, with a scale. A point is located anywhere on the graph by finding its number of scale units from each axis. Each point of the graph has two coordinates. The system of this chapter has one coordinate for each point, located on one axis.

Postulate 7 **There is a one-to-one correspondence between the set of all real numbers and the set of points of a line such that to each point there corresponds exactly one coordinate and to each coordinate there corresponds exactly one point of the line.**

A coordinate scale is applied to the points P and Q (Fig. 1). If, under one condition, the number 2 corresponds to P, and the number 9 coincides with Q, the **distance** between the pairs of matched points is 7

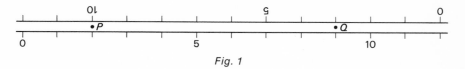

Fig. 1

units. Now, the scale may be turned around so that the smaller number is placed at Q. When this number is 3, the only number which can coincide with P is 10, and the distance between the pairs of points is 7 units. If the number $2\frac{1}{2}$ of the scale is made to coincide with one of the points, then corresponding to the other is $9\frac{1}{2}$. If the zero of the scale is placed at one point, then the number 7 is at the second point. In all cases the measure of the distance between the points is 7 units.

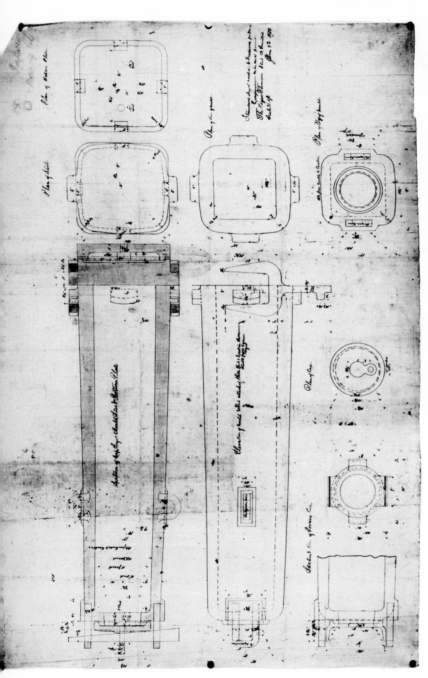

Mechanical drawings to scale accurately preserve the details of a design. This drawing of machine parts was made in 1880. The scale is 3 inches = 1 foot. Photo by Haven Bishop.

Consider the scale in Fig. 2 in which one space equals one centimeter.

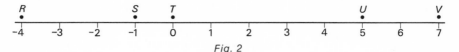

Fig. 2

Some distances between points are:

From T to $U = 5 - 0 = 5$ cm
From S to $T = 0 - (-1) = 1$ cm
From R to $S = -1 - (-4) = 3$ cm
From R to $V = 7 - (-4) = 11$ cm

If we find the distance from S to U, the difference of the coordinates is $5 - (-1) = 6$ cm. From U to S the difference of the coordinates is $-1 - 5 = -6$ cm. But if we stretch a string from U to S, we get the same positive length of string as when we stretch it from S to U. Every distance is a non-negative value whose measure is a positive number or zero. The difference of coordinates without regard to direction is the **absolute value** of the number. Only a directed movement from U to S is negative.

The absolute value is designated by putting figures between vertical bars. Thus, between the points U and S, $|5 - (-1)| = 6$. This is read: The absolute value of the difference of 5 and -1 is 6. Also $|-1 - 5| = 6$. We can write $US = 6$ or $SU = 6$. Thus: $|x| = x$ if x is zero or positive, and $|x| = -x$ if x is negative.

> DEFINITION The absolute value of the difference of the coordinates of two points is the **measure of the distance** between the points. The distance between two consecutive integers on a scale is the **unit distance**, that is, the distance between two points whose numerical difference is one.

The scale is man-made with the unit distance adopted for its convenience. As a result, all people knowing the unit can compare distances by simply finding the number of units of each. Any scale can be used, a traditional one or a new invention, each with its unique unit distance. The number of units between two given points will be different for each scale. If a sheet of paper is 11 inches long, its length is nearly 28 centimeters. For distance we usually use inches or centimeters as our scales. To each distance there corresponds exactly one positive real number in each scale.

The sequence of all real numbers is in an invariable order of succession. When a one-to-one correspondence is established between a set of points and their coordinates, the natural order of the coordinates in sequence determines the order of points. This gives a basis for the concept of betweenness. If three numbers are in the order a, b, c, then b

is **between** a and c. Also, if these numbers are the coordinates of three points A, B, and C, then the points are in the same order, and B is between A and C. If to each point there corresponds a coordinate, the order of points is known because the order of coordinates is unique.

Consider four collinear points (Fig. 3) whose names and corresponding coordinates are respectively: E, 0; F, 18; G, 13; H, 6. These points are in the order E, H, G, F or in the order F, G, H, E. Then G is between E and H.

Fig. 3

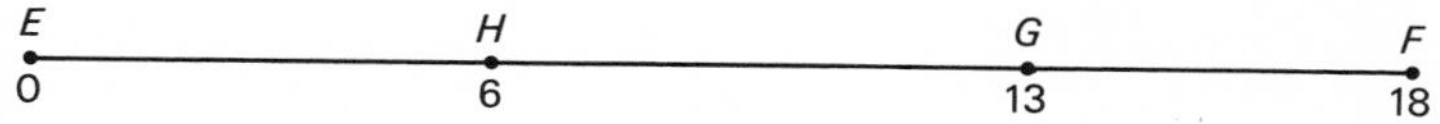

Furthermore, there is a point F beyond G from H such that G is between H and F.

EXERCISE 2.1

1. How far does a man travel on a straight road: **(a)** From 5 miles east of the center of a town to 7 miles west of it? **(b)** On the return trip?

2. The coordinate of point P is 12. What are the possible coordinates of point T if $PT = 14$?

3. The coordinates of points are as follows: E, 7; F, 2; G, 11; H, 14; J, 0.

   (a) Give the sequence of the points in two orders.
   (b) What point is between E and H?

4. GIVEN: The coordinate of A is 0, of B is 10; the distance AD is 25; $AB = BC$.

   FIND: **(a)** The coordinate of C. **(b)** The distances AC, DC, and BD.

Ex. 4

5. Make two small dots on a paper, less than a foot apart. Name them A and B.

   (a) Make the 1-inch mark of a foot ruler coincide with point A. At what number is point B? Record to the nearest sixteenth of an inch. What is the distance between the points?
   (b) Put the zero end of the ruler on B. What is the coordinate of A? What is the distance between B and A?
   (c) Make other numbers of the ruler coincide with the points. Are all measures the same within one sixteenth of an inch?

6. Make similar measurements with a ruler whose scale is in centimeters. From the above measure calculate the number of centimeters in 1 inch. It should be $2\frac{1}{2}$.

7. Complete each of the following equations.

(a) $5 - 5 =$ **(b)** $5 - (-5) =$ **(c)** $-5 - 5 =$ **(d)** $-5 - (-5) =$

(e) $|5 - 5| =$ **(f)** $|5 - (-5)| =$ **(g)** $|-5 - 5| =$ **(h)** $|-5 - (-5)| =$

8. Using the scale as a thermometer with graduations marked every 5° and letters corresponding to graduations, identify each of the following with a letter or a number or two letters.

(a) The scale value corresponding to A.
(b) The point which corresponds to $-15°$.
(c) The number of degrees from D to C.
(d) The number of degrees from D to B, directed.
(e) The number of degrees from B to D, directed.
(f) The number of degrees between B and D, undirected.
(g) The absolute value of the number of degrees from B to D.
(h) Two points whose temperature difference is 10°.
(i) Two points whose temperature difference is 40°.

Ex. 8

2.2 The Language of Sets

Probably the most basic concept of modern mathematics is that of sets. Any collection of objects can be called a **set**. The objects are usually assembled because they have some property in common. Each object is a **member** or an **element** of the set. If c is an element of set A, this is written: $c \in A$. The set may be denoted by stating the characteristic because of which the objects are related, or it may list the elements enclosed in a pair of braces. If set A contains only the elements c, d, and e, the notation is: $A = \{c, d, e\}$.

If set B is contained in set A such that every element of B is an element of A, then B is a **subset** of A. In symbols, $B \subseteq A$, which means: B is a subset of A. If B is a subset of A and there is at least one element of A which is not an element of B (Fig. 4), then B is a **proper subset** of A; this is written: $B \subset A$ or $A \supset B$. A subset may contain any number of the elements of its set from none to all of them. If there is a set which can be

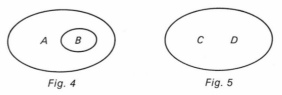

Fig. 4   Fig. 5

named, but it contains no elements, it is the **null** or **empty set**, symbolized by ∅. The empty set is a subset of any other set. Also, a set is a subset of itself.

Two sets are equal if they contain the same elements. Set C = set D if all the elements of one are elements of the other (Fig. 5). Then $D \subseteq C$, or $C \subseteq D$.

We are accustomed to the overlapping of two plane geometric figures, a part of one being also a part of the other. The same can be true of sets. Two sets which have one or more elements in common **intersect**. The set of elements common to both at once is the **intersection** of the two sets. In symbols, $G \cap H$, which is read: "G intersection H" or "G cap H." The term *intersection* is more inclusive than the term *intersect*. The intersection of two figures can contain all their points, many points, a few definite points, or no points at all. In the last case the figures do not intersect, but they have an intersection—the empty set. The intersection of parallel lines = ∅.

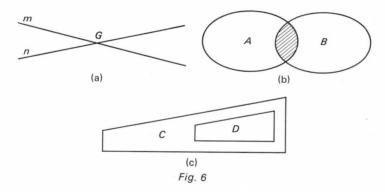

(a)   (b)

(c)

Fig. 6

In Fig. 6(a), the lines m and n intersect in the point G, and the set of points of the intersection is $\{G\}$. The intersection of sets A and B is the shaded portion in Fig. 6(b). If set D is a subset of set C, it is fully contained in C. In Fig. 6(c), D is a proper subset of C and their intersection is set D.

The set of all the elements of one or the other of two sets or of both is the **union** of the sets. If the sets overlap, as in Fig. 7(a), the union is all the points made by combining set E and set F, with no duplication of points.

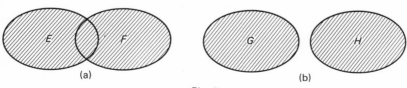

(a)   (b)

Fig. 7

If the sets do not overlap, as in Fig. 7(b), the union is all the points of the two sets. The union is written: $E \cup F$, which is read: "E union F" or "E cup F." Geometric figures are unions of sets of points. For the lines m and n in Fig. 6(a), we write $m \cup n = \{m, n\}$.

In summary, a line contains the known points P, Q, R, and S. If the set is named Z, then these and other points are elements of Z. We may denote, for example, $P \in Z$, $R \subset Z$, and $Z = \{P, Q, R, S, \ldots\}$. The three dots are to remind us that there are additional points. If m and n represent two parallel lines, then $m \cap n = \varnothing$ and $m \cup n = \{m, n\}$. If set $1 = \{A, D, G, J\}$ and set $2 = \{B, C, D, E, F, G\}$, then $1 \cap 2 = \{D, G\}$ and $1 \cup 2 = \{A, B, C, D, E, F, G, J\}$.

2.3 Subsets of a Line

Line means straight and of unlimited length. The symbol for line AB is $\overleftrightarrow{AB}$. Parts of a line have definite ends, as follows.

> DEFINITION   The subset of a line containing a point at one end as an **endpoint** and all the points of the line in the same direction from the endpoint is a **ray**. The ray RS is denoted by $\overrightarrow{RS}$.

In Fig. 8 the point R is the endpoint of each of two rays and is the point of intersection of the two rays. The second ray, $\overrightarrow{RT}$, contains point R and all the points in the opposite direction from $\overrightarrow{RS}$. In the name of a ray the

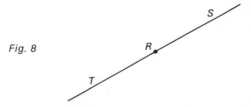

Fig. 8

first letter is always its endpoint. The arrow above it always points from left to right, away from the endpoint, regardless of the direction of the ray in the figure. Two collinear rays with only their endpoints in common are **opposite rays**. One is **opposite to** the other.

> DEFINITION   The subset of a line containing two endpoints and all the points of the line between the endpoints is a **segment**. The segment with endpoints C and D is denoted by $\overline{CD}$ or $\overline{DC}$.

> COROLLARY   A segment or ray may be extended indefinitely, forming a line.

DEFINITION   The distance between the endpoints of a segment is the **length** of the segment.

A single letter or two letters can be used to name each line. A pair of letters is usually used for a ray or segment. The marking above the letters in a symbol distinguishes each characteristic figure.

Name	*Figure*	*Symbol*
Line *m*	_____ *m*	*m*
Line *AB*	A _____ B	$\overleftrightarrow{BA}$ or $\overleftrightarrow{AB}$
Segment *CD*	C � _____ D	$\overline{DC}$ or $\overline{CD}$
Length of segment *CD*	C ⚬_____⚬ D	DC or CD
Ray *EF*	E •_____ F _____	$\overrightarrow{EF}$
Ray *FE*	 ____ E _____ F •	$\overrightarrow{FE}$

2.4   Angle Measure

DEFINITION   The union of two rays with a common endpoint is an **angle**. The common endpoint is the **vertex** and the rays are **sides** of the angle. The symbol for angle is $\angle$, plural $\angle\!s$.

The angle is the set of all points contained in the two rays. The vertex is the point of intersection of the two rays, their common endpoint. The angle at *B* (Fig. 9) is the union of $\overrightarrow{BD}$ and $\overrightarrow{BE}$. It is $\angle B$. When there are

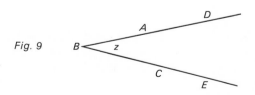

Fig. 9

more than two rays at *B*, to avoid any doubt as to what angle is meant, it is named with three letters, the first at any point of one ray, the second at the vertex, and third at a point of the other ray. It may be $\angle ABC$ or $\angle CBD$ or $\angle ABE$, etc. The vertex is always the middle letter. Or the angle can be designated by a single letter or number near the vertex between the sides, as ∠z.

An angle may be determined by segments, rays, or lines which intersect at the vertex. It is the set of points of the rays and not the surface of the plane between the sides.

Just as there is a point-coordinate system for lines, so there is a ray-coordinate system for angles. Numbers on an angular scale can be made to coincide with rays extending from a vertex and used to measure sizes of angles. The angle measure most commonly used for geometry is the degree. A measure of 30 degrees is written 30°. A set of rays in a plane with a common endpoint forms angles. The sum of the measures of these angles is 360° (Fig. 10). For precise measurements each degree is

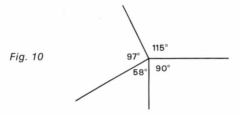

Fig. 10

divided into 60 minutes (′) and each minute is divided into 60 seconds (″). Thus the angle measure which is 10 seconds less than 20 degrees is 19° 59′ 50″.

Postulate 8   **There is a one-to-one correspondence between the set of real numbers from 0 to 360 and the set of rays with a common endpoint such that to each ray there corresponds exactly one coordinate and to each coordinate there corresponds exactly one ray.**

DEFINITION   The absolute value of the difference of the coordinates of the two rays of an angle is the **measure of the angle**. The measure of angle A is written m∠A.

The simple common angle-measuring device is the protractor. It may be a full circle measuring 360° or a half-circle containing 180°. It often has two scales with a set of numbers beginning with zero at either end, as in Fig. 11. Measured on the inner scale, $\overrightarrow{VF}$ has the coordinate 76° and $\overrightarrow{VE}$ is at 137°. The difference is m∠y = 61°. On the outer scale the coordinate of $\overrightarrow{VE}$ is 43° and that of $\overrightarrow{VF}$ is 104°, making m∠y = 61°. Either ray may be at 0°; the other will be at 61° on the same scale. To every angle there corresponds exactly one number which is its measure.

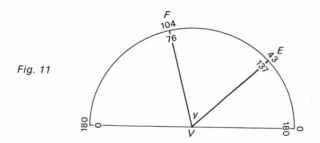

Fig. 11

Since the coordinates of rays are in a definite order, the order of their corresponding rays is determined. If four rays, $\overrightarrow{VA}$, $\overrightarrow{VB}$, $\overrightarrow{VC}$, and $\overrightarrow{VD}$, have coordinates a, b, c, and d, respectively (Fig. 12), the rays are in the order of their coordinates. If the coordinates are in the order a, b, c, d, then $\overrightarrow{VB}$ is between $\overrightarrow{VA}$ and $\overrightarrow{VC}$, $\overrightarrow{VD}$ is beyond $\overrightarrow{VC}$ from $\overrightarrow{VA}$, and $\overrightarrow{VC}$ is between $\overrightarrow{VA}$ and $\overrightarrow{VD}$.

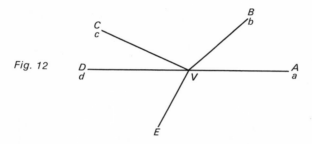

Fig. 12

Betweenness of rays can present a difficulty. For example, is $\overrightarrow{VD}$ between $\overrightarrow{VE}$ and $\overrightarrow{VA}$? Considering an angle whose measure is greater than 180°, it is. But since all the cases of betweenness for rays which we need are for angles of 180° or less, the intended betweenness will always be clear, and $\overrightarrow{VD}$ is not between $\overrightarrow{VE}$ and $\overrightarrow{VA}$.

EXERCISE 2.4

1. Which of the following are subsets of set $W = \{f, g, h, j\}$?

   (a) $\{f\}$ (b) $\{e, f, g\}$ (c) $\{\varnothing\}$ (d) $\{f, g, h, j\}$
   (e) $\{k, l\}$

2. Name the intersection and the union of each of the following pairs.

   (a) $C = \{1, 3, 5, 7, 9\}$; $D = \{4, 5, 6, 7\}$.
   (b) $C = \{1, 3, 5, 7, 9\}$; $E = \{2, 4, 6, 8\}$.

3. GIVEN: Collinear points E, F, G, H in that order. Name the intersection and the union of each of the following pairs.

(a) $\overrightarrow{EG}$ and $\overrightarrow{FG}$

Solution: Draw $\overleftrightarrow{EH}$ and the sets given so that they do not overlap.

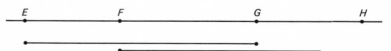

Then write the names for intersection and union. The intersection is $\overline{FG}$; the union is $\overrightarrow{EG}$.

(b) $\overrightarrow{FE}$ and $\overrightarrow{FG}$ **(c)** $\overline{GF}$ and $\overrightarrow{GH}$ **(d)** $\overline{EF}$ and $\overrightarrow{GH}$

(e) $\overline{GH}$ and $\overrightarrow{GH}$ **(f)** $\overrightarrow{FH}$ and $\overrightarrow{GE}$

4. If points $R, S,$ and T are collinear and in that order, state whether each of the following is true or false.

(a) $\overleftrightarrow{RS}$ is a subset of $\overrightarrow{RS}$.   **(b)** $\overline{RS}$ is a subset of $\overrightarrow{RS}$.

(c) $\overrightarrow{RS}$ is a subset of $\overrightarrow{RS}$.   **(d)** $\overrightarrow{SR}$ is a subset of $\overrightarrow{RS}$.

(e) $\overline{RT}$ is a subset of $\overline{RS}$.   **(f)** $\overleftrightarrow{RS}$ is a subset of $\overrightarrow{RT}$.

(g) $\overrightarrow{RS}$ is a subset of $\overline{RT}$.   **(h)** $\overline{RT}$ is a subset of $\overleftrightarrow{RS}$.

5. Add:

(a) $21°\ 30'\ 15'' + 14°\ 52'$

> *Answer:* $\quad 21°\ 30'\ 15''$
> $\quad\quad\quad\quad\ \underline{14°\ 52'\quad\quad}$
> $\quad\quad\quad\quad\ 35°\ 82'\ 15'' = 36°\ 22'\ 15''$

(b) $40°\ 27'\ 11' + 45°\ 18'\ 32''$ **(c)** $13°\ 17' + 25°\ 42'' + 48°\ 21'\ 26''$

6. Subtract:

(a) $38°\ 47'\ 20''$ from $70°\ 54''$

> *Answer:* $\quad 70°\quad\quad\ 54'' = 69°\ 60'\ 54''$
> $\quad\quad\quad\quad\ \underline{38°\ 47'\ 20'' = 38°\ 47'\ 20''}$
> $\quad\quad\quad\quad\quad\quad\quad\quad\quad\ 31°\ 13'\ 34''$

(b) $12°\ 27'\ 24''$ from $16°\ 31'\ 19''$ **(c)** $34°\ 50'$ from $90°$

7. From the figure name:

(a) A line.

(b) Two rays.

(c) The endpoint of each ray.

(d) A segment.

(e) The endpoints of the segment.

(f) An angle two ways.

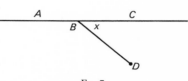

Ex. 7

8. In the segment $\overline{EH}$ the coordinate of E is 0 and of F is 8; the distance EH is 20, and $EF = FG$.

Find: **(a)** The coordinate of G. **(b)** EG. **(c)** GH. **(d)** FH.

Ex. 8

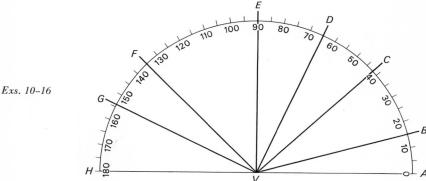

9. The ray coordinate of $\overrightarrow{VA}$ is 0; $m\angle AVB = 130°$; $m\angle BVC = 80°$; $m\angle CVD$ is 50°. Find:

(a) The coordinates of $\overrightarrow{VB}$, $\overrightarrow{VC}$, and $\overrightarrow{VD}$.

(b) $m\angle DVA$.

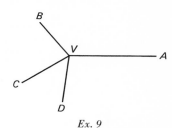

Ex. 9

The protractor is divided into units of 5°. The center is at V. Rays with endpoint V are lettered. Find the following (Exs. 10–16), estimating to the nearest whole degree.

Exs. 10–16

10. The coordinate of $\overrightarrow{VG}$.

11. The measure of each angle formed by two consecutive rays.

12. (a) $m\angle AVF$ **(b)** $m\angle CVG$ **(c)** $m\angle EVH$ **(d)** $m\angle DVF$

13. An angle whose measure is:

(a) 48°   **(b)** 64°   **(c)** 180°

14. The number of degrees in:

(a) $m\angle DVE + m\angle EVF$ **(b)** $m\angle AVB + m\angle GVH$

15. The number of degrees in:

(a) $m\angle EVG - m\angle FVG$ **(b)** $m\angle AVD - m\angle BVC$

16. (a) $2m\angle GVH$ **(b)** $\frac{1}{2}m\angle GVH$ **(c)** $3m\angle GVH$

17. Draw two intersecting lines on a paper. Measure each of the four angles twice with different locations of a protractor. Obtain the absolute values of the differences of consecutive coordinates.

18. Draw an angle of 103°. Extend one of the sides through the vertex. What is the measure of the second angle?

2.5 Simple Geometric Figures

DEFINITIONS   The union of *n* consecutive segments in a plane intersecting at and only at *n* points which are their common endpoints, with no two consecutive segments collinear, is a **polygon**. The segments are **sides**, the points of intersection are **vertices**, the angles formed by the sides are the **angles** of the polygon.

DEFINITION   The union of three segments whose common endpoints are three noncollinear points is a **triangle**. The symbol for triangle is △, plural △.

In △*FGH* (Fig. 13) the points *F*, *G*, and *H* are vertices of angles ∠*F*, ∠*G*, and ∠*H*; and $\overline{FG}$, $\overline{GH}$, and $\overline{HF}$ are sides. No two segments of a polygon have points of intersection other than their common endpoints. The polygon is the set of points of the sides and not the surface of the plane.

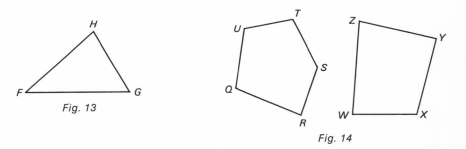

Fig. 13

Fig. 14

In Fig. 14 the polygon *QRSTU*, containing five sides, is a **pentagon**. The polygon *WXYZ*, having four sides, is a **quadrilateral**.

DEFINITIONS   A quadrilateral whose opposite sides are parallel is a **parallelogram**. A quadrilateral whose angles measure 90° is a **rectangle**. A rectangle all of whose sides have the same length is a **square**.

DEFINITIONS   The set of points of a plane a given distance from a given point is a **circle**. The given point is the **center**. A segment whose endpoints are the center and any point of the circle is the **radius**. A subset of a circle with two distinct endpoints is an **arc**. The symbol for circle is $\odot$, plural $\circledS$. The symbol for arc AB is $\overset{\frown}{AB}$.

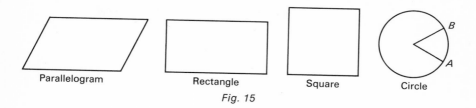

Parallelogram   Rectangle   Square   Circle

Fig. 15

2.6   Properties of Equality of Numbers

The numerical relations which determine the processes of algebra are used extensively in geometry. In algebra we manipulate symbols according to specific principles, the logical consequences of a few basic definitions and laws. Once the principles are determined, they remain inviolate. A few of these, properties of equality of real numbers, are necessary in geometry. We begin by assuming them for numerical quantities, and then later will apply them to relationships of geometric figures. Here is given a set of these properties, each with its statement and its title, followed by examples of its use.

Property 1   **A number equals itself.**   Reflexive property

The number 3 in one expression equals the number 3 in every other, and $a = a$ in each relationship.

This was traditionally called the property of **identity**.

Property 2   **If one number equals a second number, the second number equals the first.**   Symmetric property

If $a = b$, then $b = a$ and the two numbers can be interchanged.

Property 3   **If one number equals a second number and the second equals a third number, the first equals the third.**   Transitive property

If $a = b$ and $b = c$, then $a = c$.

This applies for any number of equalities. Therefore the property can be applied in two other ways:

Corollary   **In a series of equal numbers the first equals the last.**

Corollary   **A number may be substituted for its equal in any relationship.**

The traditional statement of this property is:

Two numbers equal to the same number equal each other.

Property 4   If equal numbers are added to equal numbers, the results are equal numbers.   Addition property

Subtraction is included in this property, since subtraction is the addition of the negative of a number. If $d = e$ and $f = g$, then $d + f = e + g$ or $f - d = g - e$ or $d + 5 = e + 5$ or $6 - f = 6 - g$.

Property 5   If equal numbers are multiplied by equal numbers, the results are equal numbers.   Multiplication property

Division is the multiplication of the reciprocal of a number. Note that a number cannot be divided by zero. If $d = e$ and $f = g$, then $df = eg$ or $7f = 7g$ or $d/f = e/g$ or $8/d = 8/e$ if no denominator is 0.

Two special cases of this property are useful in relation to bisectors:

Corollary   **Halves of equal numbers are equal numbers.**

Corollary   **Doubles of equal numbers are equal numbers.**

Other properties of numerical relationships are listed in Chapter 5 and Appendix C. The basic properties are postulates. Theorems derived from them are summarized in Appendix B (sections B.1 and B.2).

EXERCISE 2.6

1. If $a = 14$, $b = 16$, and $c = 20$, find:

    (a) $a + b + c$ (b) $a + b - c$ (c) $(a + b)c$
    (d) $(a + b) \div c$

2. If $d = 22$, find:

    (a) $2d$ (b) $d/2$ (c) $3d$ (d) $3d/2$

3. If $f = p$ and $h = q$, substitute a number for its equal in $f + h = 20$ and give an equation relating p and q.

4. A trellis is made of 4-foot pieces of lath. Find the length of: (a) Half a piece. (b) 3 pieces laid end to end. (c) $2\frac{1}{2}$ pieces end to end.

5. The coordinate of A is 5 and of D is 25. Find: **(a)** The coordinate of B if $AB = \frac{1}{5}AD$. **(b)** The coordinate of C if $AC = \frac{3}{4}AB$. **(c)** The distance BC.

6. State the property which is the reason for each of the following equations, using the given and the equations in previous parts of the question as necessary.

GIVEN: $\overline{AF}$; $BC = 2AB$; $CD = 2DE$; $BC = CD$; $BC = EF$.

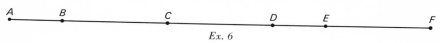

Ex. 6

(a) $CD = BC$	**(b)** $2AB = 2DE$	**(c)** $AB = DE$	**(d)** $CE = AC$
(e) $CD = EF$	**(f)** $DE = DE$	**(g)** $CE = DF$	**(h)** $\frac{1}{2}BC = AB$

7. GIVEN: $9x - 5 = 7x + 11$. State the property used in each of the following:

(a) $9x - 5 - 7x = 11$ **(b)** $9x - 7x = 11 + 5$ **(c)** $2x = 16$
(d) $x = 8$

8. Find the value(s) of x in each of the following equations:

(a) $|x - 8| = 14$.

Solution: The number x for which $x - 8 = 14$, and the number x for which $-(x - 8) = 14$; $x = 22$ and -6.

(b) $|x| - 8 = 14$.

Solution: The numbers whose positive values satisfy the equation $x - 8 = 14$; $x = +22$ and -22.

(c) $|x + 5| = 16$ **(d)** $|x + a| = 16$ **(e)** $|x + 7| = 3$
(f) $|x - 8| = 2$ **(g)** $|x| + 9 = 15$ **(h)** $|x| + b = 15$
(i) $|x| + 6 = 1$ **(j)** $|x| - 10 = 0$

2.7 **Summary Test**

After each number on answer sheet write T if the statement is true, F if it is false. If a statement is false, make a corresponding statement which is true.

1.   When a scale is laid on a plane, each point of the scale has one-to-one correspondence with exactly one point of the plane.

2.   The coordinate of point R is 5, of S is 15, of T is 12; the points can be in the order S, T, R.

3.   The distance between a point with a positive coordinate and a point with a negative coordinate is always a positive number.

4.   If two points are 12 units apart on one scale, they are 12 units apart on every kind of scale.

5.   If the coordinate of $\overrightarrow{DA}$ is 20°, of $\overrightarrow{DB}$ is 85°, and of $\overrightarrow{DC}$ is 48°, then $\overrightarrow{DB}$ is between $\overrightarrow{DA}$ and $\overrightarrow{DC}$.

6.   If two plane figures are covered with glue and made to partly overlap, the part of each figure which sticks to the other is their union.

7.   A segment can be extended in both directions and produce a line.

8.   If two points of one segment are identical with two points of another segment, the two segments are collinear.

9.   An endpoint of $\overleftrightarrow{AB}$ is B.

10.   An endpoint of $\overrightarrow{CD}$ is D.

11.   An endpoint of $\overline{EF}$ is F.

12.   A one-to-one correspondence between numbers on a ruler and the endpoints of a segment provides a means of measuring the length of the segment.

13.   A ray is the part of a line joining two endpoints.

14.   A line has a definite length.

15.   An angle is the intersection of two rays at a common endpoint.

16.   The measure of an angle depends on the length of its sides.

17.   An angle is the part of a plane which is between two rays with a common endpoint.

18.   A triangle is the union of an angle and a segment.

19.   A triangle is the intersection of three segments which intersect at their endpoints.

20. The three vertices of a triangle are noncollinear.

21. The three vertices of a triangle are noncoplanar.

22. If $R = S$ and $S = T$ and $U = V$, then $R = V$.

23. If G is between F and H, then $FG + GH = FH$.

24. Two opposite rays with a common endpoint are collinear.

25. The intersection of two sets is a subset of each.

26. A set is a subset of its union with another set.

chapter **3**

The Logic of Proof

3.1 Reasoning Better Than Usual

The great strength of geometry as an important discipline through the centuries lies in its careful use of logic. The whole spirit of the *Elements* was to use fully this technique developed so thoroughly in Greek culture. Logic is a system of intellectual honesty, the same mental attitude which has made the development of modern science possible. But logic is grossly misused in our modern culture. Reasoning in heated arguments or in advertising is sadly illogical. Advertising claims by inference that every new development is effected only with the best interest of the customer at heart. Scientific research on the product may indicate that this is not true. In our scientific age it is part of our training to test every new idea with the evidence of facts, but people continue to believe all sorts of ideas not supported by fact or by good judgment, and to defend them with emotional fervor.

One of the real problems in logical thinking comes from the obscurity of the meaning of the word *truth*. Philosophy has reached no final truth but has found many truths. In logical reasoning it is a relationship rather than a fact which is true. An argument is composed of statements, any one of which may, or may not, conform to the facts of real experience. A statement which could not be true to scientific fact can still be part of a valid argument. The requirement is that each statement conforms to the others. One does not refute any other. A system of reasoning must be consistent — no part of it may contradict any other part.

3.2   Inductive Reasoning

The development of scientific knowledge follows a logical sequence. First there is **inductive reasoning** by which one accumulates facts from observation. The mind of man slowly evolves generalizations which seem to fit the evidence of the facts. The scientist thus forms a theory which he then tests by every means available, and submits it to others that they may check his data and his reasoning. Theories with this substantial a beginning have been trusted enough to be used as the basis for new industries with millions of dollars invested.

The weakness of induction is that one cannot investigate all the cases, and he cannot recognize all the implications of his findings, but the technique has a worthy history of success in discovering theories which do conform to fact. Often in the past when theories were changed, they were not found to be wrong and discarded. They were just modified.

A person may develop a theorem of geometry by trying many cases. Thus he may come to the conclusion that his statement is correct. He could test "If two lines are parallel to a third line, they are parallel to each other," or "The sum of the measures of the angles of a triangle equals 180°." But in geometry he will still need to prove that it conforms to the accepted concepts which he already has verified and to the total system.

3.3   Deductive Reasoning

If we accept the supposition that certain ideas are true, then certain results emerge through logical reasoning. The accepted ideas may have come from inductive thought or from the imagination of man, but a body of knowledge is built which is used to test a new insight proposed as an expression of truth. This is **deductive reasoning**. If the new insight does not agree with formerly accepted knowledge, it must be convincing enough to replace or modify the old.

A deductive argument is **valid** when each step in the process is solidly supported by the previous steps, each one deduced from formerly proved propositions, until the argument is pushed back to the original definitions and postulates.

But deduction cannot supply the initial affirmations from which the others are derived. Induction is called upon to provide the first principles upon which deduction is built. Then deduction tests new evidence which is submitted, to strengthen or refute the conclusions of induction. We might think of the two types of reasoning thus: induction places new conclusions in the stock of knowledge; deduction borrows from the stock the statements which are needed to test a proposed conclusion.

The body of knowledge in geometry is composed of statements organized into a consistent system. The most basic are definitions, postulates, and properties of numbers. They are accepted without proof. Geometry is different from physical science in that we do not prove the truth of the postulates which determine our foundation. And so geometry is more theoretical than practical. But its successful logical structure is the envy of other sciences.

A deductive argument is a sequence of three sentences. The first is a **general statement** or **proposition**, the statement of a condition which is either true or false. The second is a **specific statement**, the assertion that a given case is a specific instance of the proposition. The third is the **conclusion** that the instance is consequently true to the proposition.

"Two points determine" is not a proposition; it is neither true nor false. "Two points determine exactly one line" is true, while "Two points determine exactly one plane" is false. A specific statement is "Two points, A and B, are located" (as on a chalkboard). The conclusion reports that of all the possible lines which can be drawn on the chalkboard "Exactly one line is $\overrightarrow{AB}$."

The general proposition contains two parts: the **hypothesis**, which establishes the condition to be discussed, and the **conclusion**, which asserts the consequence of the condition. The hypothesis implies the conclusion.

These statements can be written as sentences of two clauses, beginning with the conjunctions *if* and *then*. The hypothesis is the if-clause and the conclusion is the then-clause. Using H and C as the initials of these terms, we write the statement: "If H, then C." A theorem which we are to prove in this chapter reads: "If two distinct lines intersect, then their intersection is exactly one point." The H is: "Two distinct lines intersect." The C is: "Their intersection is exactly one point." This statement of the theorem is the **conditional** form of the sentence.

The other form of the proposition is a **declarative** sentence in which the subject is the source of the hypothesis and the predicate expresses the conclusion. In this form the theorem is worded: "Two distinct intersecting lines have exactly one point of intersection." This book uses the declarative sentence when the other is not preferable. If the conditional form makes the meaning more clear, it should be used.

A sequence of three statements in deductive reasoning is valid when the general statement expresses a hypothesis and a conclusion, and when the specific statement refers to the hypothesis of the general statement. The conclusion follows inevitably. In the first illustration of this section the hypothesis as a complete clause may be stated: "Two points are located." Then the conclusion is: "They determine exactly one line." The sequence may be visualized in a diagram (Fig. 16).

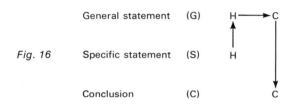

Fig. 16

Some arguments erroneously make the specific statement a case of the conclusion of the general. Then there is no valid concluding statement. To illustrate, a general proposition is: "For every three noncollinear points there is exactly one plane containing them." A specific statement can be: "Points *E*, *F*, and *G* are contained in one plane." The specific, applying to the conclusion of the general, produces no conclusion statement. It does not prevent the three points from being collinear, in which case they could be contained in other planes. To be valid in this case, the specific statement would need to read: "Points *E*, *F*, and *G* are noncollinear." The student should supply the valid conclusion resulting from this.

If a specific statement is a negation of the hypothesis, the concluding statement expresses the fact that the specific is not a case of the general. A sample general proposition is: "All the facts about mathematics known to Euclid were assembled in the *Elements*." Referring to this, a specific statement may be: "Algebra had not been developed in Euclid's time." This means that Euclid did not know algebra except in a rudimentary form. Therefore, the conclusion is that "A well-developed algebra was not included in the *Elements*." This is the inverse discussed below.

A valid sequence is shown by:

General: "The set of points common to two figures is their intersection."
Specific: "Lines *m* and *n* have a common point, *X*."
Conclusion: "The point *X* is the intersection of lines *m* and *n*."

3.4 Expressions of a Proposition

The general proposition used in logical deduction is the **reason** employed in each step of proof in geometry. Different forms of these statements are used for different purposes. The original form is the proposition. Three other forms are variations derived from it. They are expressions of H and C, thus:

Proposition:	If H, then C	Converse:	If C, then H
Inverse:	If not H, then not C	Contrapositive:	If not C, then not H

The proposition with H and C interchanged is the **converse**. The original C becomes the if-clause, and the H becomes the then-clause. The negation of both parts of the proposition is the **inverse**. The negation of both parts of the converse is the **contrapositive**.

With the definition of collinear points in Section 1.4 is the statement: "All points not of one line are noncollinear points." This is the inverse of the definition.

One proposition is: "A square is a rectangle." Given in the form of a conditional sentence, it reads: "If a figure is a square, then it is a rectangle." The four expressions of the proposition can be stated, whether they are true or false.

A square is a rectangle	True	A rectangle is a square	False
A figure which is not a square is not a rectangle	False	A figure which is not a rectangle is not a square	True

The necessary clue to the falsity of the two parts is that all squares have all the requirements for rectangles, but there are many shapes of rectangles which are not squares. The set of all squares is a subset of all rectangles. The inverse and converse are true in only a part of the cases, and so must be called false. The contrapositive is true because if a figure is not a rectangle, it is excluded from being a square. In Fig. 17, *ABCD* is a square and also a rectangle; *EFGH* is a rectangle which is not a square.

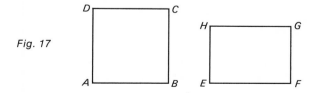

Fig. 17

A case in which all four of the expressions are true has the proposition: "All equilateral triangles are equiangular." A triangle which has all sides of equal length is **equilateral**, and one with all angles of equal measure is **equiangular**. To formulate the four sentences is an exercise left to the student.

The theory of logic shows that the contrapositive is always true or false the same as the proposition is true or false, and the converse and inverse are true or false together. With all our geometric theorems which are not just statements of algebraic expressions, it is required to prove the converse of each theorem before we can accept it.

When a proposition and its converse are true, both facts can be expressed in a single statement. A proposition in the conditional form of the sentence begins with *if*. The converse does not need to have H and C reversed if the hypothesis is begun with *only if*. And both are true together after *if and only if*. One proposition is: "If a triangle is equilateral, then it is equiangular." One form of the converse is: "Only if a triangle is equilateral, it is equiangular." Both are included in the expression: "If and only if a triangle is equilateral, it is equiangular." Furthermore, the alternate expression of the statement is consistently true: "If and only if a triangle is equiangular, it is equilateral."

EXERCISE 3.4

Identify the hypothesis and the conclusion of each proposition in Exs. 1–12, and restate the proposition in the if-then conditional form.

1. The absolute value of the difference of the coordinates of points equals the distance between the points.

   Answer: The hypothesis is: The absolute value of the difference of the coordinates of points is found. The conclusion is: The value equals the distance between the points. The conditional sentence is: If the absolute value of the difference of coordinates of points is found, then it equals the distance between the points.

2. A plane which contains two points of a line contains the entire line.
3. The sum of the measures of two angles which are complements is 90°.
4. Angles which are complements of the same angle are congruent.
5. Lines of one plane which do not intersect are parallel lines.
6. Corresponding parts of congruent triangles are congruent.
7. A triangle which has two congruent sides is isosceles.
8. An angle whose measure is less than 90° is an acute angle.
9. Two lines parallel to the same line are parallel to each other.
10. The diagonals of a parallelogram bisect each other.
11. In a circle, chords with the same endpoints as congruent arcs are congruent.

12. A line which intersects a circle at exactly one point is a tangent.

Give the converse of each proposition in Exs. 13–23.

13. If three collinear points are in the order first, second, third, the second is between the first and the third.

> *Answer:* If of three collinear points the second is between the first and the third, they are in the order first, second, third. (NOTE: They may also be in the order third, second, first.)

14. The set of points common to two figures is their intersection.

15. Angles with the same measure are congruent.

16. A triangle all of whose sides are congruent is equilateral.

17. To each ray there corresponds exactly one coordinate.

18. Sides of a right angle are perpendicular.

19. A ray which separates an angle into two congruent halves bisects the angle.

20. Every point of the bisector of an angle is equidistant from the sides of the angle.

21. The side of a triangle opposite a greater angle is the greater side.

22. A quadrilateral whose opposite sides are parallel is a parallelogram.

23. The measure of an angle inscribed in a circle is half the measure of its intercepted arc.

3.5   Form for a Proof

Geometric proofs are necessarily of different types, their procedure depending upon the resources available to secure the statements used in the proofs. And they may be organized in a formal or an informal manner. The reasons which can be used for steps in a proof are definitions, postulates, properties of numbers, and theorems already accepted. These items constitute the stock of reasons at our command. When we have appropriate reasons available, we use a direct method of proof. When the supply is insufficient for direct proof, we have alternatives which are discussed in Section 3.7.

In both methods there is a proposition to be proved. It may be stated in general form in a sentence. In all cases it is expressed in the specific form of one example. The example is displayed in a **diagram** which shows the geometric figure(s) referred to in the hypothesis of the proposition and conforms to all the conditions of the hypothesis. Accompanying the diagram is the **given**, which expresses the hypothesis in a short lettered form, matching the letters of the diagram. Next is **prove**, which puts the conclusion in terms of the diagram.

The diagram allows us to visualize the conditions of the problem. But the proof is independent of the drawing. The diagram cannot be used to justify any step not implied by the hypothesis. And so the diagram is made to be as general as possible. The ideal geometric object exists in the mind. The figure is a representation of it.

We shall infer from the diagram some things which are assumed in the hypothesis. A line is straight. A point which should be on a line is on the line. A point of a segment is between endpoints. A letter labels a point of intersection. On the other hand, two figures do not have equal size simply because they are drawn equal. We must know the equality from some other criterion. Sometimes figures overlap in a diagram. When they do, we assume that they are plane figures whose points of overlapping coincide perfectly. Their common points are an intersection. In summary, the diagram is made to be the servant of the proof, and not to play tricks on the student.

When a theorem is being proved, the method is to give an example in which the conditions of the hypothesis have been met and to prove that the conclusion fits the example. The theorem is a general statement of the form: "If H, then C." The GIVEN for the proof is: "This is an example of H." The PROVE is: "C follows in this example." If the available resources prove the example and if the example is general enough to represent all cases of the theorem, then the conclusion is inescapable. If it is not proved, the theorem is not valid. Furthermore, a proposition cannot be used to prove itself.

3.6   Direct Proof

Whether written in a formal or an informal style, the direct proof collects in a reasonable order a series of facts needed to supply all the steps which form a bridge between the hypothesis and the conclusion. Some steps may be chosen which are not absolutely necessary, but they make the proof clearer and smoother. Choosing the necessary steps and excluding those which do not contribute to the proof is a matter of experience.

The following proof is direct and formal. The steps are numbered in order. Each one is a unit of the bridge, secured by a reason describing why the step is justified and based soundly on the facts which precede it. The wording of the reason is condensed and abbreviated as much as is possible without obscuring the meaning (see Section 3.8). We will proceed through the complete proof and then analyze it.

THEOREM 1   Points between the ends of a segment separate it into parts, the sum of whose lengths equals the length of the whole.

GIVEN: Segment $\overline{DG}$; points E and F between D and G in the order D, E, F, G.

D ————————— E ————————————— F ——— G

PROVE: $DE + EF + FG = DG$.

Statements	*Reasons*
1. D, E, F, G points of a segment in that order.	1. Given.
2. Let the coordinates of the points be $d, e, f,$ and g, respectively.	2. To each point corresp 1 coord.
3. $DE = \|e - d\|$: $EF = \|f - e\|$; $FG = \|g - f\|$.	3. Diff of coord = distance.
4. $DE + EF + FG = \|e - d\| + \|f - e\| + \|g - f\| = \|g - d\|$.	4. Equals + equals are equals.
5. $DG = \|g - d\|$.	5. Reason 3.
6. $DE + EF + FG = DG$.	6. First = second = third.

COROLLARY 1.1   The length of a part of a segment equals the length of the whole minus the length of the remainder of the segment.

A corollary of a theorem is so closely related to the theorem from which it is derived that it is proved by the process developed in the original theorem. It often is a special case of the original.

In Theorem 1, segments, geometric figures, are related by resorting to known facts about their lengths expressed in numbers. Each coordinate is a number. Numbers are added and subtracted. The resulting relation of coordinates determines the relation of points and segments.

Step 1 repeats the part of the given which is needed. Step 2 introduces coordinates as an instrument used in accomplishing the purpose of the proof. Its reason is from Postulate 7: "To each point there corresponds exactly one coordinate." The other steps are algebra. Reason 3 is the definition of the measure of a distance. Reason 4 is a property of equality of numbers. When reason 3 needs to be repeated in step 5, it does not need to be rewritten. Step 6 is a copy of the PROVE, showing that the goal of the process has been reached. Reason 6 means that, since $DE + EF + FG = \|g - d\|$, and since $\|g - d\| = DG$, then $DE + EF + FG = DG$, all of these being numerical measures of lengths.

In every step of a proof, the reason has a simple grammatical relationship with the statement. With few exceptions, every reason is a general proposition of which its step is a specific case. The hypothesis of the reason (see Section 3.3) refers to something which precedes its step. The conclusion refers to the step of which it is the reason. Specifically, the verb of the step matches the verb of its reason. One exception is in a step taken from the given or one introducing new material, implicit in the given, to implement the proof. Here the source of the hypothesis of the reason is only implied. In Theorem 1, step 2 is the introduction of a measuring scale as a means of proving the case. The verb "corresponds" matches the verb "be" of its step. In the last four steps the verb is "=."

NOTE: In the condensation of a property the word "equals" means *equal numbers*; the symbol "=" represents verb forms *equal(s)* or *is (are) equal (to)* or adjective *equal*.

THEOREM 2   Rays from the vertex of an angle between its sides separate it into parts, the sum of whose measures equals the measure of the whole.

COROLLARY 2.1   The measure of a part of an angle equals the measure of the whole minus the measure of the remainder of the angle.

The proof of this theorem is like that of Theorem 1, with "angle" instead of "segment" and "measure" in place of "length." The proof of Theorem 2 is left to the student.

3.7   Indirect Proof

When we do not have reasons with which we can prove a proposition directly, we resort to a roundabout method of indirect proof. In one technique we assume the opposite or denial of the conclusion. If a hypothesis is accepted but the conclusion is not proved, the proposition is not valid. But if we find that this opposite contradicts the hypothesis or one of the statements already accepted, the opposite is false and the conclusion is true. It is impossible for a statement and one contradicting it both to be true. We learned in Section 3.4 that a proposition and its contrapositive are true or false together. The technique just described shows how the proof of the contrapositive makes the proposition true. The proof of Theorem 22 (Section 6.1) will use the contrapositive.

A second technique lists all the possible conditions. For instance, one measure can be either greater than, equal to, or less than a second measure. These are the only possibilities. Then if all but one of them is proved false, the remaining one is declared true. We must be sure to include all cases. By way of illustration, an alternative to the statement: "All students do well in geometry" is not only the statement: "No students do well in geometry," but also: "Some students do well in geometry."

In Theorem 3 the proposition is: "If two distinct lines intersect, then their intersection is exactly one point." Other possible statements could be: ". . . their intersection is no points," or ". . . their intersection is more than one point." To refute the possibility of no points is to prove existence; to eliminate more than one point is to prove uniqueness (see Section 1.5).

The following is an informal paragraph form of proof. This form is exceedingly convenient for indirect proof.

THEOREM 3 **If two distinct lines intersect, then their intersection is exactly one point.**

GIVEN: Lines m and n intersecting.

PROVE: The intersection is at least one point; at most one point.

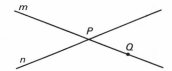

Lines m and n intersect at at least one point, since it is only when two sets do not intersect that their intersection is the empty set.   (Existence)

Let P be the point of intersection. P is an element of each line. Let Q be a second point of m which may intersect n. There would be two distinct lines through P and Q, but for every two distinct points in space there is exactly one line containing them. The intersection is exactly one point. (Uniqueness)

In this proof the possibility of *no points* was removed with a reason from the definition of *intersect* and the definition of the *empty set*. The possibility of *two points* was removed by assuming that a second point is located on one line and proving that it could not be a point of intersection. Then *exactly one point* was the only alternative remaining. The second point was not possible because its presence contradicted the fact that for every two distinct points there is exactly one line, from Postulate 1.

IN SUMMARY: The method of proof may be either direct or indirect; the way of writing it may be either formal or informal. The first two theorems proved in this text by each of the possibilities are:

	Formal	*Informal*
Direct	Theorems 1, 4	Theorems 5, 6
Indirect	Theorems 11, 12	Theorems 3, 16

EXERCISE 3.7

Argue pro or con each proposition in Exs. 1 and 2. Give a definite, clear statement of opinion. Support it with reasons which are factual and defensible.

1. The purpose of studying geometry is more to develop facility in abstract reasoning than to learn applications of geometry to engineering problems.
2. When a person studies logic, he improves his ability to analyze propaganda.

Even when a statement cannot be true in a life situation, it can contribute to a valid deduction.

3. Give a valid conclusion which follows from these two statements: (1) He who does not practice consistently can be a champion. (2) Paul plays tennis occasionally.
4. If the groundhog sees his shadow in Punxsutawney, Pennsylvania, on February 2, there will be six more weeks of cold weather before spring sets in. Last year there was sunshine part of the day on February 2 in Punxsutawney. By the end of the month the days were warm. March came in like a lamb.
   (a) Do the statements above constitute a deductive argument? If so, identify the general statement, the specific statement, and the conclusion.
   (b) Argue the correctness of the statements as a true logical sequence regardless of their accuracy in relation to natural phenomena.
   (c) Argue the correctness of these statements as true expressions of scientific fact in nature.

In Exs. 5–15, (G) is the general statement, (S) is the specific statement, and (C) is the conclusion. Provide the correct missing part of each deduction.

5. (G) For every two points in space there is exactly one line containing them.
   (C) In the figure there is exactly one line $\overleftrightarrow{GH}$.
6. (S) The points E and F are points of plane J.
   (C) Plane J contains the line $\overleftrightarrow{EF}$.
7. (G) The absolute value of the difference of their coordinates is the measure of the angle between two rays.
   (S) Ray $\overrightarrow{VR}$ has the coordinate $18°$ and $\overrightarrow{VS}$ has the coordinate $52°$.
8. (G) All the points of a line are collinear.
   (C) The points $C, D,$ and E are collinear.

9. (S) R, S, and T are three noncollinear points.
   (C) The union of $\overline{RS}$, $\overline{ST}$, and $\overline{TR}$ is $\triangle RST$.
10. (S) The points C and D correspond to 2 and 16 on a ruler.
    (C) The distance between C and D is 14 units.
11. (G) A set contained within a second set is a subset of the second.
    (S) A polygon of three sides is a triangle.
12. (G) If three rays with a common endpoint are in the order first, second, third, the second is between the first and the third.
    (S) The coordinate of $\overrightarrow{VC}$ is 25°, of $\overrightarrow{VB}$ is 0°, of $\overrightarrow{VA}$ is 38°.
13. (G) A point of a line separates the line into two opposite collinear rays.
    (C) Rays $\overrightarrow{GE}$ and $\overrightarrow{GF}$ are opposite collinear rays.
14. (G) The intersection of two sets is an element of each set.
    (C) Point P is a point of each line, m and n.
15. (S) The figure contains rays $\overrightarrow{VE}$ and $\overrightarrow{VF}$.
    (C) The union of $\overrightarrow{VE}$ and $\overrightarrow{VF}$ is $\angle EVF$.

For Exs. 16–24, GIVEN: *(G) general statement and (S) specific statement. If a valid conclusion follows logically, state it. When a conclusion does not follow, explain why.*

16. (G) The Egyptians put their knowledge of geometry to practical use.
    (S) The Egyptians knew about the 3–4–5 right triangle.
17. (G) Certain Greek philosophers developed deductive reasoning to a high degree of perfection.
    (S) Archimedes was a Greek philosopher.
18. (G) A few basic terms in our study are accepted without definition.
    (S) The set of elements common to two sets is the intersection of the sets.
19. (G) A postulate is accepted without proof.
    (S) The statement "The set of all elements of one or the other of two sets or of both is the union of the sets" is accepted without proof.
20. (G) An accepted theorem does not contradict a postulate or a definition.
    (S) The Pythagorean Theorem has always been included in geometry.
21. (G) The order of coordinates of points determines the order of their corresponding points.
    (S) The coordinate of A is 7, of E is 11, of G is 9.
22. (G) If equal numbers are added to equal numbers, the results are equal numbers.
    (S) $a = 3$; $b = 5$.
23. (G) Sides of an angle are rays.
    (S) The given figure includes $\angle GVH$.
24. (G) Two segments which have the same length are congruent.
    (S) $\overline{QR}$ is not congruent to $\overline{ST}$. NOTE: This is contrapositive.

25. (G) Two lines which intersect forming right angles are perpendicular.
(S) Lines $\overleftrightarrow{AB}$ and $\overleftrightarrow{CD}$ are perpendicular.

26. Many expressions of ideas play tricks on our logical reasoning. Many drawings play tricks on our habits of visualization. Try this optical illusion. Cover up the left half, then cover up the right half, then move the cover from one end to the other and describe the cause of the illusion.

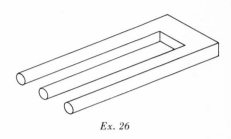

Ex. 26

3.8   Condensations of Reasons

In this text the reason for each step is a statement, not a title referring to a statement. But to write out all reasons in full is an unnecessary drudgery. Therefore, the reasons in formal proofs are condensations. Those from Chapters 1–3 which are needed in problems are given here. The others are assembled at the ends of the chapters in which they originate. Each statement is identified as a definition, postulate, property, or theorem. Also the condensed postulates are listed in Appendix A and the condensed theorems are in Appendix B, grouped by subject to show their relatedness.

As soon as a reason is used in writing a proof, it should be memorized.

The first three properties of equality—the reflexive, symmetric, and transitive properties—have so many applications that these are pointed out throughout the text. Whenever a relationship is introduced which is an application of one of these properties, it is labeled with the appropriate initial: (R), (S), or (T).

NOTE: In the properties the word "equals" stands for *equal numbers*. The symbol "=" represents verb forms *equal(s)* or *is (are) equal (to)* or adjective *equal.*

CONDENSATIONS

2 points, 1 line.   (Post 1)

To each point corresp 1 coord; to each coord corresp 1 point.   (Post 7)

Diff of coord = distance.   (Def)

To each ray corresp 1 coord; to each coord corresp 1 ray.   (Post 8)

Diff of coord = m∠.   (Def)

Number = itself.   (Property 1) (R)

First = second = third. Number sub for equal.   (Property 3) (T)

Equals + (×, −, ÷) equals are equals.   (Properties 4, 5)

Halves of equals =.   (Property 5)

Points separate segment into parts, sum lengths = length of whole.   (Thm 1)

Rays separate ∠ into parts, sum m = m whole.   (Thm 2)

Part = whole − part.   (Thms 1, 2)

chapter **4**

Angles
and Triangles

4.1 Congruence

Congruent figures play a very important part in our lives. Our system of mass production is based on congruence of plane and solid figures. Every automobile can have any part replaced by referring to specifications in a record. The accuracy of interchangeable parts makes possible the quantity and variety of machines that we have.

The word *congruent* comes from Latin meaning "together agree." Two geometric figures which have the same size and shape are **congruent**. One figure is **congruent to** the other. The symbol for congruent is ≅.

Thus two segments are congruent when they have the same size. All segments, being straight, have the same shape. They have the same size if they have the same length. This can be determined by comparing the two with each other by means of a compass, or with a third line such as a ruler having a scale of measure. Two segments are congruent when their lengths are the same number of a unit length.

DEFINITION   Two segments which have the same length are **congruent segments**.

All angles have the same characteristic makeup of two intersecting rays, and so their congruence depends upon their sizes. Relative size can be determined by comparing two angles with each other by construction, or with a protractor.

DEFINITION   Two angles which have the same measure are **congruent angles**.

COROLLARY   Expressions for the congruence of figures and the equality of their measures can be interchanged at will.

We can say that sides or angles of a triangle are equal only if they are identical. In $\triangle ABC$ and $\triangle ADC$ (Fig. 18) it is correct to write $\overline{AC} = \overline{AC}$, since $\overline{AC}$ is first a side of one triangle and then a side of the other. In like manner, $\angle CAB = \angle CAD$, each one an angle of a different triangle.

Fig. 18

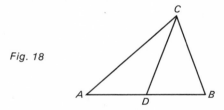

When the figures are not identical, we have separate symbols for equality of numbers and congruence of figures. In Fig. 18 we write for numerical measures: $CD = CB$ and m$\angle CDB$ = m$\angle CBD$ and for the corresponding congruence: $\overline{CD} \cong \overline{CB}$ and $\angle CDB \cong \angle CBD$.

We can determine the congruence of two triangles by means of correspondence. We match in pairs the vertices of one triangle with the vertices of the other. As a result, pairs of sides and pairs of angles correspond. In triangles ABC and DEF (Fig. 19), the one-to-one correspondence between the vertices is: $A \leftrightarrow D$, $B \leftrightarrow E$, $C \leftrightarrow F$. The symbol $\leftrightarrow$ is read "corresponds to." Then the corresponding sides and angles are:

$$\overline{AB} \leftrightarrow \overline{DE} \qquad \overline{BC} \leftrightarrow \overline{EF} \qquad \overline{CA} \leftrightarrow \overline{FD}$$

$$\angle A \leftrightarrow \angle D \qquad \angle B \leftrightarrow \angle E \qquad \angle C \leftrightarrow \angle F$$

and the correspondence between the triangles is $\triangle ABC \leftrightarrow \triangle DEF$. We name triangles by placing the vertices in order to indicate correspondence; we can locate all the corresponding parts from the names. If $\triangle RST \leftrightarrow \triangle UVW$, $\overline{RS} \leftrightarrow \overline{UV}$, $\overline{TR} \leftrightarrow \overline{WU}$, or $\angle S \leftrightarrow \angle V$. If the pairs of corresponding

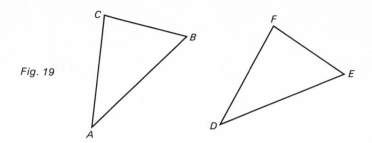

Fig. 19

sides and the pairs of corresponding angles are congruent, the correspondence becomes a congruence. To each point of one figure there
corresponds exactly one point of the second figure.

DEFINITION   Triangles, all of whose corresponding parts are congruent, are
congruent triangles.

CONVERSE   Corresponding parts of congruent triangles are congruent.

DEFINITION   Two polygons whose vertices can be paired so that corresponding parts — angles and sides — are congruent are **congruent polygons**.

4.2   Kinds of Angles and Triangles

DEFINITION   The union of two opposite rays with a common endpoint is a
straight angle. The two rays are collinear. The measure of a straight angle
is 180°. Abbreviation: st $\angle$.

DEFINITION   Two angles in one plane whose intersection is exactly one ray
between the two other rays are **adjacent angles**. One angle is **adjacent to**
the other.

DEFINITION   Two angles, the sum of whose measures is 180°, are **supplementary angles**. One is the **supplement of** the other or **supplementary
to** the other. Abbreviation: supp.

COROLLARY   Two adjacent angles whose noncommon sides form a straight
angle are **supplementary angles**.

CONVERSE   The sum of the measures of two supplementary angles is the
measure of one straight angle.

In Fig. 20, $\angle AVB$ is a straight angle, and $\angle AVC$ and $\angle CVB$ are adjacent
and supplementary. The angle EGF is also supplementary to $\angle CVB$.

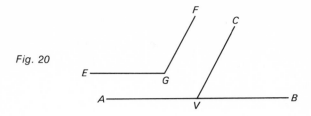

Fig. 20

DEFINITION An angle whose measure is 90° is a **right angle**. Abbreviation: rt ∠.

DEFINITION Two lines which intersect forming right angles are **perpendicular lines**. The symbol for perpendicular is ⊥.

COROLLARY The sides of a right angle are perpendicular.

NOTE: When the three terms *line*, *ray*, and *segment* may all be appropriate in a given usage, the word *line* is used.

Angle *EDG* (Fig. 21) is a right angle. The square at *D* is the symbol for a right angle. $\overline{DG} \perp \overline{EF}$. Also, ∠*FDG* is a right angle.

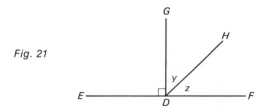

Fig. 21

DEFINITION Two angles, the sum of whose measures is 90°, are **complementary angles**. One is **complementary to** the other or **the complement of** the other. Abbreviation: comp.

COROLLARY Two adjacent angles whose noncommon sides form a right angle are **complementary angles**.

CONVERSE The sum of the measures of two complementary angles is the measure of one right angle.

In Fig. 21, ∠*y* is the complement of ∠*z*.

An angle whose measure is less than 90° is an **acute angle**. An angle whose measure is greater than 90° but less than 180° is an **obtuse angle**. An angle whose measure is greater than 180° but less than 360° is a **reflex angle**. In Fig. 21, ∠*HDF* is an acute angle and ∠*EDH* is an obtuse angle.

DEFINITION   Two angles with a common vertex whose sides are pairs of opposite rays are **vertical angles**. One angle is **vertical to** the other.

COROLLARY   Where two lines intersect, the pairs of nonadjacent angles formed are **vertical angles**.

In Fig. 22, ∠*s* is vertical to ∠*t* and ∠*u* is vertical to ∠*v*; ∠*s* is adjacent to ∠*u*, and ∠*s* is the supplement of ∠*u*.

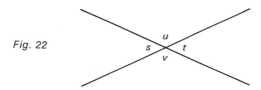

Fig. 22

A triangle, all of whose angles are acute, is an **acute triangle**. If one angle is a right angle, the triangle is a **right triangle**. An **obtuse triangle** has one obtuse angle. A triangle which has two sides congruent is an **isosceles triangle**. One which has no two sides congruent is **scalene**. If all three sides are congruent, it is an **equilateral triangle**. If all three angles are congruent, the triangle is **equiangular**.

In a triangle a side is **opposite** an angle of which it is not a side, and an angle is **opposite** the side of the triangle which is not a side of the angle. In a right triangle the side opposite the right angle is the **hypotenuse**. The sides which form the right angle are **legs**.

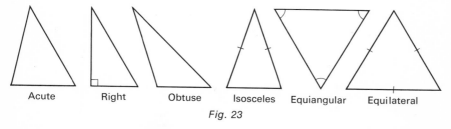

Acute   Right   Obtuse   Isosceles   Equiangular   Equilateral

Fig. 23

The triangles in Fig. 23 are named according to their characteristics, and typical marks indicate congruent sides and angles: a tick mark across the sides, an arc inside the angle, or a right angle square. The first three triangles are scalene.

EXERCISE 4.2

1. GIVEN: $\triangle ABC \leftrightarrow \triangle DEF$ with corresponding vertices in order. What part of the second triangle corresponds with each of the following in the first?

(a) $\angle ABC$ (b) $\angle A$

(c) $\angle C$ (d) Side $\overline{CA}$

(e) Side $\overline{BC}$ (f) Side $\overline{AB}$

(g) Point R (h) Segment $\overline{BQ}$

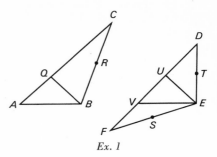

Ex. 1

2. GIVEN: $\overline{QU}$ containing points R, S, and T, with coordinates as shown. State whether each of the following is true or false.

Ex. 2

Q	R	S	T	U
0	6	12	21	24

(a) $QR = RS$ (b) $SU = \overline{QS}$ (c) $ST = SU$ (d) $\overline{QR} = \overline{RS}$

(e) $SU \cong \overline{QS}$ (f) $\overline{QR} \cong \overline{RS}$ (g) $\overline{QS} \cong \overline{SQ}$ (h) $ST + TU = SU$

(i) $SU = 2RS$ (j) $QR = \frac{1}{2}SU$ (k) $UT + TS = US$ (l) $SU - TU = ST$

3. GIVEN: $\overleftrightarrow{AB}$ and $\overleftrightarrow{EF}$ intersect at C; $\overrightarrow{CD} \perp \overleftrightarrow{AB}$; $m\angle BCF = 25°$. Identify the relationship between the angles in each of the following pairs.

(a) $\angle ECA$ and $\angle FCB$

(b) $\angle ACE$ and $\angle ECD$

(c) $\angle BCF$ and $\angle FCA$

(d) $\angle ECD$ and $\angle DCB$

(e) $\angle ECD$ and $\angle BCF$

4. Find the measure of each angle as follows:

(a) $m\angle DCF$ (b) $m\angle ACD$

(c) $m\angle ACE$ (d) $m\angle ECD$

(e) $m\angle FCA$ (f) $m\angle ECF$

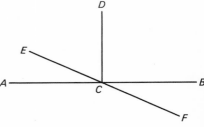

Exs. 3, 4

5. In the figure $\overline{ZV} \perp \overline{ZX}$. Name parts of the figure as follows:

(a) A line   (b) A ray

(c) A straight angle

(d) An obtuse angle

(e) A right angle

(f) An acute angle

(g) Two adjacent angles

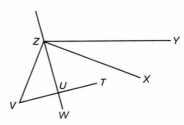

Ex. 5

(h) Two supplementary angles
(i) Two complementary angles
(j) Two vertical angles
(k) Three collinear points

6. In the figure the measure of each angle is given. Name:

(a) An angle adjacent to ∠CVD
(b) An angle nonadjacent to ∠AVE
(c) The complement of ∠AVB
(d) The supplement of ∠AVE

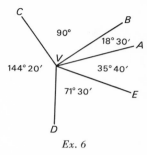

Ex. 6

7. Find the number of degrees in each of the following:

(a) The complement of 33° 50′   **(b)** The complement of 68° 25′ 30″
(c) The supplement of 110° 428   **(d)** The supplement of 54° 16′ 20″
(e) The angle which is twice its complement
(f) The angle which is one fourth its supplement
(g) The angle which is the same size as its complement

4.3 Properties Applied to Figures

There are relationships in geometry which are theoretical and go beyond the obvious, but we do not encounter them in an elementary course. Here two figures are compared in relations that are apparent enough so that a student is tempted to say: "This is so obvious; why do we have to prove it?" But one of our responsibilities is to see that appearances are checked with minute accuracy through a series of logical steps.

   In this course we touch only a few of the many relationships which are part of the geometric system. We relate segments, angles, and arcs and simple geometric figures composed of them. Two figures are compared by means of the correspondence of their parts. Conversely, if the figures have definite correspondence, then their parts do.

   The relating of sizes of figures is, whether expressed or implied, the relating of their measures. Segments are geometric figures; their lengths are numerical quantities. When we relate halves or doubles of congruent angles, for instance, it is because we have already recognized that halves or doubles of their measures are equal. The same reasoning is used when adding "congruent" segments or angles. We add, subtract, multiply, or divide measures. We should not say that a segment equals the sum of its parts. It is numerical measures that are terms of the equation. However, we do readily alternate between equality of measures and congruence of figures without writing the transition step.

THEOREM 4 **If a triangle is congruent to a second triangle and the second is congruent to a third triangle, then the first is congruent to the third.** (T)

GIVEN: $\triangle RST \cong \triangle UVW$ and $\triangle UVW \cong \triangle XYZ$ with consecutive vertices corresponding.

PROVE: $\triangle RST \cong \triangle XYZ$.

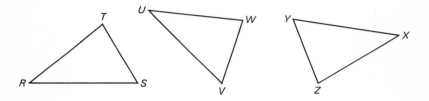

1. $\triangle RST \cong \triangle UVW$; $\triangle UVW \cong \triangle XYZ$.	1. Given.
2. $\overline{RS} \cong \overline{UV}$; $\overline{UV} \cong \overline{XY}$; $\overline{ST} \cong \overline{VW}$; $\overline{VW} \cong \overline{YZ}$; $\overline{TR} \cong \overline{WU}$; $\overline{WU} \cong \overline{ZX}$.	2. Corresp parts $\cong$ ⧍ $\cong$.
3. $RS = UV = XY$; $ST = VW = YZ$; $TR = WU = ZX$.	3. $\cong$ segments have the same m. First = second = third.
4. $\angle R \cong \angle U$; $\angle U \cong \angle X$; $\angle S \cong \angle V$; $\angle V \cong \angle Y$; $\angle T \cong \angle W$; $\angle W \cong \angle Z$.	4. Reason 2.
5. $m\angle R = m\angle U = m\angle X$; $m\angle S = m\angle V = m\angle Y$; $m\angle T = m\angle W = m\angle Z$.	5. $\cong$ ⧍ have the same m. First = second = third.
6. $\triangle RST \cong \triangle XYZ$.	6. All corresp parts $\cong$, ⧍ $\cong$.

COROLLARY 4.1 **A triangle is congruent to itself.** (R)

COROLLARY 4.2 **If a triangle is congruent to a second triangle, then the second is congruent to the first.** (S)

COROLLARY 4.3 **A segment is congruent to itself.** (R)

Properties of Equality Applied to Segments, Angles, and Triangles

	Numbers	*Segments*	*Angles*	*Triangles*
Reflexive	$a = a$	$\overline{AB} \cong \overline{AB}$	$\angle w \cong \angle w$	$\triangle QRS \cong \triangle QRS$
Symmetric	$a = b$: $b = a$	$\overline{AB} \cong \overline{CD}$: $\overline{CD} \cong \overline{AB}$	$\angle w \cong \angle x$: $\angle x \cong \angle w$	$\triangle QRS \cong \triangle TUV$: $\triangle TUV \cong \triangle QRS$
Transitive	$a = b$; $b = c$: $a = c$	$\overline{AB} \cong \overline{CD}$; $\overline{CD} \cong \overline{EF}$: $\overline{AB} \cong \overline{EF}$	$\angle w \cong \angle x$; $\angle x \cong \angle y$: $\angle w \cong \angle y$	$\triangle MNP \cong \triangle QRS$, $\triangle QRS \cong \triangle TUV$: $\triangle MNP \cong \triangle TUV$
Addition	$d = e$; $f = g$: $d + f = e + g$ $d - f = e - g$	$\overline{AB} \cong \overline{CD}$; $\overline{EF} \cong \overline{GH}$: $AB + EF = CD + GH$ $EF - AB = GH - CD$	$\angle w \cong \angle x$; $\angle y \cong \angle z$: $m\angle w + m\angle y = m\angle x + m\angle z$ $m\angle w - m\angle y = m\angle x - m\angle z$	
Multiplication	$d = e$; $f = g$: $3d = 3e$ $\dfrac{f}{2} = \dfrac{g}{2}$	$\overline{AB} \cong \overline{CD}$; $\overline{EF} \cong \overline{GH}$: $3AB = 3CD$ $\dfrac{EF}{2} = \dfrac{GH}{2}$	$\angle w \cong \angle x$; $\angle y \cong \angle z$: $3m\angle w = 3m\angle x$ $\dfrac{m\angle y}{2} = \dfrac{m\angle z}{2}$	

COROLLARY 4.4 If a segment is congruent to a second segment, then the second is congruent to the first. (S)

COROLLARY 4.5 If a segment is congruent to a second segment and the second is congruent to a third segment, then the first is congruent to the third. (T)

COROLLARY 4.6 An angle is congruent to itself. (R)

COROLLARY 4.7 If an angle is congruent to a second angle, then the second is congruent to the first. (S)

COROLLARY 4.8 If an angle is congruent to a second angle and the second is congruent to a third angle, then the first is congruent to the third. (T)

COROLLARY 4.9 Doubles or halves of congruent segments or angles are congruent.

COROLLARY 4.10 The name of a figure may be substituted for the name of another to which it is congruent.

The properties of equality of numbers as applied to segments, angles, and triangles are summarized in the preceding table. Note that we do not add or multiply triangular figures.

4.4 Bisectors

Theorem 1 states that "Points between the ends of a segment separate it into parts the sum of whose lengths equals the length of the whole." In every segment there is one so located that the two parts have equal length.

> DEFINITIONS A point of a segment which separates it into two segments of the same length is a **midpoint**. A point or line which separates a segment into two congruent segments **bisects** the given segment. It is a **bisector**.

> CONVERSE A midpoint or bisector separates a segment into two congruent halves.

> DEFINITION Two equal parts of a whole are **halves**. Two congruent parts of a figure are **halves**.

A ray in an angle between its sides, sharing a common endpoint with the sides, divides the angle into two parts. A certain one of these rays causes the parts to have the same measure.

DEFINITION   A ray which separates an angle into two congruent angles **bisects** the given angle. It is a **bisector**.

CONVERSE   A bisector separates an angle into two congruent halves.

The bisector of a segment or an angle may be a ray, a segment, or a line. If C in Fig. 24(a) is the midpoint of $\overline{AB}$, then any line, such as l, passing through C bisects the segment. If $\overrightarrow{DG}$ separates $\angle EDF$ in Fig. 24(b) such that m$\angle EDG$ = m$\angle FDG$, then $\overrightarrow{DG}$ is the angle bisector and $\angle EDG \cong \angle FDG$.

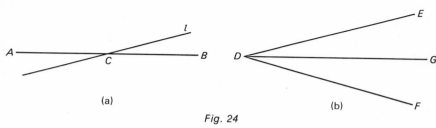

(a)

(b)

Fig. 24

EXERCISE 4.4

In Exs. 1–8, indicate which one of the statements is not a valid conclusion from the GIVEN. *Practice visualizing the relations without drawing the figures.*

1. GIVEN: $\overrightarrow{AB} \perp \overrightarrow{AC}$; $\overrightarrow{AD}$ is between $\overrightarrow{AB}$ and $\overrightarrow{AC}$.

   (a) $\angle BAC$ is a rt $\angle$.   (b) $\angle BAD$ comp $\angle DAC$.
   (c) $\overrightarrow{AD} \perp \overrightarrow{AC}$ (d) m$\angle BAD$ + m$\angle DAC$ = 90°.

2. GIVEN: $\overrightarrow{EG}$ contains point F; $\overrightarrow{FH}$ is a ray not contained in $\overleftrightarrow{EG}$.

   (a) $\angle EFG$ is a st $\angle$.   (b) m$\angle EFH$ + m$\angle HFG$ = 180°.
   (c) $\angle EFH$ supp $\angle HFG$.   (d) $\angle HFG$ is a rt $\angle$.

3. GIVEN: $\angle QRS$ is a st $\angle$; $\angle QRT$ is a rt $\angle$; $\overrightarrow{RU}$ is between $\overrightarrow{RQ}$ and $\overrightarrow{RT}$.

   (a) $\angle QRU$ is an acute $\angle$.   (b) $\angle URT$ is an obtuse $\angle$.
   (c) $\angle URS$ is an obtuse $\angle$.   (d) $\overrightarrow{RT} \perp \overleftrightarrow{QS}$.

4. GIVEN: $\overleftrightarrow{AB}$ and $\overleftrightarrow{CD}$ intersect at X.

   (a) $\angle AXC$ is vertical to $\angle BXD$.   (b) $\angle BXD$ supp $\angle CXB$.
   (c) $\angle AXD$ is a st $\angle$.   (d) $\angle DXA$ is adjacent to $\angle CXA$.

5. GIVEN: $\overrightarrow{VG}$ bisects $\angle EVF$.

(a) $\angle EVG$ comp $\angle GVF$. (b) $m\angle EVG = \frac{1}{2}m\angle EVF$.

(c) $m\angle EVG = m\angle GVF$. (d) $m\angle EVG + m\angle GVF = m\angle EVF$.

6. GIVEN: $\overleftrightarrow{QR}$ bisects $\overline{ST}$ at X.

(a) $QX = XR$. (b) $\overline{SX} \cong \overline{XT}$.

(c) $SX = \frac{1}{2}ST$. (d) $SX + XT = ST$.

7. GIVEN: Scalene $\triangle ABC \cong \triangle DEF$. Their vertices are corresponding in order.

(a) $\overline{AB} \cong \overline{DE}$. (b) $m\angle C = m\angle F$.

(c) $\overline{CA}$ corresponds to $\overline{FD}$. (d) $\angle B \cong \angle D$.

8. GIVEN: $\angle x \cong \angle y$; $\angle y \cong \angle z$.

(a) $\angle x \cong \angle x$. (b) $2m\angle z = 2m\angle x$.

(c) $\angle x \cong \angle z$. (d) $m\angle x + m\angle y = m\angle z$.

In Exs. 9–21, the statement in the left column is given and that in the right column is proved in one step. State the reason for the step.

Exs. 9–21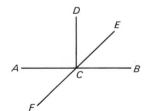

9. $\angle ACD \cong \angle DCB$. $m\angle ACD = m\angle DCB$.

10. C is a point of $\overline{AB}$. $\angle ACB$ is a st $\angle$.

11. $\overrightarrow{CE}$ intersects $\overline{AB}$ at C. $\angle ACE$ is adjacent to $\angle ECB$.

12. $\angle ACF$ supp $\angle FCB$. $m\angle ACF + m\angle FCB = 180°$.

13. $\angle DCB$ is a rt $\angle$. $\overline{CD} \perp \overline{AB}$.

14. $\overline{CD} \perp \overline{AB}$. $\angle DCB$ is a rt $\angle$.

15. $m\angle BCD = 90°$; $\overrightarrow{CE}$ between $\overrightarrow{CD}$ and $\overrightarrow{CB}$. $\angle DCE$ comp $\angle BCE$.

16. $\overline{FE}$ intersects $\overline{AB}$ at C. $\angle ACF$ is vertical to $\angle BCE$.

17. $\angle ACF \cong \angle BCE$; $\angle BCE \cong \angle DCE$. $\angle ACF \cong \angle DCE$.

18. $CE = \frac{1}{2}FE$; $CB = \frac{1}{2}AB$; $\overline{FE} \cong \overline{AB}$. $\overline{CE} \cong \overline{CB}$.

19. $\angle BCE$ comp $\angle DCE$; $\angle ACF \cong \angle BCE$. $\angle ACF$ comp $\angle DCE$.

20. C is midpoint of $\overline{AB}$. $\overline{AC} \cong \overline{CB}$.

21. $\angle DCE \cong \angle BCE$. CE bisects $\angle BCD$.

4.5   Relations of Angles

THEOREM 5   **Angles which are supplements of congruent angles are congruent.**

GIVEN: $\angle x$ supp $\angle w$; $\angle y$ supp $\angle z$; $\angle w \cong \angle z$.

PROVE: $\angle x \cong \angle y$.

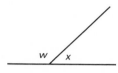 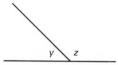

1. $\angle x$ supp $\angle w$; $\angle y$ supp $\angle z$; $\angle w \cong \angle z$.	1. Given.
2. $m\angle x + m\angle w = 180°$; $m\angle y + m\angle z = 180°$.	2. Sum m supp $\angle s = 180°$.
3. $m\angle x + m\angle w = m\angle y + m\angle z$.	3. First = second = third.
4. $m\angle w =$ $m\angle z$.	4. $\cong \angle s$ have same m.
5. $m\angle x$ $= m\angle y$.	5. Equals − equals are equals.
6. $\angle x$ $\cong$ $\angle y$.	6. $\angle s$ with same m $\cong$.

COROLLARY 5.1   **Angles which are supplements of the same angle are congruent.**

THEOREM 6   **Angles which are complements of congruent angles are congruent.**

GIVEN: $\angle s$ comp $\angle t$; $\angle u$ comp $\angle v$; $\angle t \cong \angle v$.

PROVE: $\angle s \cong \angle u$.

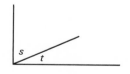 

The proof is left to the student.

COROLLARY 6.1   **Angles which are complements of the same angle are congruent.**

THEOREM 7   Angles which are vertical angles are congruent.

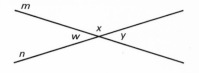

GIVEN: Intersecting lines *m* and *n* forming vertical ∡ *w* and *y*.

PROVE: ∠*w* ≅ ∠*y*.

1. ∠*w* is vertical to ∠*y*.
2. m∠*w* + m∠*x* = 180°; m∠*y* + m∠*z* = 180°.
3. ∠*w* supp ∠*x*; ∠*y* supp ∠*x*.
4. ∠*w* ≅ ∠*y*.

1. Given.
2. Rays separate ∠ into parts: sum m = m whole.
3. ∡ sum m = 180° are supp.
4. Supp same ∠ ≅.

In the two proofs presented above the converse statements of a definition are used. In Theorem 5 the supplements were given and "the sum of the measures of supplementary angles = 180°" resulted as the reason for step 2. In Theorem 7 the sum of the measures was found first and then the fact of supplements followed; that is, the reason for step 3 began with the sum of the measures and progressed to supplementary angles. A statement and its converse are reasons for two different kinds of steps. In each case the predicate of the reason matched the predicate of its step. The verb *equals* and the verb *is* are interchangeable.

THEOREM 8   Two lines which intersect forming congruent adjacent angles are perpendicular.

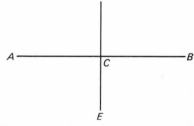

GIVEN: $\overleftrightarrow{AB}$ and $\overleftrightarrow{DE}$ intersect at *C*; ∠*ACD* ≅ ∠*BCD*.

PROVE: $\overleftrightarrow{DE}$ ⊥ $\overleftrightarrow{AB}$.

1. ∠*ACD* ≅ ∠*BCD*.
2. ∠*ACB* is a st ∠ of 180°.

3. m∠*ACD* + m∠*BCD* = 180°.

4. m∠*ACD* = m∠*BCD*.
5. 2m∠*ACD* = 180°.
6. m∠*ACD* = 90°.
7. $\overleftrightarrow{DE}$ ⊥ $\overleftrightarrow{AB}$.

1. Given.
2. Union opposite rays with common endpoint is a st ∠ of 180°.
3. Rays separate ∠ into parts; sum m = m whole.
4. ≅ ∡ have same m.
5. Number sub for equal.
6. Equals × equals are equals.
7. Sides of 90° ∠ ⊥.

COROLLARY 8.1 **Two lines which intersect forming congruent supplementary angles are perpendicular.**

COROLLARY 8.2 **The supplement of a right angle is a right angle.**

COROLLARY 8.3 **Two angles which are congruent and supplementary are right angles.**

COROLLARY 8.4 **The measure of a straight angle is two times the measure of a right angle; the measure of a right angle is half the measure of a straight angle.**

COROLLARY 8.5 **Two lines which intersect forming one right angle form four right angles.**

There are several variations of the way in which a proof can be organized. Each step in the process may be the antecedent for several consequences. We have a choice which is directed both by the hypothesis from which the proof is launched and by the conclusion toward which it is aimed. The proof eventually chosen must be a smooth consistent course from the hypothesis to the conclusion. Each step grows out of—is implied by—what precedes it and is pointed in the direction of the final goal.

Some steps are omitted in a usual proof, accepted without being written. They are often steps of definition. For instance, in Theorem 8, between steps 6 and 7 there could be a step: "$\overrightarrow{CD}$ and $\overrightarrow{CA}$ are sides of $\angle ACD$." Or, in a less rigorous proof, step 2 might be omitted without destroying the sequence.

Whatever the method of proof, all the reasons following GIVEN are obtained from the stock of reasons already accepted. We rely upon any statement in the stock which contributes to our progress, choosing the sequence which seems the most satisfactory.

It is possible to use the topic of a reason instead of the expression in sentence form. The topic matches the correct general statement with the step but does not distinguish between a proposition and the converse thereof, only one of which is the correct reason for a given step. Furthermore, it does not make clear the smooth flow of thought from the first step to the last. In the second proof of Ex. 2 (below) the reason, "Two angles the sum of whose measures equals the measure of a right angle are complementary," expresses more meaning than, "Definition of complementary angles." It shows its hypothesis emerging right out of steps 2 and 3, and its conclusion matching step 4.

The choosing of the correct reason for each step is somewhat of an art, requiring considerable practice. Usually there is one reason superior to all others as support for the logic which allows for the chosen step. But experience develops ability and insight grows with each attempt.

In each of the illustrative exercises that follow, a **plan** is written. It is a brief informal discussion of the requirements for the proof by one method.

EXERCISE 4.5

1. GIVEN: $AB = FG$; $CD = GH$; B the midpoint of $\overline{AC}$; F the midpoint of $\overline{EG}$.

PROVE: $AD = EH$.

Ex. 1

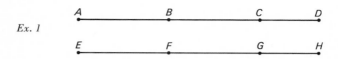

Solution

Plan: The separate parts constitute the whole of each segment. If corresponding parts have equal lengths, the whole segments have equal lengths.

1. B is the midpoint of $\overline{AC}$; F is the midpoint of $\overline{EG}$.	1. Given.
2. $AB = BC$; $EF = FG$.	2. Midpoint separates segment into 2 ≅ halves of equal measure.
3. $AB = FG$.	3. Given.
4. $BC = EF$.	4. First = second = third = fourth.
5. $CD = GH$.	5. Given.
6. $AB + BC + CD = AD$; $EF + FG + GH = EH$.	6. Points separate segment into parts; sum lengths = length of whole.
7. $AD = EH$.	7. Equals + equals are equals.

A simple chart of the sequence of steps shows how each one receives from what has gone before and contributes to what follows. Each step taken from the GIVEN begins a new line.

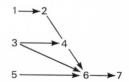

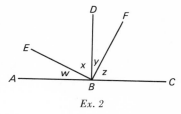

Ex. 2

2. GIVEN: $\overrightarrow{BD} \perp \overleftrightarrow{AC}$; rays $\overrightarrow{BE}$ and
$\overrightarrow{BF}$; $\angle w \cong \angle y$.
PROVE: $\angle x \cong \angle z$.

Often there are "two ways around the bush" to formulate a proof.
When two good methods are available, we have free choice between
them.

First Solution

Plan: If m$\angle w$ and m$\angle y$ are subtracted from 90°, the measures
remaining are m$\angle x$ and m$\angle z$.

1. $\overrightarrow{BD} \perp \overleftrightarrow{AC}$, $\angle w \cong \angle y$.	1. Given.
2. $\angle ABD$ is a rt $\angle$; $\angle CBD$ is a rt $\angle$.	2. $\perp$ lines form rt $\angle\!s$.
3. m$\angle w$ + m$\angle x = 90°$; m$\angle y$ + m$\angle z = 90°$.	3. Rays separate $\angle$ into parts, sum m = m whole.
4. m$\angle w$ + m$\angle x$ = m$\angle y$ + m$\angle z$.	4. First = second = third.
5. m$\angle w$ = m$\angle y$.	5. $\cong$ $\angle\!s$ have same m.
6. m$\angle x$ = m$\angle z$.	6. Equals − equals are equals.
7. $\angle x \cong$ $\angle z$.	7. $\angle\!s$ with same m $\cong$.

Second Solution

Plan: $\angle x$ and $\angle z$ are complements of angles which are congruent.

1. $\overrightarrow{BD} \perp \overleftrightarrow{AC}$.	1. Given.
2. $\angle ABD$ and $\angle CBD$ are rt $\angle\!s$.	2. $\perp$ lines form rt $\angle\!s$.
3. m$\angle w$ + m$\angle x$ = m$\angle ABD$; m$\angle y$ + m$\angle z$ = m$\angle CBD$.	3. Rays separate $\angle$ into parts; sum m = m whole.
4. $\angle w$ comp $\angle x$; $\angle y$ comp $\angle z$.	4. $\angle\!s$ sum m = m rt $\angle$ are comp.
5. $\angle w \cong \angle y$.	5. Given.
6. $\angle x \cong \angle z$.	6. Comp $\cong$ $\angle\!s$ $\cong$.

3. Supply the reason for each of the steps in the proof.

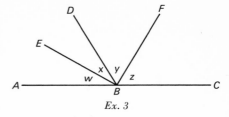

GIVEN: $\overrightarrow{BD}$ intersects $\overleftrightarrow{AC}$ at B;
$\overrightarrow{BE}$ bisects $\angle ABD$; $\overrightarrow{BF}$
bisects $\angle DBC$.
PROVE: $\overrightarrow{BE} \perp \overrightarrow{BF}$.

Ex. 3

Plan: The sum of the measures of the four angles is 180°. If the sum of the two in $\angle EBF$ is 90°, then $\overrightarrow{BE} \perp \overrightarrow{BF}$.

1. $\overrightarrow{BE}$ bisects $\angle ABD$; $\overrightarrow{BF}$ bisects $\angle DBC$.
2. $m\angle w = m\angle x$; $m\angle y = m\angle z$.
3. $m\angle w + m\angle x + m\angle y + m\angle z = 180°$.
4. $m\angle x + m\angle x + m\angle y + m\angle y = 180°$.
5. $2m\angle x + 2m\angle y = 180°$.
6. $m\angle x + m\angle y = 90°$.
7. $m\angle x + m\angle y = m\angle EBF$.
8. $\angle EBF$ is a rt $\angle$.
9. $\overrightarrow{BE} \perp \overrightarrow{BF}$.

4. GIVEN: $\overline{AB}$ and $\overline{CD}$ intersect at H;
$AH = CH$; $BH = DH$.
PROVE: $AB = CD$.

5. GIVEN: $\overline{AB}$ and $\overline{CD}$ intersect at H;
$AB = CD$; $AH = CH$.
PROVE: $BH = DH$.

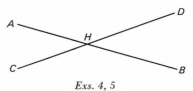

Exs. 4, 5

6. GIVEN: $m\angle RST = m\angle XWV$:
$m\angle UST = m\angle YWV$.
PROVE: $m\angle RSU = m\angle XWY$.

7. GIVEN: $m\angle RSU = m\angle XWY$:
$m\angle UST = m\angle YWV$.
PROVE: $m\angle RST = m\angle XWV$.

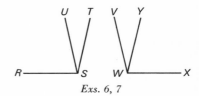

Exs. 6, 7

8. GIVEN: $\angle ABE$ supp $\angle DCF$.
PROVE: $\angle ABE \cong \angle DCG$.

9. GIVEN: $\angle EBC \cong \angle FCD$.
PROVE: $\angle EBC$ supp $\angle FCB$.

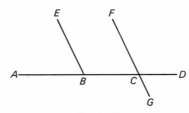

Exs. 8, 9

10. **GIVEN:** $\overleftrightarrow{EF}$ and $\overleftrightarrow{CD}$ intersect at X; $\overrightarrow{AB}$ bisects $\angle EXC$.
    PROVE: $\overrightarrow{AB}$ bisects $\angle DXF$.

11. **GIVEN:** $\overleftrightarrow{EF}$ and $\overleftrightarrow{CD}$ intersect at X; $\angle s \cong \angle u$.
    PROVE: $\angle t \cong \angle v$.

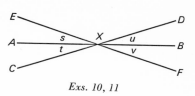

Exs. 10, 11

12. **GIVEN:** Intersecting lines l, m, and n; $m\angle v + m\angle x = 180°$.
    PROVE: $m\angle w = m\angle x$.

13. **GIVEN:** Intersecting lines l, m, and n; $\angle u \cong \angle z$.
    PROVE: $\angle w \cong \angle x$.

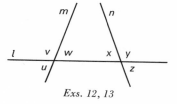

Exs. 12, 13

14. **GIVEN:** $\overrightarrow{BD}$ and $\overrightarrow{BE}$ intersect $\overleftrightarrow{AC}$ at B; $\angle y$ is rt $\angle$.
    PROVE: $\angle x$ comp $\angle z$.

15. **GIVEN:** $\overrightarrow{BD}$ and $\overrightarrow{BE}$ intersect $\overleftrightarrow{AC}$ at B; $\angle x$ comp $\angle z$.
    PROVE: $\angle y$ is a rt $\angle$.

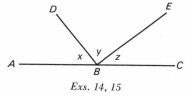

Exs. 14, 15

16. **GIVEN:** $\overline{BA} \perp \overline{BC}$; $\overline{FE} \perp \overline{FG}$; $m\angle x = m\angle y$.
    PROVE: $m\angle w = m\angle z$.

17. **GIVEN:** $\overline{BA} \perp \overline{BC}$; $\angle EFG$; $\angle w \cong \angle z$; $\angle x \cong \angle y$.
    PROVE: $\overline{FE} \perp \overline{FG}$.

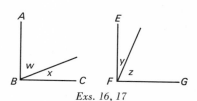

Exs. 16, 17

18. **GIVEN:** $\overrightarrow{RV}$, $\overrightarrow{RT}$, $\overrightarrow{RU}$ intersect $\overleftrightarrow{QS}$ at R; $\angle w \cong \angle y$; $\angle x \cong \angle z$.
    PROVE: $\overrightarrow{RT} \perp \overleftrightarrow{QS}$.

19. **GIVEN:** $\overrightarrow{RT} \perp \overleftrightarrow{QS}$ at R; $\overrightarrow{RV} \perp \overrightarrow{RU}$.
    PROVE: $\angle x \cong \angle z$.

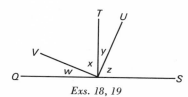

Exs. 18, 19

4.6   Construction

Some proofs require extra lines not given in the hypothesis. The figures do not contain enough material to allow for a proof. We are free to draw these **auxiliary lines** as necessary. Only two rules are mandatory: (1) an auxiliary line does not change any requirement of the hypothesis, and (2) the conditions which determine an auxiliary line are minimum. Usually the line contains one known point and satisfies only one other condition.

Auxiliary lines are drawn with the techniques of construction. Compass marks may be shown or not, but are implied with each drawing. The new line is an authentic part of each figure because the validity of its construction is proved by a postulate or theorem containing the term *exactly one* or *every*. The theorem is used as a reason for a step which calls for construction. If many students are given the same figure and construct an auxiliary line according to the same directions, all will produce the same line. There is *exactly one* line which satisfies the conditions of the construction.

Since the time of Greek geometry the accepted tools for construction were only a straightedge and a compass. We shall be limited to these. We can use a ruler and a protractor if figures of measured size are required, but not to produce figures which illustrate general cases. The setting between points of a compass is found from points of a figure or from numbers on a ruler. It then can mark off any number of points at a distance equal to the given distance. To complete any figure, a line may be extended indefinitely in either direction.

Postulate 9   **With a given point as center and a given length of radius exactly one circle can be drawn in one plane.**

Corollary   **All radii of a circle are congruent.**

DEFINITION   Circles which have congruent radii are **congruent circles**.

CONVERSE   All radii of congruent circles are congruent radii.

Construction 1   *Construct a segment congruent to a given segment.*

GIVEN: Segment $\overline{EF}$; line m.

CONSTRUCT: Segment $\overline{AB} \cong \overline{EF}$.

Let A be a point of line m. With A as a center and with length of radius $=$ EF, construct an arc which intersects m at B. $\overline{AB}$ is the required segment.

This process may be duplicated to give any multiple of the unit length.

THEOREM 9   From a point of a line there is exactly one point of each ray such that the length of the segment from the given point is a constant.

GIVEN: Line m with point A; segment $\overline{EF}$ whose length is k units.

PROVE: There is exactly one point of each ray such that its distance from $A = k$.

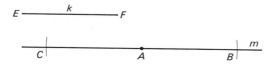

Let the coordinate of A be a. There is exactly one number which equals $a + k$ and one number $a - k$. There is exactly one point whose coordinate is $a + k$ and one point whose coordinate is $a - k$. Construct them. Let the points be B and C, respectively. B is the only point of $\overrightarrow{AB}$ whose distance from $A = k$, and C is the only point of $\overrightarrow{AC}$ whose distance from $A = k$; to every coord 1 point, diff $=$ distance. (NOTE: For uniqueness of numbers see Appendix C.)

COROLLARY 9.1   From a point of a line there is exactly one point of each ray such that the segment determined by the two points is congruent to a given segment.

COROLLARY 9.2   From a point of a line there is exactly one point of each ray such that the distance from the given point is a given multiple of a given distance measure.

COROLLARY 9.3   A segment has exactly one midpoint.

Construction 2   *Construct an angle congruent to a given angle.*

GIVEN: $\angle ABC$; line m.

CONSTRUCT: $\angle DEF$ with one side on m and $\cong \angle ABC$.

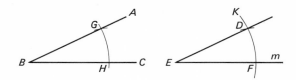

With B as a center and any convenient radius, construct an arc intersecting $\overrightarrow{BA}$ at G and $\overrightarrow{BC}$ at H. Let E be a point of m. With E as a center and a radius $= BH$, construct arc $\overset{\frown}{FK}$ intersecting m at F. With F as a center and radius $= HG$, construct an arc intersecting $\overset{\frown}{FK}$ at D. Construct $\overrightarrow{ED}$. $\angle DEF$ is the required angle.

This process may be duplicated to give any multiple of $m\angle ABC$. To each angle there corresponds a unique positive real number which is its measure.

THEOREM 10   **On each side of a given ray there is exactly one ray in one plane having a common endpoint with the given ray such that the measure of the angle formed by the rays is a constant.**

GIVEN: Line m; $\angle ABC$ whose measure is k units.

PROVE: There is exactly one ray on each side of m such that the measure of the angle $= k$.

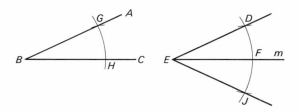

Let the ray coordinate of $\overrightarrow{EF}$ be a. There is exactly one ray whose coordinate is $a + k$ and one ray whose coordinate is $a - k$. Construct them. Let the rays be $\overrightarrow{ED}$ and $\overrightarrow{EJ}$, respectively. $\overrightarrow{ED}$ is the only ray on one side of $\overrightarrow{EF}$ such that $m\angle FED = k$, and $\overrightarrow{EJ}$ is the only ray on the other side of $\overrightarrow{EF}$ such that $m\angle FEJ = k$; to each coord corresp 1 ray, diff $= m\angle$.

COROLLARY 10.1 On each side of a given ray there is exactly one ray having a common endpoint with the given ray such that the angle formed by the two rays is congruent to the given angle.

COROLLARY 10.2 On each side of a given ray there is exactly one ray having a common endpoint with the given ray such that the measure of the angle formed by the two rays is a given multiple of the given measure.

EXERCISE 4.6

1. GIVEN: Draw segment a, segment b longer than a; $\angle C$, $\angle D$ greater than $\angle C$. Showing the arcs of construction, construct:

   (a) A segment whose length $= a + b$
   (b) A segment whose length $= b - a$
   (c) A segment whose length $= 2a - b$
   (d) An angle whose measure $= \mathrm{m}\angle D - \mathrm{m}\angle C$
   (e) An angle whose measure $= \mathrm{m}\angle D + \mathrm{m}\angle C$
   (f) An angle whose measure is $2\mathrm{m}\angle C$
   (g) A triangle in which a and b are sides of $\angle C$
   (h) A triangle in which $\angle C$ and $\angle D$ are at the ends of side b

2. Construct triangles with sides of the given lengths:

   (a) 2, 2, and 3 inches   (b) $1\frac{1}{2}$, 2, and $2\frac{1}{2}$ inches
   (c) $1\frac{1}{2}$, 2, and 3 inches   (d) $1\frac{1}{2}$, 2, and $3\frac{1}{2}$ inches

4.7   Congruence of Triangles

Before proving theorems of triangles, we need another postulate. When there is a one-to-one correspondence between the vertices of two triangles, Postulate 7 leads to proving corresponding sides congruent. But in order to be certain that angles are congruent, we adopt the following postulate. With this we can prove that two triangles are congruent if other sets of three of their corresponding parts are congruent.

Postulate 10   **If two triangles have two sides and the included angle of one congruent to the corresponding parts of the other, then the triangles are congruent.**   (SAS $\cong$ SAS)

The side of a triangle which is a common side of two angles is **included** between the two angles. An angle formed by two sides is **in-**

cluded between the sides. A side which does not include a given angle is **opposite to** the angle, and the angle is **opposite** to the side. In $\triangle RST$, $\angle S$ is included between $\overline{SR}$ and $\overline{ST}$; side $\overline{TR}$ is included between $\angle T$ and $\angle R$: $\angle S$ is opposite to $\overline{RT}$; side $\overline{RS}$ is opposite to $\angle T$ (Fig. 25).

Fig. 25

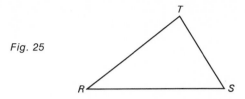

THEOREM 11 If two triangles have two angles and the included side of one congruent to the corresponding parts of the other, then the triangles are congruent.   (ASA $\cong$ ASA)

GIVEN: $\triangle ABC$ and $\triangle DEF$; $\angle CAB \cong \angle FDE$; $\overline{AB} \cong \overline{DE}$; $\angle ABC \cong \angle DEF$.

PROVE: $\triangle ABC \cong \triangle DEF$.

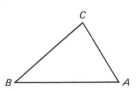
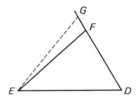

1. $\angle CAB \cong \angle FDE$.	1. Given.
2. If $\overline{DF}$ is not $\cong \overline{AC}$, there is a point G on $\overrightarrow{DF}$ such that $\overline{AC} \cong \overline{DG}$. Construct it.	2. 1 point, segment $\cong$ segment.
3. Draw $\overline{EG}$.	3. 2 points, 1 line.
4. In $\triangle ABC$ and $\triangle DEG$, $\overline{AB} \cong \overline{DE}$; $\angle CAB \cong \angle GDE$.	4. Given.
5. $\triangle ABC \cong \triangle DEG$.	5. SAS $\cong$ SAS.
6. $\angle ABC \cong \angle DEG$.	6. Corresp parts $\cong$ ⚠ $\cong$.
7. $\angle ABC \cong \angle DEF$.	7. Given.
8. $\angle DEG \cong \angle DEF$.	8. First $\cong$ second $\cong$ third.
9. $\overline{EF}$ and $\overline{EG}$ coincide.	9. 1 coord, $\angle \cong \angle$.
10. $G = F$.	10. 2 lines, intersection is 1 point.
11. $\overline{DF} = \overline{DG}$.	11. Diff of coords = length.
12. $\overline{AC} \cong \overline{DF}$.	12. Reason 8.
13. $\triangle ABC \cong \triangle DEF$.	13. SAS $\cong$ SAS.

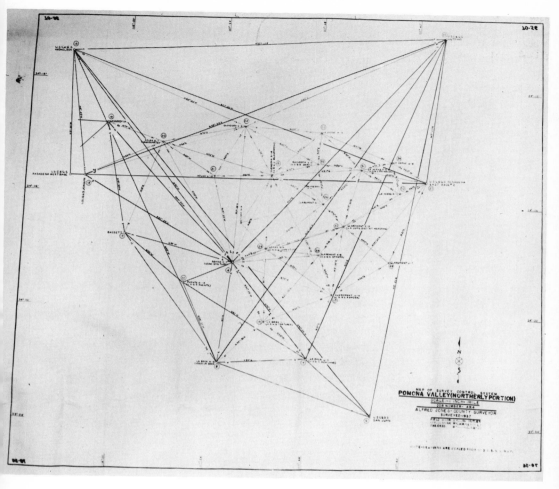

With a surveyor's transit, which is a telescope mounted on a protractor, one can accurately measure coordinates of rays. What is said to be the most precise engineering survey ever made was a series of measurements from the valleys to determine the distance between points on Mount Wilson (upper left) and Mount San Antonio (upper right) in California. Knowing this distance accurately, Professor Albert Michelson was able to conduct his famous experiment to determine the speed of light.

COROLLARY 11.1   If two right triangles have a leg and an adjacent acute angle of one congruent to the corresponding parts of the other, then the triangles are congruent.

EXERCISE 4.7

1. In $\triangle RUT$:

   (a) What side is opposite to $\angle R$?
   (b) What angle is opposite to $\overline{RU}$?

2. In $\triangle RST$:

   (a) What side is opposite to $\angle R$?
   (b) What angle is opposite to $\overline{TR}$?

3. Name an angle opposite to side $\overline{RS}$.

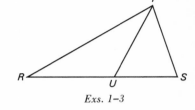

Exs. 1–3

4. If $\triangle ABC \cong \triangle DEF$, with corresponding vertices in order, state the pairs of corresponding angles and sides.

The pairs of triangles in Exs. 5–17 are labeled with the symbols of congruency: tick marks across the sides, arcs inside the angles, or right angle squares. Where the same side or angle is a part of two triangles, the mark is a cross to show the reflexive property or identity. For each pair of triangles, indicate whether the SAS postulate, the ASA theorem, or neither can be used to prove the two triangles congruent. Where an identity mark is not shown, assume it.

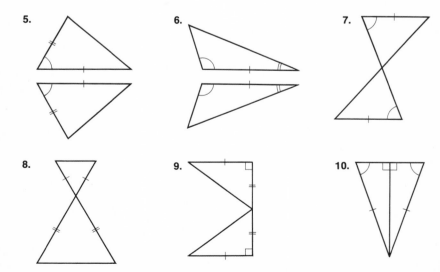

5.

6.

7.

8.

9.

10.

11. 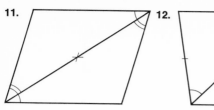 **12.**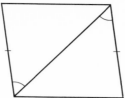

13. 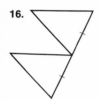 **14.** 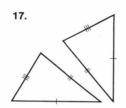 **15.**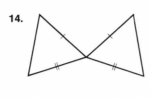

16. **17.**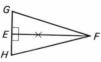

18. In each of the figures name the other parts needed to be congruent in order to prove triangles congruent by: **(a)** SAS ≅ SAS. **(b)** ASA ≅ ASA.

Ex. 18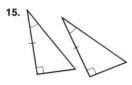

19. In the figure name:

   (a) The sides which include ∠G
   (b) The angles which include $\overline{FH}$
   (c) The angle included by $\overline{HF}$ and $\overline{FG}$
   (d) The side included by ∠G and ∠H

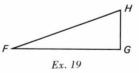

Ex. 19

20. GIVEN: ∠GAB ≅ ∠HBA; ∠GAH ≅ ∠HBG.
   PROVE: ∠G = ∠H; $\overline{GA} = \overline{HB}$. (Solution on page 76)

Ex. 20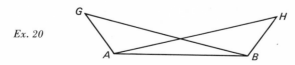

Solution

1. ∠*GAB* ≅ ∠*HBA*; ∠*GAH* ≅   1. Given.
   ∠*HBG*.
2. m∠*GAB* ≅ m∠*HBA*; m∠*GAH* ≅   2. ≅ ∠ have same m.
   m∠*HBG*.
3. m∠*BAH* ≅ m∠*ABG*.   3. Equals − equals are equals.
4. ∠*BAH* ≅ ∠*ABG*.   4. ∠ with same m ≅.
5. $\overline{AB}$ ≅ $\overline{AB}$.   5. Segment ≅ itself.
6. △*GAB* ≅ △*HBA*.   6. ASA ≅ ASA.
7. ∠*G* ≅ ∠*H*; $\overline{GA}$ ≅ $\overline{HB}$.   7. Corresp parts ≅ △ ≅.

21. GIVEN: $\overline{GH}$ and $\overline{EF}$ bisect each other at *X*.
PROVE: △*GXE* ≅ △*HXF*.

22. GIVEN: $\overline{GX}$ ≅ $\overline{HX}$; ∠*EGX* ≅ ∠*FHX*.
PROVE: △*EGX* ≅ △*FHX*.

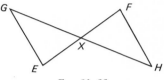

Exs. 21, 22

23. GIVEN: $\overline{RQ}$ ≅ $\overline{RS}$; ∠*Q* ≅ ∠*S*.
PROVE: △*RQU* ≅ △*RST*.

24. GIVEN: $\overline{RT}$ ≅ $\overline{RU}$; $\overline{RQ}$ ≅ $\overline{RS}$.
PROVE: △*RUQ* ≅ △*RTS*.

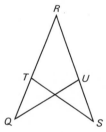

Exs. 23, 24

25. GIVEN: $\overline{WZ}$ ⊥ $\overline{VX}$; $\overline{WV}$ ≅ $\overline{WY}$; ∠*V* ≅ ∠*XYW*.
PROVE: △*VWZ* ≅ △*YWX*.

26. GIVEN: $\overline{WZ}$ ⊥ $\overline{VX}$; $\overline{WV}$ ≅ $\overline{WY}$; $\overline{WZ}$ ≅ $\overline{WX}$.
PROVE: △*WZV* ≅ △*WXY*.

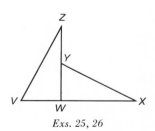

Exs. 25, 26

27. GIVEN: $\overline{CD}$ and $\overline{AB}$ intersect at *E*; $\overline{AB}$ ≅ $\overline{CD}$; $\overline{EB}$ ≅ $\overline{ED}$.
PROVE: ∠*A* ≅ ∠*C*.

28. GIVEN: $\overline{EB}$ ≅ $\overline{ED}$; $\overline{DA}$ ⊥ $\overline{DC}$; $\overline{BC}$ ⊥ $\overline{BA}$.
PROVE: $\overline{AD}$ ≅ $\overline{CB}$.

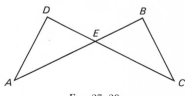

Exs. 27, 28

29. GIVEN: Quad $VYWX$; diagonals $\overline{VW} \perp \overline{XY}$; $\overline{ZX} \cong \overline{ZY}$.
PROVE: $\overline{VX} \cong \overline{VY}$; $\overline{WX} \cong \overline{WY}$.

30. GIVEN: Quad $VYWX$; diagonals $\overline{VW} \perp \overline{XY}$; $\angle WVZ \cong \angle YVZ$.
PROVE: $\overline{ZX} \cong \overline{ZY}$.

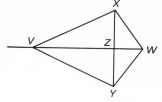

Exs. 29, 30

31. GIVEN: Square $ABCD$; E is the midpoint of $\overline{AD}$.
PROVE: $\angle x \cong \angle y$.

32. GIVEN: Square $ABCD$; $\angle x \cong \angle y$.
PROVE: E is the midpoint of $\overline{AD}$.

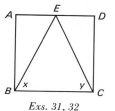

Exs. 31, 32

33. GIVEN: Line $\overleftrightarrow{RT}$; $\angle URS \cong \angle VRS$; $\angle UST \cong \angle VST$.
PROVE: $\overline{RU} \cong \overline{RV}$.

34. GIVEN: Line $\overleftrightarrow{RT}$; $\overline{RU} \cong \overline{RV}$; $\angle URS \cong \angle VRS$.
PROVE: $\angle UST \cong \angle VST$.

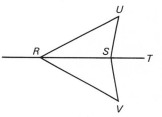

Exs. 33, 34

35. GIVEN: $\triangle EDH$; $\overline{ED} \cong \overline{HD}$; $\angle E \cong \angle H$; $\angle EDF \cong \angle HDG$.
PROVE: $\angle EGD \cong \angle HFD$.

36. GIVEN: $\triangle EHD$; $\overline{ED} \cong \overline{HD}$; $\angle E \cong \angle H$; $\overline{EF} \cong \overline{HG}$.
PROVE: $\angle EDG \cong \angle HDF$.

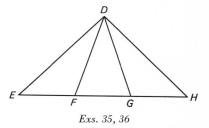

Exs. 35, 36

37. Surveyors cannot get to points A and B, but they find m$\angle ADC =$ m$\angle BDC$ and m$\angle ACD =$ m$\angle BCD$.
PROVE: $AC = BC$.

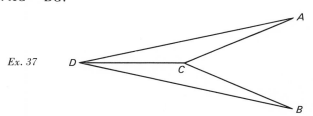

Ex. 37

4.8   Other Congruent Triangles

Some triangles can be congruent to each other in more than one way.

> DEFINITIONS   A triangle which has two congruent sides is an **isosceles triangle**. The third side is the **base**. Angles which include the base are **base angles**. The angle opposite the base is sometimes specifically called the **vertex angle**.

Fig. 26

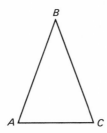

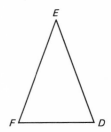

An isosceles triangle can be congruent to itself or to another isosceles triangle in two ways. Consider the triangles *ABC* and *DEF* in Fig. 26. GIVEN: $\overline{AB} \cong \overline{CB}$; $\overline{DE} \cong \overline{FE}$; $\overline{AB} \cong \overline{DE}$; then $\overline{CB} \cong \overline{FE}$. If $\angle B \cong \angle E$, then $\triangle ABC \cong \triangle DEF$. But also $AB \cong FE$ and $CB \cong DE$ and $\triangle ABC \cong \triangle FED$. The first triangle is congruent to the second and to the third, and by the same method the second is congruent to the third.

A triangle which has three sides congruent is equilateral. Drawing the triangle six ways and showing how any two of these six triangles are congruent is an exercise left to the student.

THEOREM 12   If two sides of a triangle are congruent, then the angles opposite the sides are congruent.

GIVEN: $\triangle ABC$; $\overline{AC} \cong \overline{BC}$.

PROVE: $\angle A \cong \angle B$.

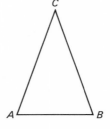
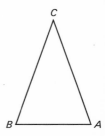

1. $\overline{AC} \cong \overline{BC}$.
2. $\overline{BC} \cong \overline{AC}$.
3. $\angle C \cong \angle C$.
4. $\triangle ABC \cong \triangle BAC$.
5. $\angle A \cong \angle B$.

1. Given.
2. First $\cong$ second $\cong$ first.
3. $\angle \cong$ itself.
4. SAS $\cong$ SAS.
5. Corresp parts $\cong \triangle \cong$.

COROLLARY 12.1 An equilateral triangle is also equiangular.

COROLLARY 12.2 The base angles of an isosceles triangle are congruent.

THEOREM 13 If two angles of a triangle are congruent, then the sides opposite the angles are congruent.

The proof is an exercise left to the student.

COROLLARY 13.1 An equiangular triangle is also equilateral.

THEOREM 14 If two triangles have three sides of one congruent to the corresponding sides of the other, then the triangles are congruent. (SSS $\cong$ SSS)

GIVEN: $\triangle ABC$ and $\triangle DEF$; $\overline{AB} \cong \overline{DE}$; $\overline{BC} \cong \overline{EF}$; $\overline{CA} \cong \overline{FD}$.

PROVE: $\triangle ABC \cong \triangle DEF$.

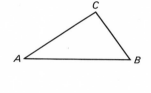 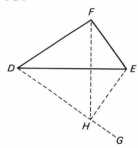

1. There is a ray $\overrightarrow{DG}$ on the opposite side of $\overline{DE}$ from F such that $\angle EDG \cong \angle A$. Construct it.
2. On $\overrightarrow{DG}$ there is a point H such that $\overline{DH} \cong \overline{AC}$. Construct it.
3. Construct $\overline{EH}$.
4. $\overline{AB} \cong \overline{DE}$.
5. $\triangle ABC \cong \triangle DEH$.
6. Draw $\overline{FH}$.
7. $\overline{AC} \cong \overline{DF}$.
8. $\overline{DH} \cong \overline{DF}$.
9. $\overline{EH} \cong \overline{BC}$.
10. $\overline{BC} \cong \overline{EF}$.
11. $\overline{EH} \cong \overline{EF}$.
12. $\angle DFH \cong \angle DHF$; $\angle EFH \cong \angle EHF$.
13. $\angle DFE \cong \angle DHE$.

14. $\triangle DEF \cong \triangle DEH$.
15. $\triangle ABC \cong \triangle DEF$.

1. 1 ray, $\angle \cong \angle$.
2. 1 point, segment $\cong$ segment.
3. 2 points, 1 line.
4. Given.
5. SAS $\cong$ SAS.
6. Reason 3.
7. Given.
8. First $\cong$ second $\cong$ third.
9. Corresp parts $\cong$ $\triangle$ $\cong$.
10. Given.
11. Reason 8.
12. Sides of $\triangle$ $\cong$, $\triangle$ opp $\cong$.
13. $\cong$ $\triangle$ have same m. Equals + equals are equals.
14. SAS $\cong$ SAS.
15. Reason 8.

Theorems 11 and 14 are the same for triangles of all shapes. The diagram for proving obtuse triangles congruent in Theorem 14 is shown below.

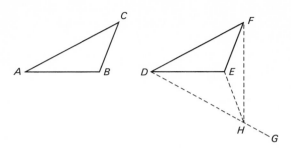

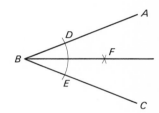

Construction 3 *Bisect a given angle.*

GIVEN: $\angle ABC$.

CONSTRUCT: The bisector of $\angle ABC$.

With B as a center and any convenient radius, construct an arc intersecting $\overrightarrow{BA}$ at D and $\overrightarrow{BC}$ at E. With D and E as centers and any convenient radius greater than half the distance DE, construct arcs which intersect at F. Construct the ray $\overrightarrow{BF}$. $\overrightarrow{BF}$ is the bisector of $\angle ABC$.

THEOREM 15 An angle has exactly one bisector.

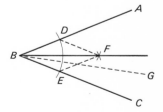

GIVEN: $\angle ABC$; $\overrightarrow{BF}$ from Construction 3.

PROVE: $\overrightarrow{BF}$ is the bisector of $\angle ABC$; $\overrightarrow{BF}$ is the only bisector of $\angle ABC$.

Draw $\overline{DF}$ and $\overline{EF}$. Radii of the same circle: $\overline{BD} \cong \overline{BE}$ and $\overline{DF} \cong \overline{EF}$. $\overline{BF} \cong$ itself, and $\triangle BDF \cong \triangle BEF$ by SSS $\cong$ SSS. Corresp parts $\angle ABF \cong \angle CBF$. $\overline{BF}$ bisects $\angle ABC$; a ray which separates $\angle$ into $\cong$ parts bisects.

(Existence)

Let $\overrightarrow{BG}$ be another ray such that m$\angle CBG = \frac{1}{2}$m$\angle ABC$, but $\overrightarrow{BG} = \overrightarrow{BF}$

since there is exactly one ray such that the angle is a multiple of the given angle.   (Uniqueness)

A carpenter can bisect an angle by means of his square. He measures convenient equal distances from the vertex on each side. He then moves his square until its vertex is equidistant from the marked points of the sides (Fig. 27). The vertex of the square is a point of the bisector.

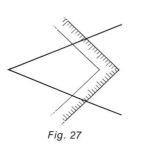

Fig. 27

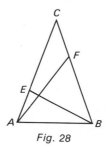

Fig. 28

NOTE: Theorems 12 and 13 apply only to congruent sides and angles of a single triangle, not parts of two triangles. If $\overline{AC} \cong \overline{BC}$ in Fig. 28, that does not indicate that $\angle AFC \cong \angle BEC$. What angles are congruent here?

EXERCISE 4.8

NOTE: When a proposition to be proved is given in sentence form, the student is required to make a diagram and to provide statements of what is given and what is to be proved related to the diagram. This complete form should be used in all such cases, beginning with Ex. 11 below.

1. $\overleftrightarrow{AB}$ and $\overleftrightarrow{CD}$ intersect at V. $\overrightarrow{VE}$ bisects $\angle CVB$. The ray coordinate of $\overrightarrow{VB} = 0$, of $\overrightarrow{VD} = 50°$. Find the ray coordinates of: **(a)** $\overrightarrow{VA}$. **(b)** $\overrightarrow{VC}$. **(c)** $\overrightarrow{VE}$.

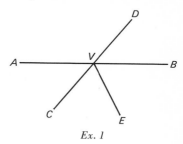

Ex. 1

2. Construct an equilateral triangle. Each angle measures 60°. Extend one side of the triangle through a vertex.

   (a) What is the measure of the new angle formed?
   (b) At this vertex construct an angle of 30°.
   (c) Find an angle of 150°.
   (d) Construct an angle of 75°.

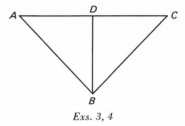

Exs. 3, 4

3. GIVEN: $\triangle ABC$; $\overline{DB} \perp \overline{AC}$; $\overline{DB}$ bisects $\angle ABC$.
   PROVE: $\triangle ADB \cong \triangle CDB$.

4. GIVEN: $\triangle ABC$; $\overline{DB}$ bisects $\overline{AC}$; $\overline{AB} \cong \overline{BC}$.
   PROVE: $\triangle ADB \cong \triangle CDB$.

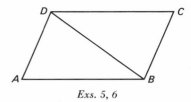

Exs. 5, 6

5. GIVEN: $\overline{AB} \cong \overline{CD}$; $\overline{DA} \cong \overline{BC}$.
   PROVE: $\triangle ABD \cong \triangle CDB$.

6. GIVEN: $\overline{AB} \cong \overline{CD}$; $\angle ABD \cong \angle CDB$.
   PROVE: $\triangle ABD \cong \triangle CDB$.

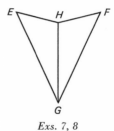

Exs. 7, 8

7. GIVEN: $\overline{EG} \cong \overline{FG}$; $\overline{EH} \cong \overline{FH}$.
   PROVE: $\triangle EGH \cong \triangle FGH$.

8. GIVEN: $\overline{EG} \cong \overline{FG}$; $\overline{GH}$ bisects $\angle EGF$.
   PROVE: $\triangle EHG \cong \triangle FHG$.

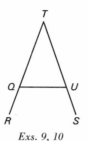

Exs. 9, 10

9. GIVEN: $\overline{RT} \cong \overline{ST}$; $QT = 0.7RT$; $UT = 0.7ST$.
   PROVE: $\angle TQU \cong \angle TUQ$.

10. GIVEN: $\overline{RT} \cong \overline{ST}$; $\angle TQU \cong \angle TUQ$.
   PROVE: $\overline{RQ} \cong \overline{SU}$.

11. Two poles of equal length make equal angles with a line on the ground between them. They are supported by braces from the base of one to the top of the other. Prove that the braces are of the same length.

12. Find the distance across a hole in the ground with measurements made on the ground. Given stakes A and B, tell where others should be placed and what measurements should be made. Prove that two measures are equal.

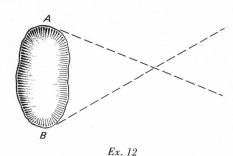

Ex. 12

13. GIVEN: $\triangle ABC$; $\overline{AC} \cong \overline{BC}$; $\overline{AF}$ bisects $\angle CAB$; $\overline{BE}$ bisects $\angle CBA$.
PROVE: $\overline{AF} \cong \overline{BE}$.

14. GIVEN: $\triangle ABC$; $\overline{AC} \cong \overline{BC}$; E is midpoint of $\overline{AC}$; F is midpoint of $\overline{BC}$.
PROVE: $\overline{AF} \cong \overline{BE}$.

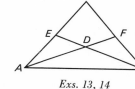

Exs. 13, 14

15. GIVEN: $\triangle RST$; $\overline{UT} \cong \overline{VT}$; $\angle RTU \cong \angle STV$.
PROVE: $\triangle RTV \cong \triangle STU$.

16. GIVEN: $\triangle RST$; $\overline{RU} \cong \overline{SV}$; $\overline{UT} \cong \overline{VT}$.
PROVE: $\overline{RT} \cong \overline{ST}$.

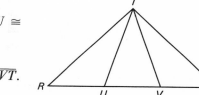

Exs. 15, 16

17. GIVEN: $\triangle ABC$; $\overline{AC} \cong \overline{BC}$; $CE = \frac{2}{3}CA$; $CF = \frac{2}{3}CB$.
PROVE: $\angle BEC \cong \angle AFC$.

18. GIVEN: $\triangle ABC$; $\overline{AC} \cong \overline{BC}$; $\overline{AF}$ bisects $\angle CAB$; $\overline{BE}$ bisects $\angle CBA$.
PROVE: $\overline{AG} \cong \overline{BG}$.

Exs. 17, 18

19. GIVEN: Quad $ABCD$; $\overline{AB} \cong \overline{AD}$; $\overline{BC} \cong \overline{DC}$.
PROVE: $\angle BCA \cong \angle DCA$.

20. GIVEN: Quad $ABCD$; $\overline{BA} \perp \overline{BC}$; $\overline{DA} \perp \overline{DC}$; $\overline{AB} \cong \overline{AD}$.
PROVE: $\triangle ABC \cong \triangle ADC$.

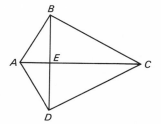

Exs. 19, 20

21. GIVEN: $\triangle RTS$; $\overline{RT} \cong \overline{ST}$; $\overline{TQ}$ bisects $\angle RTS$.
    PROVE: $\angle QRS \cong \angle QSR$.

22. GIVEN: $\triangle RST$; $\overline{RT} \cong \overline{ST}$; $m\angle TRQ = \frac{2}{5}m\angle TRS$; $m\angle TSQ = \frac{2}{5}m\angle TSR$.
    PROVE: $\overline{TQ}$ bisects $\angle RTS$.

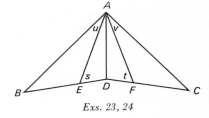

Exs. 21, 22

23. GIVEN: $\triangle ADB$, ADC; $\overline{AB} \cong \overline{AC}$, $\overline{BD} \cong \overline{CD}$; $\angle u \cong \angle v$.
    PROVE: $\angle EAD \cong \angle FAD$.

24. GIVEN: $\triangle ADB$, ADC; $\overline{AE} \cong \overline{AF}$; $\overline{BE} \cong \overline{CF}$; $\angle s \cong \angle t$.
    PROVE: $\overline{AB} \cong \overline{AC}$.

Exs. 23, 24

25. GIVEN: $\triangle ABC$; $\overline{AC} \cong \overline{BC}$; midpoints: D of $\overline{AB}$; E of $\overline{AC}$; F of $\overline{BC}$.
    PROVE: $\angle CED \cong \angle CFD$.

26. GIVEN: $\triangle ABC$; $\overline{AC} \cong \overline{BC}$; $\overline{ED} \cong \overline{FD}$; midpoints: E of $\overline{AC}$; F of $\overline{BC}$.
    PROVE: $\angle AED \cong \angle BFD$.

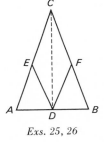

Exs. 25, 26

27. PROVE: Lines joining the three midpoints of the sides of an equilateral triangle form another equilateral triangle. (NOTE: Prove three triangles congruent to each other.)

28. Prove Theorem 13.

29. State a theorem proved by Ex. 3 in Exercise 4.5.

4.9 Summary Test

For each of the following statements write A if it is always true, S if it is sometimes true under some of the possible conditions, and N if it is never true.

1. A triangle is the intersection of three segments which intersect at their endpoints.

2. In a proof the hypothesis of a reason applies directly to the step of which it is a reason.

3. Segment $\overline{AB} \cong \overline{CD}$; $\overline{CD}$ is extended to E; $\overline{AB}$ is still $\cong \overline{CD}$.

4. The size of an angle depends upon the length of its sides.

5. Congruent triangles remain congruent regardless of the positions to which they are moved.

6. $\angle w$ supp $\angle x$; $\angle x$ vertical to $\angle y$; $\angle w$ supp $\angle y$.

7. If two angles are supplements, one is obtuse.

8. Two complementary angles are congruent.

9. The ray $\overrightarrow{BD}$ separates $\angle ABC$ such that $m\angle ABD + m\angle DBC = m\angle ABC$.

10. If two figures are congruent to a third figure, they are congruent to each other.

11. The introduction of an auxiliary line changes the congruence of the angles in the original figure.

12. Exactly one circle can be constructed with a given radius.

13. If $\triangle ABC \cong \triangle FGH$ with corresponding vertices in order, then $\overline{AB} \cong \overline{GH}$.

14. If $\triangle DEF \cong \triangle EDF$ with corresponding vertices in order, then the triangle is equilateral.

15. In $\triangle RST$, side $\overline{RS}$ is opposite to $\angle S$.

16. In $\triangle UVW$, $\angle V$ is included between sides $\overline{UV}$ and $\overline{VW}$.

17. If an obtuse angle is bisected, two acute angles are formed.

18. Existence means "at most one."

19. The bisector of an angle forms congruent angles with the sides of the given angle.

20. Corresponding sides of congruent angles are congruent.

21. A line that intersects a segment bisects the segment.

22. A segment that intersects a line bisects the line.

23. Two supplementary angles are adjacent.

24. The complement of an angle measures $90° - x$; the measure of the angle is $x°$.

25. One triangle can be congruent to a second triangle without having the same shape.

26. Congruences between triangles have the reflexive, symmetric, and transitive properties.

27. The ray coordinate of $\overrightarrow{VW}$ is 95°; the coordinate of the ray opposite to $\overrightarrow{VW}$ is 275°.

CONDENSATIONS

Segments with same length ≅; ≅ segments have same length.   (Def)

≰ with same m ≅; ≅ ≰ have same m.   (Def)

Corresp parts ≅ △ ≅.   (Def)

Union of opp rays with common endpoint is a st ∠.   (Def)

m st ∠ = 180°; ∠ whose m = 180° is a st ∠.   (Def)

2 ≰, sum m = 180°, are supp; sum m supp ≰ = 180°.   (Def)

2 adjacent ≰, sides form st ∠, are supp.   (Def)

m rt ∠ = 90°; ∠ whose m = 90° is a rt ∠.   (Def)

⊥ lines form rt ≰; sides of rt ∠ ⊥.   (Def)

2 ≰, sum m = 90°, are comp; sum m comp ≰ = 90°.   (Def)

△ with 2 ≅ sides is isosceles; 2 sides of isosceles △ ≅.   (Def)

First ≅ second ≅ third; segment (∠) ≅ itself.   (Thm 4)

Name sub for name of ≅; halves of ≅ segments (≰) ≅.   (Thm 4)

Point (line, ray) which separates into ≅ halves bisects.   (Def)

Bisector separates into 2 ≅ halves.   (Def)

With given center and radius, 1 ⊙; radii of a ⊙ ≅.   (Post 9)

Radii of ≅ Ⓢ ≅.   (Def)

Supp ≅ ∡ ≅; supp same ∠ ≅.   (Thm 5)

Comp ≅ ∡ ≅; comp same ∠ ≅.   (Thm 6)

Vertical ∡ ≅.   (Thm 7)

2 lines forming ≅ adjacent ∡ ⊥; 2 lines forming ≅ supp ∡ ⊥; supp of rt ∠ is a rt ∠.
(Thm 8)

1 point, segment ≅ segment.   (Thm 9)

1 ray, ∠ ≅ ∠.   (Thm 10)

SAS ≅ SAS.   (Post 10)

ASA ≅ ASA.   (Thm 11)

Sides of △ ≅, ∡ opp ≅.   (Thm 12)

∡ of △ ≅, sides opp ≅.   (Thm 13)

SSS ≅ SSS.   (Thm 14)

chapter **5**

Inequalities

5.1 A Sense of Order

The order of numbers in a fixed pattern gives us the basis for establishing that any number is greater than or less than any other number. This is the concept of **inequality**. We know from experience this relationship for positive numbers, since 50 pounds weighs more than 20 pounds and 5 miles is a longer distance than 2 miles. On the negative side of a number line that number closer to the positive, or in the increasing positive direction from another, is the greater number, although the absolute value of the number in the increasing negative direction is greater. The symbols for inequality are: $\neq$ does not equal, or are unequal; $>$ is greater than; $<$ is less than; $\not<$ is not less than. Thus we write

$$50 \neq 20 \qquad 5 > 2 \qquad -5 < 0 \qquad -111 < -2 \qquad -8 \not< -20$$

Another way of interpreting inequality is that if $c > d$, then $c - d$ is a positive number and $d - c$ is a negative number. A positive number is any number greater than zero: a negative number is less than zero. For example, if $c = -2$ and $d = -10$, then $-2 - (-10) = +8$ and $-10 - (-2) = -8$, since $-2 > -10$.

The concept of inequality is admirably suited to expressing the relations of a **variable**, a symbol used to represent any number of a set. If a segment has endpoints with coordinates f and g, one point of the segment corresponds to each number from f to g. If x represents any coordinate of the set of points, then we can write: $x \geq f$ and $x \leq g$. This states that x is equal to or greater than f and equal to or less than g. The two expressions can be put together in one statement: $f \leq x \leq g$, in which x is a variable number from f to g inclusive.

The sense of order applies to two or more inequalities as well as to sets of numbers in one inequality.

DEFINITION   If the first of a pair of numbers in set A is greater than the second, and the first number in set B is greater than the second, then the two inequalities are **in the same order**. If in set A the first is greater than the second and in set B the first is less than the second, then the inequalities are **in the reverse order**.

5.2   Properties of Inequalities

The properties of equality are true for equal numbers. There is a corresponding group of properties for the relations of equal and unequal numbers.

Property 6   **One number is either less than, equal to, or greater than another number.**   Property of trichotomy.

Either $b < c$ or $b = c$ or $b > c$.

Property 7   **If the first of two numbers is greater than the second, then the second is less than the first.**   Linear property.

If $b > c$, then $c < b$; $11 > 7$ and $7 < 11$.

Property 8   **Of three numbers if the first is greater than the second and the second is greater than the third, then the first is greater than the third.**   Transitive property.

If $b > c$ and $c > d$, then $b > d$. Since $11 > 7$ and $7 > 5$, then $11 > 5$.

A second possibility of this property is that one of the relations may be an equality. If $b = c$ and $c > d$, then $b > d$. Here we use the corollary of the transitive property of equality:

A number may be substituted for its equal in any relationship.

The number b is substituted for c in $c > d$, and $b > d$.

Property 9 **If equal numbers and unequal numbers are added, then the results are unequal in the same order.** Addition property.

If $e > f$, then $e + g > f + g$. Since $15 > 9$, $15 + 3 > 9 + 3$.

Property 10 **If equal numbers are subtracted from unequal numbers, then the results are unequal in the same order.** Subtraction property.

If $e > f$, then $e - h > f - h$. Since $15 > 9$, then $15 - 3 > 9 - 3$.

Property 11 **If unequal numbers are subtracted from equal numbers, then the results are unequal in the reverse order.** Subtraction property.

If $e > f$, then $g - e < g - f$. Subtracting 15 and 9 from 17 gives $2 < 8$.

In the following properties multiplication and division by zero are not possible.

Property 12 **If positive equal numbers and unequal numbers are multiplied, then the results are unequal in the same order.**

Multiplication property.

If $h > j$, then $hi > ji$ or $5h > 5j$.

Property 13 **If unequal numbers are divided by positive equal numbers, then the results are unequal in the same order.** Division property.

If $h > j$, then $h/k > j/k$ or $9/4 > 6/4$.

Property 14 **If positive equal numbers are divided by unequal numbers, than the results are unequal in the reverse order.** Division property.

If $h > j$, then $k/h < k/j$ or $4/9 < 4/6$.

THEOREM 16 The sum of positive numbers is greater than any one of them.

GIVEN: Positive numbers b, c, and e; $b + c = e$.

PROVE: $e > b$.

From $b + c = e$ subtract $b = b$. Then $c = e - b$ and $e > b$, for $e - b = $ a positive number.

COROLLARY 16.1   The whole is greater than any of its parts. (The traditional wording.)

EXERCISE 5.2

1. Make a table like the following and complete it:

	Add	*Subtract*	*Multiply*	*Divide*
	(a)	**(b)**	**(c)**	**(d)**
Equals	$12 = 12$	$12 = 12$	$12 = 12$	$12 = 12$
Unequals	$2 < 4$	$2 < 4$	$2 < 4$	$2 < 4$
Results	$14 < 16$			
Order	same			

	(e)	**(f)**	**(g)**	**(h)**
Unequals	$20 < 26$	$20 < 26$	$20 < 26$	$20 < 26$
Equals	$2 = 2$	$2 = 2$	$2 = 2$	$2 = 2$
Results				
Order				

2. Make a second table in which the equals are made negative: $-12 = -12$ and $-2 = -2$. Find the order of each result and compare with those of Ex. 1.

3. If $r > s > 0$, give the symbol to be used in place of each question mark:

   (a) $s \; ? \; r$ (b) $r - s \; ? \; 0$ (c) $s - r \; ? \; 0$
   (d) $r + 2 \; ? \; s + 2$ (e) $r - 3 \; ? \; s - 3$ (f) $10 - r \; ? \; 10 - s$
   (g) $5r \; ? \; 5s$ (h) $r/s \; ? \; 1$ (i) $s/r \; ? \; 1$
   (j) $r/4 \; ? \; s/4$ (k) $8/r \; ? \; 8/s$

5.3   Separation

One of the fallacies into which we can stumble in geometry is to develop a completely wrong proof because we try to locate a point in a place where it cannot be. With our modern numerical relations of coordinates we have a means by which to prevent such a mistake. With coordinates in a definite numerical order we can describe the locations of their corresponding points or rays in an order, between others or in the interior or exterior of a figure.

DEFINITIONS   The set of all points of a ray except its endpoint is the **interior of the ray**. Each is an **interior point** of the ray. The set of all points of a segment except its endpoints is the **interior of the segment**. The set of all the interior points of the rays with the vertex of an angle as the common end-point and between the sides of the angle is the **interior of the angle**. The intersection of the interiors of the angles of a triangle is the **interior of the triangle**. The set of all points whose distance from the center of a circle is less than the length of the radius is the **interior of the circle**.

A plane geometric figure separates its plane into three sets of points: the set in the interior of the figure, the set of the figure, and the set in the **exterior** of the figure. The union of the interior set and the set of points of the figure is the **region** of the figure.

Line and angle relationships are expressed in terms of coordinates (Fig. 29). If the coordinate of point P of a line is c, the coordinates of

Fig. 29

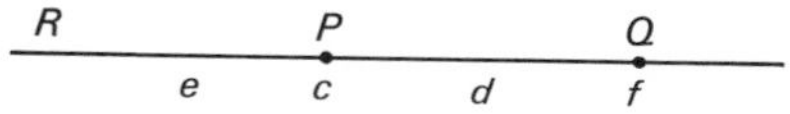

the points of one ray are greater than c, and those in the opposite direction are less than c. If the coordinate of any point of $\overrightarrow{PQ}$ is d, then $d \geq c$, meaning that d is equal to or greater than c. If the coordinate of any point of $\overrightarrow{PR}$ is e, then $e \leq c$; that is, e is equal to or less than c. If the coordinate of point Q is f, then the coordinates of the points of segment $\overline{PQ}$ are equal to or greater than c and equal to or less than f. This is written $c \leq d \leq f$.

Now, if the interior of a ray or segment is wanted, all the points are included except the endpoints, and the coordinate of any interior point is not that of an endpoint. Thus for the interior of $\overrightarrow{PQ}$, $d > c$; of $\overrightarrow{PR}$, $e < c$; and of $\overline{PQ}$, $c < d < f$.

If $0 \leq x \leq 6$, x is any coordinate from 0 to 6 inclusive. If $0 < x < 6$, x is any coordinate between 0 and 6.

Rays and segments with definite coordinates can be plotted on a number line. In Fig. 30(a), if the coordinate of the endpoint of $\overrightarrow{PQ}$ is 5, the ray is the set of points whose coordinates d satisfy the condition $d \geq 5$. The interior of the ray is the set $d > 5$. A black circle is the endpoint where $d = 5$, and the empty circle is the endpoint where $d \neq 5$. In Fig. 30(b), the plot of the segment $\overline{RS}$, whose coordinates are $0 \leq e \leq 6$, is shown first, and the second is the interior in which $0 < e < 6$.

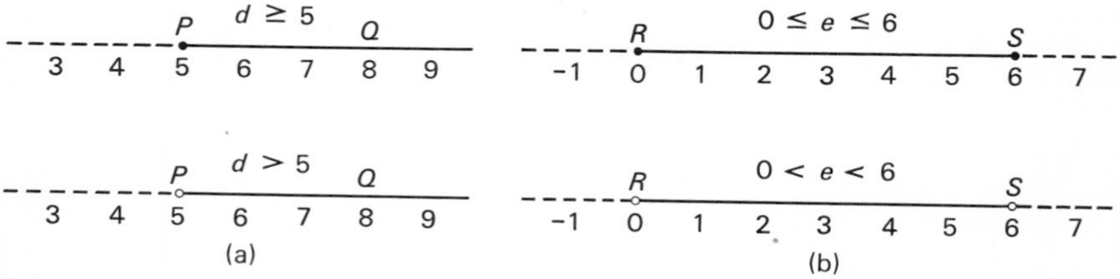

Fig. 30

The points of intersection of $\overrightarrow{PQ}$ and $\overline{RS}$ have coordinates y such that $5 \leq y \leq 6$. The points of their union have coordinates z such that $0 \leq z$.

In like manner, in $\angle STU$ (Fig. 31), if the coordinate of $\overrightarrow{TS}$ is g and the

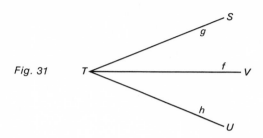

Fig. 31

coordinate of $\overline{TU}$ is h, all the rays of the interior of the angle have coordinates f such that $h < f < g$ or $g < f < h$. The interior of a ray, such as $\overrightarrow{TV}$, is the set of all the points of the ray except its endpoint. All rays between $\overrightarrow{TU}$ and $\overrightarrow{TS}$ are interior rays of the angle. The interior of the angle is the union of the interiors of all the interior rays.

Separation for two-dimensional figures often employs another concept. A line separates a plane into two **half-planes**, one on each side of the line. The line is the **edge** of each and is contained in neither.

Each side of a figure separates its plane. In Fig. 32, side $\overline{AB}$ extended is a line. One of its half-planes is shaded. One half-plane of $\overleftrightarrow{AC}$ is also shaded. The intersection of the two half-planes is the **interior** of the angle $\angle CAB$. The interior of the triangle is the intersection of the three half-planes described thus: that on the same side of $\overleftrightarrow{AB}$ as C, that on the same side of $\overleftrightarrow{BC}$ as A, and that on the same side of $\overleftrightarrow{CA}$ as B. When the interior of the figure is exactly the intersection of the half-planes, one formed by each side, the figure is **convex**. And each half-plane alone is convex.

A figure of four or more sides may not be convex. A part of the quadrilateral $DEFG$ (Fig. 33) is not contained in the half-plane on the same

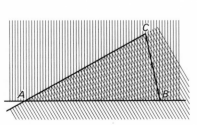

Fig. 32

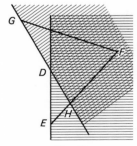

Fig. 33

side of $\overleftrightarrow{GD}$ as F, namely, $\triangle DEH$. Thus $DEFG$ does not satisfy the conditions of convexity.

Postulate 11   **A line contained in a plane separates the plane into two convex sets of points such that every segment joining a point of one set to a point of the other intersects the line at exactly one point.**

Postulate 12   **A convex geometric figure separates a plane into two regions, interior and exterior, such that a segment joining a point of one region to a point of the other intersects the figure at exactly one point.**

When a figure is convex, a segment which joins a point in the interior to a point in the exterior intersects the figure at exactly one point, as segment $\overline{UV}$ in Fig. 34(b). When a figure is not convex, its interior contains some points such that a segment joining them intersects the figure at two or more points. Segment $\overline{RS}$ in Fig. 34(a) intersects the figure at two points, and $\overline{RT}$, joining the interior and the exterior, at three points.

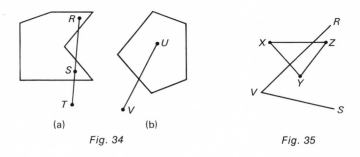

(a)   (b)

Fig. 34   Fig. 35

Point Z is in the interior of $\angle RVS$ (Fig. 35). If point Y is in the interior, then $\overline{YZ}$ is entirely in the interior of the angle. If X is in the exterior of the angle, then both $\overline{XZ}$ and $\overline{XY}$ intersect a side of the angle.

In Theorem 17 (page 98), since A is in the exterior of $\angle CBD$ and $\overline{AF}$ intersects $\overrightarrow{CB}$, then F is in the interior $\angle CBD$ and $\overrightarrow{BF}$ is a ray of the interior. This seems like a complicated and perhaps unnecessary routine just to be sure that a point, a ray, or a segment is precisely located. But it is an illustration of the routine through which Euclid did not go to secure a rigorous proof, as discussed in Section 2.1. This is part of the reason why several postulates were added to the traditional work.

DEFINITION   The union of the extension of one side of a triangle and the second side with the same vertex is an **exterior angle** of the triangle.

Thus, in Fig. 36, there are six exterior angles: u, v, w, x, y, and z. Two angles whose intersection is one ray between the two other rays are adjacent angles. One interior angle is adjacent to each exterior angle.

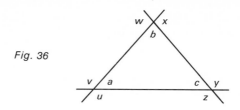

Fig. 36

The two other interior angles are **nonadjacent** to the given exterior angle. In Fig. 36, $\angle c$ is adjacent to $\angle y$. The nonadjacent interior angles are $\angle a$ and $\angle b$.

EXERCISE 5.3

1. The collinear points A, B, and C have the coordinates 6, 12, and 20, respectively. Write an expression for the coordinates of the variable point x of each of the following.

   (a) The union of $\overline{AB}$ and $\overrightarrow{BC}$

   Answer: $x \geq 6$

   (b) The intersection of $\overline{AB}$ and $\overrightarrow{BG}$

   Answer: $x = 12$

   (c) Segment $\overline{BC}$
   (e) Ray $\overrightarrow{BA}$
   (g) The union of $\overrightarrow{BC}$ and $\overline{BC}$
   (i) The intersection of the interiors of $\overrightarrow{BC}$ and $\overrightarrow{BC}$

   (d) The interior of $\overleftrightarrow{BC}$
   (f) The interior of $\overrightarrow{BA}$
   (h) The intersection of $\overline{BC}$ and $\overrightarrow{BC}$

2. Describe the condition of set X with coordinates x when:

   (a) $x > 6$

   Answer: X is the set of points of the interior of a ray whose endpoint is 6, extending in a positive direction.

   (b) $x \geq 20$ **(c)** $x \nless 4$ **(d)** $0 < x < 50$ **(e)** $5 \geq x \geq 2$

   Use the ray $\overrightarrow{AD}$ to answer Exs. 3–12.

Exs. 3–12   A———B———————C———D

3. Compare the lengths of $\overline{AB}$ and $\overline{AC}$, knowing that B is between A and C.

4. If C is a point of the interior of segment $\overline{BD}$, write an equation relating BC, CD, and BD.

5. Give two general rules relating the lengths of segments when one of three collinear points is between the other two.

6. If $BC > AB$, where must a point E be located along the ray so that $BE = AB$?

7. If E is between A and D, compare the lengths AE and ED.

8. What is the location of point E if $AE = AD$?

9. Give the relationship of AB to CD if we know that AB is neither $>$ nor $= CD$.

10. Give the relationship of BC to AB if $BC \not< AB$.

11. Give the relationship of AB to CD if $AB < BC$ and $BC > CD$.

12. Give the relationship of AC to BD if $AB < CD$.

13. Without drawing segments and visualizing the inequalities, supply the correct sign ($>$, $=$, $<$, or blank if none applies) in place of each question mark.

    GIVEN: $AB = BC$; $CD > BC$; $DE > CD$; $EF > DE$.

    (a) $AB \; ? \; BA$ (b) $BC \; ? \; CD$
    (c) $DE \; ? \; BC$ (d) $CD + AB \; ? \; CD + BC$
    (e) $BC + CD \; ? \; DE + CD$ (f) $DE - CD \; ? \; CD - AB$
    (g) $DE - AB \; ? \; EF - BC$ (h) $EF - BC \; ? \; EF - CD$
    (i) $3CD \; ? \; 3DE$ (j) $CD + BC \; ? \; CD$
    (k) $EF/4 \; ? \; DE/4$ (l) $CD/3 \; ? \; CD/2$

14. For each part of Ex. 13 give a property of which it is a case.

15. GIVEN: $m\angle AVB = 70°$; $m\angle BVC = 30°$.
    FIND: $m\angle AVC$ if:

    (a) C is in the interior of $\angle AVB$
    (b) C is in the exterior of $\angle AVB$
    (c) $\overrightarrow{VC}$ is between $\overrightarrow{VA}$ and $\overrightarrow{VB}$
    (d) $\overrightarrow{VB}$ is between $\overrightarrow{VA}$ and $\overrightarrow{VC}$
    (e) $\angle AVB$ and $\angle BVC$ are adjacent with the common side $\overrightarrow{VB}$

16. If the ray coordinate of $\overrightarrow{VR}$ is 0, of $\overrightarrow{VS}$ is 25°, and of $\overrightarrow{VT}$ is 45°, give the expression for all the coordinates (u) of rays:

    (a) Of $\angle RVS$
    (b) In the interior of $\angle SVT$
    (c) In the interior of $\angle RVT$ and not in the interior of $\angle SVT$
    (d) Between $\overrightarrow{VR}$ and $\overrightarrow{VS}$

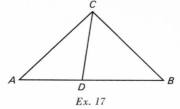

Ex. 17

17. Name the exterior angle and the two nonadjacent interior angles of
  (a) $\triangle ADC$ **(b)** $\triangle DBC$

18. Give a general rule for the maximum size of each interior angle of a convex polygon.

19. Give a general rule for the maximum size of at least one interior angle of a polygon which is not convex.

5.4   Inequality of Some Measures

THEOREM 17   The measure of an exterior angle of a triangle is greater than the measure of either nonadjacent interior angle.

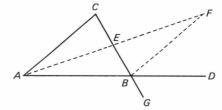

GIVEN: $\triangle ABC$; $\overline{AB}$ extended to D, forming exterior $\angle CBD$.

PROVE: $m\angle CBD > m\angle C$.

Let E be the midpoint of $\overline{BC}$. On $\overrightarrow{AE}$ there is a point F such that $\overline{AE} \cong \overline{EF}$. $\overline{EB} \cong \overline{EC}$ since midpoint separates segment into $\cong$ halves. Point A is on the opposite side of $\overline{CG}$ from D and in the exterior of $\angle CBD$. Since $\overline{AF}$ intersects $\overline{BC}$, F is in the interior of $\angle CBD$. Then $\overline{BF}$ is between $\overline{BC}$ and $\overline{BD}$. With $\angle AEC \cong \angle FEB$, vertical $\angle s \cong$, $\triangle AEC \cong \triangle FEB$ by SAS $\cong$ SAS. Corresponding parts, $\angle C \cong \angle EBF$. Now $m\angle CBD = m\angle CBF + m\angle FBD$ and $m\angle CBD > m\angle CBF$; sum of numbers $>$ any one. Substituting, $m\angle CBD > m\angle C$. In like manner, $m\angle ABG > m\angle A$.

Just as an isosceles triangle has a definite relationship between two congruent sides and two congruent angles, so in a scalene triangle there are definite relations of inequality between the sizes of angles and the lengths of opposite sides. Proofs of these relations are developed from the equalities of isosceles triangles.

THEOREM 18   If the lengths of two sides of a triangle are unequal, then the measures of the angles opposite these sides are unequal in the same order.

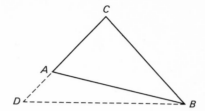

GIVEN: $\triangle ABC$; $BC > AC$.

PROVE: $m\angle CAB > m\angle CBA$.

On $\overrightarrow{CA}$ there is a point D such that $CD = CB$. Construct it; one point, length is constant. Draw $\overline{BD}$ forming an isosceles $\triangle$. $\overline{BA}$ is in the interior of $\angle CBD$. In $\triangle ABD$, $m\angle CAB > m\angle ADB$. m exterior $\angle >$ m nonadjacent interior $\angle$. $m\angle ADB = m\angle CBD$; sides $\cong$, $\measuredangle$ opp $\cong$. $m\angle CBD > m\angle CBA$; sum of numbers $>$ any one. $m\angle CAB > m\angle CBA$; number sub for equal.

COROLLARY 18.1 The angle opposite a longer side of a triangle is a greater angle; the angle opposite a shorter side is a smaller angle.

THEOREM 19 If the measures of two angles of a triangle are unequal, then the lengths of the sides opposite these angles are unequal in the same order.

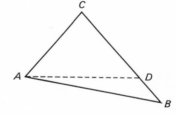

GIVEN: $\triangle ABC$; $m\angle CAB > m\angle CBA$.

PROVE: $BC > AC$.

If $BC = AC$, then $m\angle CAB = m\angle CBA$; sides of $\triangle \cong$, $\measuredangle$ opp $\cong$. If $BC < AC$, then $m\angle CAB < m\angle CBA$; $\angle$ opp greater side is greater $<$. $BC > AC$, for one number is either $<$, $=$, or $>$ another number.

COROLLARY 19.1 The side opposite a greater angle of a triangle is a longer side; the side opposite a smaller angle is a shorter side.

Two theorems, not used in this text, are given here without proof. They involve inequalities of corresponding parts of two triangles.

THEOREM If two triangles have two sides of one congruent to the corresponding sides of the other and the third sides not congruent, then the angle opposite the longer third side is larger than the angle opposite the shorter.

The geometry involved in the building of one complex freeway intersection staggers the imagination. Changes of direction and of elevation, along with differences in the force which vehicles apply to roadways when they turn, require an enormously varied design. Photo courtesy of California Division of Highways.

THEOREM If two triangles have two sides of one congruent to the corresponding sides of the other and the included angles not congruent, then the side opposite the larger included angle is longer than the side opposite the shorter.

THEOREM 20 The sum of the lengths of two sides of a triangle is greater than the length of the third side.

GIVEN: $\triangle ABC$.

PROVE: $BA + AC > BC$.

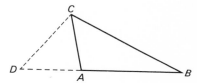
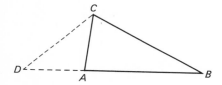

The case is given for both an acute and an obtuse $\triangle$. Extend one side, $\overline{BA}$. On $\overrightarrow{BA}$ there is a point D such that $AD = AC$. One point, length = length. Then $BA + AD = BD$; point separates into parts, sum lengths = length of whole. $BA + AC = BD$; number substituted for equal. $m\angle DCB >$ $m\angle DCA$; sum of numbers > any one. $m\angle DCA = m\angle CDA$; sides $\cong$, $\underline{\angle s}$ opp $\cong$. By substitution, $m\angle DCB > m\angle CDA$. Now $BD > BC$, since the side opp the greater $\angle$ is longer. By substitution, $BA + AC > BC$.

COROLLARY 20.1 The length of a segment joining two points is the shortest distance between the two points.

EXERCISE 5.4

1. When the sides of a triangle have the lengths given, name the angles in order from the smallest to the largest.

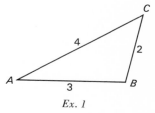

Ex. 1

2. When the angles of a triangle have the measures given, name the sides in order from the shortest to the longest.

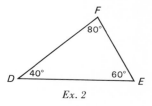

Ex. 2

3. Which of the following sets of numbers could not be used as lengths of the sides of a triangle?

   (a) 2, 11, 11   **(b)** 2, 2, 11   **(c)** 3, 4, 5   **(d)** 7, 6, 12

4. Two sticks are hinged together at ends. One is 16 inches long and the other 11 inches. Find the minimum and maximum lengths of a third stick which would make a triangle with the two.

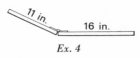

Ex. 4

5. GIVEN: $\triangle QRS$; $\overline{QS} \cong \overline{QR}$; $\overline{QR}$ extended to U.
   PROVE: $SU > SR$.

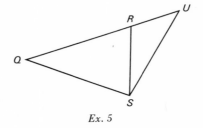

Ex. 5

Solution

1. $\overline{QS} \cong \overline{QR}$.
2. In $\triangle QRS$, m$\angle URS >$ m$\angle QSR$.

3. m$\angle QSR =$ m$\angle QRS$.
4. In $\triangle RSU$, m$\angle QRS >$ m$\angle SUR$.
5. m$\angle URS >$ m$\angle SUR$.

6. $SU > SR$.

1. Given.
2. m ext $\angle >$ m either nonadjacent int $\angle$.
3. Sides of $\triangle \cong$, opp $\angle$s $\cong$.
4. Reason 2.
5. First $>$ second $>$ third. Number sub for equal.
6. $\angle$s $\neq$, sides $\neq$ in same order.

6. Supply the reasons.
   GIVEN: $\triangle VWT$; $\overline{VY} \cong \overline{WY}$; $WT > VT$; WY bisects $\angle VWT$.
   PROVE: m$\angle TVY >$ m$\angle WVY$.

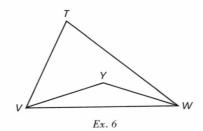

Ex. 6

1. $\overline{VY} \cong \overline{WY}$.
2. m$\angle WVY =$ m$\angle VWY$.
3. $\overline{WY}$ bisects $\angle VWT$.
4. m$\angle VWY =$ m$\angle TWY$.
5. m$\angle WVY =$ m$\angle TWY$.
6. $WT > VT$.
7. m$\angle WVT >$ m$\angle VWT$.
8. m$\angle TVY >$ m$\angle TWY$.
9. m$\angle TVY >$ m$\angle WVY$.

7. GIVEN: $\triangle ABC$; $m\angle A > m\angle CBA$; $\overline{BD}$ between $\overline{BA}$ and $\overline{BC}$.
PROVE: $BC > AD$.

8. GIVEN: $\triangle ABC$; $BC = BD$; $m\angle C > m\angle A$.
PROVE: $BA > BD$.

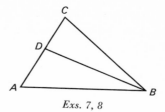
Exs. 7, 8

9. GIVEN: $\overline{RQ} \perp \overline{RS}$; $\overline{UT} \perp \overline{UV}$; $m\angle w > m\angle y$.
PROVE: $m\angle x < m\angle z$.

10. GIVEN: $\overline{RQ} \perp \overline{RS}$; $\overline{UT} \perp \overline{UV}$; $m\angle x < m\angle z$.
PROVE: $m\angle w > m\angle y$.

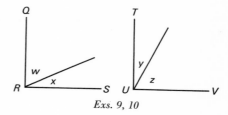
Exs. 9, 10

11. GIVEN: $EG = FG$; $EH > FJ$.
PROVE: $m\angle GHJ > m\angle GJH$.

12. GIVEN: $EG = FG$; $m\angle GJH < m\angle GHJ$.
PROVE: $EH > FJ$.

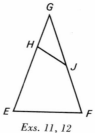
Exs. 11, 12

13. GIVEN: $AC > BC$; $\overline{AD}$ bisects $\angle CAB$; $\overline{BD}$ bisects $\angle CBA$.
PROVE: $AD > BD$

14. GIVEN: $AD > BD$; $\overline{AD}$ bisects $\angle CAB$; $\overline{BD}$ bisects $\angle CBA$.
PROVE: $AC > BC$.

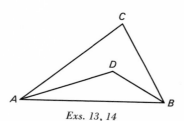
Exs. 13, 14

15. GIVEN: $QS = RS$; $\overline{RT}$ between $\overline{RQ}$
and $\overline{RS}$.
PROVE: $RT > QT$.

16. GIVEN: $QT = RT$; $\overline{RT}$ between $\overline{RQ}$
and $\overline{RS}$.
PROVE: $QS > RS$.

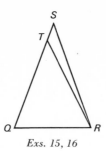

Exs. 15, 16

17. GIVEN: $AC = BC$; B between A
and D.
PROVE: $CD > CB$.

18. GIVEN: $AC = BC$; E between A
and B.
PROVE: $CB > CE$.

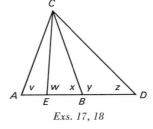

Exs. 17, 18

19. GIVEN: $\overline{EF} \perp \overline{EH}$; $EH > EG$.
PROVE: $HF > GF$.

20. PROVE: The shortest distance from
a point to a line is the perpendicular distance.

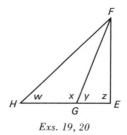

Exs. 19, 20

21. GIVEN: $m\angle BAD = m\angle BCD$; $AB >$
BC.
PROVE: $CD > DA$.

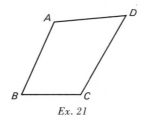

Ex. 21

22. GIVEN: $EH = EF$; m$\angle EHG >$ m$\angle EFG$.
PROVE: $FG > GH$.

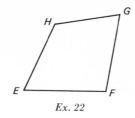

Ex. 22

23. The image I of a subject S in a mirror $\overline{MQ}$ appears to the viewer V to be behind the mirror such that $\overline{SI} \perp \overline{MQ}$ and $SM = MI$ because the light has followed the shortest path from S to A to V. VI is a segment.
PROVE: $SA + AV < SC + CV$.

24. The rays of light form congruent angles with the mirror.
PROVE: $\angle SAM \cong \angle VAQ$.

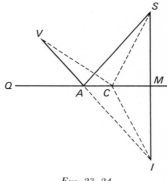

Exs. 23, 24

5.5   Summary Test

After each number on an answer sheet write T if the statement is always true and F if it is not always true.

1. The set of the whole numbers, x, which satisfy the condition $4 < x \le 8$ is $\{5, 6, 7\}$.
2. The expression $d \ge 12$ means: "d is greater than 12."
3. If $b > 3$ and $c < 9$, the intersection of b and c is $\{4, 5, 6, 7, 8\}$.
4. The intersection of $x \ge 0$ and $x < 0$ is 0.

5. If $a > 8$, then $a - 8 > 0$.
6. If $x < y$ and $y < z$, then $z > x$.
7. $-6 + 3 > 6 - 4$.
8. $|-6 + 3| > |6 - 4|$.
9. $(-7)(3) > (7)(3)$.
10. If $-5 < x < 3$, then x can have the value 4.
11. Point A has the coordinate a; point B has the coordinate b; $AB = |b - a|$.
12. Rays $\overrightarrow{VX}$, $\overrightarrow{VY}$, and $\overrightarrow{VZ}$ have coordinates x, y, and z, respectively, such that $x < z < y$. The rays are in the order $\overrightarrow{VX}$, $\overrightarrow{VY}$, $\overrightarrow{VZ}$.
13. In No. 12, $\overrightarrow{VY}$ is between $\overrightarrow{VX}$ and $\overrightarrow{VZ}$.
14. In No. 12, $m\angle XVY = m\angle XVZ + m\angle ZVY$.
15. If the endpoints of a segment have coordinates 0 and 16, then the coordinates, x, of the interior points of the segment are represented by $0 < x < 16$.
16. If the coordinate of E is 12 and the coordinate of F is 23, then the coordinates, x, of the ray $\overrightarrow{FE}$ are represented by $x \leq 23$.
17. If the coordinate of $\overrightarrow{VA}$ is 10° and the coordinate of $\overrightarrow{VB}$ is 70°, then the coordinate of the bisector of $\angle AVB$ is 35°.
18. In No. 17, the coordinates, x, of all the rays in the interior of the angle are represented by $10 \leq x \leq 70$.
19. A side of an angle is in the interior of the angle.
20. A segment joining a point in the interior of an angle and a point in the exterior of the angle intersects the angle.
21. The interiors of adjacent angles do not intersect.
22. A point can be in the exterior of a triangle and in the interior of an angle of the triangle.
23. A point in the interior of two angles of a triangle is in the interior of the triangle.
24. Every triangle is convex.
25. An exterior angle of a triangle is the supplement of one of the interior angles of the triangle.
26. If two distinct points are contained in one half-plane, then the segment joining the two points intersects the edge of the half-plane.
27. If the lengths of two sides of a triangle are 9 and 14, then the length of the third side must be greater than 5.
28. In No. 27, the length of the third side must be less than 15.
29. In $\triangle UVW$ if the $m\angle U = 40°$, $m\angle V = 60°$, and $m\angle W = 80°$, then the longest side is $\overline{WU}$.
30. In $\triangle ABC$ if $AB = 8$ and $BC = 13$ and $CA = 18$, then the greatest angle is $\angle B$.

CONDENSATIONS

First > second > third.   (Property 8) (T)

Unequals + (−, ×, ÷) equals ≠ in same order.   (Properties 9, 10, 12, 13)

Equals − (÷) unequals ≠ in reverse order.   (Properties 11, 14)

Sum of numbers > any one.   (Thm 16)

m ext ∠ > m nonadjacent int ∠.   (Thm 17)

∠ opp longer side is > ∠.   (Thm 18)

Side opp > ∠ is longer side.   (Thm 19)

chapter **6**

Parallels and
Perpendiculars

6.1 Parallel Lines and Transversals

Parallel and perpendicular lines find countless uses in our culture, not
only for esthetic reasons but for practical structural purposes.

> DEFINITION Two distinct lines which are contained in the same plane
> and do not intersect are **parallel lines**. One line is **parallel to** the other.
> The symbol for parallel is ‖.

It follows that all segments of parallel lines are parallel and all rays of
parallel lines are parallel. Parallel segments can be extended and the
resulting rays or lines are parallel.

In Chapter 10 we will prove that two parallel lines and two intersecting lines are contained in exactly one plane. In this chapter we will
state that they are in one plane as part of a definition, postulate, or theorem.
We are assuming that, unless otherwise stated, all parts of each figure are
coplanar.

The following is the *Parallel Postulate* which stimulated so much of the modern research in geometry:

Postulate 13   **Through a point not of a line in one plane there is exactly one line parallel to the given line.**

DEFINITIONS   One line which intersects two other distinct lines at exactly two distinct points is a **transversal.** The two lines **intercept** the segment of the transversal whose endpoints are the points of intersection.

The transversal can intersect three or more lines at one point of each line. In Fig. 37, line q is a transversal of lines m and n and lines m and k, but not of lines n and k.

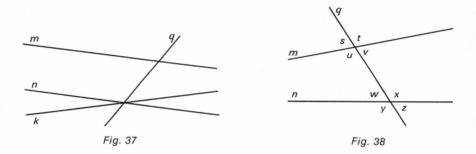

Fig. 37   Fig. 38

DEFINITION   Two angles on the opposite sides of a transversal, one at each point of intersection, are **alternate angles.**

DEFINITIONS   The region of a plane between two distinct coplanar lines is the **interior of the lines.** The region of the plane not the interior nor the lines is the **exterior of the lines.**

In Fig. 38, the two distinct lines are m and n, while the transversal is q. Angles v and w are alternate interior. Angles s and z are alternate exterior. The student should name the other pairs of alternate angles in the figure.

DEFINITION   When a transversal intersects two distinct lines, angles whose sides extend in the same general directions from the vertices are **corresponding angles.**

Angle s is corresponding to $\angle w$. The student should name three other pairs. In our usage the lines m and n will usually be parallel, and the sides of corresponding angles will extend exactly in the same directions. We specify that they are due to parallel lines to distinguish them from corresponding parts of triangles.

In Fig. 39, with transversals intersecting parallel lines *m* and *n*, one pair of each kind of angle is emphasized. The student should name them in order.

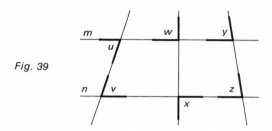

Fig. 39

THEOREM 21   Two lines parallel to the same line are parallel to each other.

GIVEN: Line *k* ∥ line *n*; line *m* ∥ line *n*.

PROVE: Line *k* ∥ line *m*.

If *k* and *m* are not ∥, they intersect at some point *P*. Then there are two lines through *P* ∥ *n*. But there can be only one line through *P* ∥ *n*, and so *k* and *m* do not intersect and are parallel.

COROLLARY 21.1   If one line is parallel to a second line, the second is parallel to the first.   (S)

COROLLARY 21.2   If one line is parallel to a second line and the second is parallel to a third line, then the first is parallel to the third.   (T)

NOTE: The symbol for parallel lines in a diagram is an arrowhead at some point of each line, the two pointing in the same direction, as shown in Construction 4.

Construction 4 *Construct a line through a given point parallel to a given line.*

GIVEN: Line *m*; point *P*.

CONSTRUCT: Line *n* through *P* ∥ *m*.

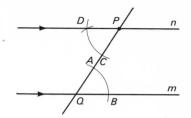

Through *P* draw any convenient line intersecting *m* at *Q*. With *Q* as a center and any convenient radius draw an arc intersecting $\overrightarrow{PQ}$ at *A* and *m* at *B*. With *P* as a center and the same radius draw an arc intersecting $\overrightarrow{PQ}$ at *C*. With *C* as a center and radius *AB* draw an arc intersecting arc *P* at *D*. Draw line *n* through *PD*. Line *n* ∥ *m*.

THEOREM 22 If two lines form congruent alternate interior angles with a transversal, the lines are parallel.

GIVEN: Lines *m* and *n*; transversal *q* intersects *m* in *A* and *n* in *B*; ∠*x* ≅ ∠*y*.

PROVE: *m* ∥ *n*.

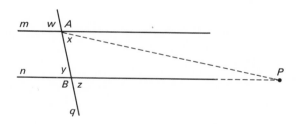

If *m* and *n* are not ∥, they intersect at some point *P*, and form △*ABP*. Then, since ∠*y* is an exterior ∠ of the △, m∠*y* > m∠*x*. But ∠*y* ≅ ∠*x*; lines *m* and *n* cannot intersect and are ∥.

COROLLARY 22.1 If two lines form congruent corresponding angles with a transversal, the lines are parallel.   (∠*z* ≅ ∠*x*)

COROLLARY 22.2 If two lines form congruent alternate exterior angles with a transversal, the lines are parallel.   (∠*w* ≅ ∠*z*)

THEOREM 23 If a transversal intersects two parallel lines, alternate interior angles are congruent.

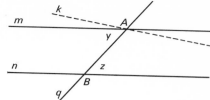

GIVEN: Line $m \parallel$ line n; $\angle y$ and $\angle z$
        alternate interior $\angle$s.

PROVE: $\angle y \cong \angle z$.

If $\angle y$ is not $\cong \angle z$, then there is a line k through A which forms $\angle w \cong \angle z$; one ray, $\angle \cong \angle$. Lines k and n, forming $\cong$ alternate interiors $\angle$s, are $\parallel$. Then $k = m$ and $k \parallel n$, since through a point there is 1 line $\parallel$ a given line. Then $\angle y = \angle w$ and $\angle y \cong \angle z$; first $\cong$ second $\cong$ third.

COROLLARY 23.1 If a transversal intersects two parallel lines, corresponding angles are congruent.

COROLLARY 23.2 If a transversal intersects two parallel lines, alternate exterior angles are congruent.

EXERCISE 6.1

1. GIVEN: $\overline{AB} \parallel \overline{CD}$; $\overline{AB}$, $\overline{EF}$, and $\overline{GH}$ intersect at K; m$\angle y = 100°$; m$\angle z = 140°$.

   (a) Name an angle alternate interior to $\angle x$.

   (b) Name an angle corresponding to $\angle AKF$.

   (c) Name an angle alternate exterior to $\angle z$.

   (d) Name a transversal of $\overline{EF}$ and $\overline{GH}$.

   (e) Give the number of degrees in each angle: s, t, u, v, and w.

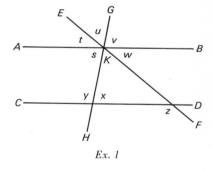

Ex. 1

2. GIVEN: $\overline{AB} \parallel \overline{DC}$; $\overline{AD} \parallel \overline{BC}$; transversal $\overline{EF}$. Name the angle congruent to **(a)** $\angle EDA$. **(b)** $\angle EDC$. **(c)** $\angle ADB$. **(d)** $\angle CDB$.

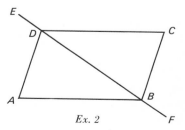

Ex. 2

3. GIVEN: Line q is a transversal of lines m and n. What are the following pairs of angles called?

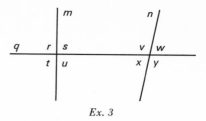

Ex. 3

   (a) $\angle r$ and $\angle t$ **(b)** $\angle r$ and $\angle y$
   (c) $\angle u$ and $\angle v$ **(d)** $\angle s$ and $\angle w$

4. State a theorem proved by each of the following in this section.

   (a) Ex. 7   **(b)** Ex. 9   **(c)** Ex. 10   **(d)** Ex. 15

5. GIVEN: $\overrightarrow{AB} \parallel \overrightarrow{DE}$; transversal $\overleftrightarrow{BG}$;
   $m\angle CBE = 0.6m\angle ABE$;
   $m\angle FEG = 0.6m\angle DEG$.
   PROVE: $\angle CBE \cong \angle FEG$.

6. GIVEN: $\overrightarrow{AB} \parallel \overrightarrow{DE}$; transversal $\overleftrightarrow{BG}$;
   $m\angle CBE = 0.6m\angle ABE$;
   $m\angle FEG = 0.6m\angle DEG$.
   PROVE: $\angle CBE$ supp $\angle BEF$.

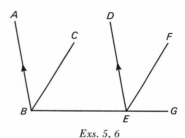

Exs. 5, 6

7. GIVEN: $\overleftrightarrow{AB} \parallel \overleftrightarrow{CD}$; $\overrightarrow{EG}$ bisects $\angle AEF$; $\overrightarrow{FH}$ bisects $\angle DFE$.
   PROVE: $\overrightarrow{EG} \parallel \overrightarrow{FH}$.

8. GIVEN: $\overleftrightarrow{AB} \parallel \overleftrightarrow{CD}$; $\overrightarrow{EG} \parallel \overrightarrow{FH}$.
   PROVE: $\angle AEG \cong \angle DFH$.

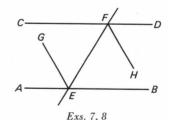

Exs. 7, 8

9. GIVEN: $\overline{AD} \parallel \overline{BC}$; $\overline{AD} \cong \overline{BC}$.
   PROVE: $\overline{AB} \parallel \overline{DC}$; $\overline{AB} \cong \overline{DC}$.

10. GIVEN: $\overline{AD} \cong \overline{BC}$; $\overline{AB} \cong \overline{DC}$.
   PROVE: $\overline{AD} \parallel \overline{BC}$; $\overline{AB} \parallel \overline{DC}$.

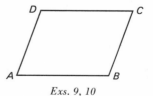

Exs. 9, 10

11. GIVEN: $\overleftrightarrow{HB} \parallel \overleftrightarrow{CG}$; $\angle AFC \cong \angle DEB$.
   PROVE: $\overline{AF} \parallel \overline{DE}$.

12. GIVEN: $\overline{AF} \parallel \overline{DE}$; $\angle AFD \cong \angle DEA$.
   PROVE: $\overleftrightarrow{AB} \parallel \overleftrightarrow{CD}$.

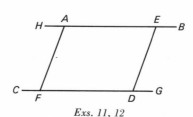

Exs. 11, 12

13. GIVEN: $\overline{AC} \cong \overline{BC}$; $\overline{DG} \parallel \overline{AC}$;
$\overline{EF} \parallel \overline{BC}$; $\overline{AD} \cong \overline{BE}$.
PROVE: $\overline{DG} \cong \overline{EF}$.

14. GIVEN: $\overline{DG} \parallel \overline{AC}$; $\overline{AD} \cong \overline{BE}$;
$\overline{AF} \cong \overline{BG}$; $\overline{AC} \cong \overline{BC}$.
PROVE: $\overline{EF} \parallel \overline{BC}$.

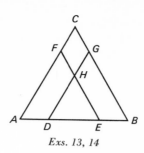

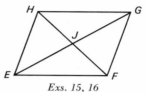

Exs. 13, 14

15. GIVEN: $\overline{HJ} \cong \overline{JF}$; $\overline{EJ} \cong \overline{JG}$.
PROVE: $\overline{EF} \parallel \overline{HG}$; $\overline{EH} \parallel \overline{FG}$.

16. GIVEN: $\overline{EF} \cong \overline{HG}$; $\overline{EF} \parallel \overline{HG}$.
PROVE: $\overline{HJ} \cong \overline{JF}$; $\overline{EJ} \cong \overline{JG}$.

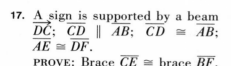

Exs. 15, 16

17. A sign is supported by a beam
$\overrightarrow{DC}$; $\overline{CD} \parallel \overline{AB}$; $\overline{CD} \cong \overline{AB}$;
$\overline{AE} \cong \overline{DF}$.
PROVE: Brace $\overline{CE} \cong$ brace $\overline{BF}$.

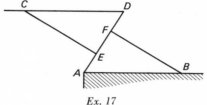

Ex. 17

18. An ironing board is adjustable
for height with one leg attached
to the board at S and the two
legs attached at their centers, T.
Prove informally that the board
is parallel to the floor.

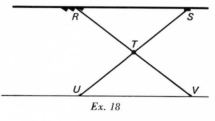

Ex. 18

19. PROVE: If the bisector of an
exterior angle of a triangle is
parallel to the nonadjacent side,
the triangle is isosceles.

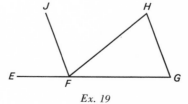

Ex. 19

6.2   Parallel Lines in Angles and Triangles

Rays have direction. Two rays in one line extend from a point of the line
in opposite directions. This concept is appropriate for parallel lines. When

a transversal intersects parallel lines, corresponding angles have the same corresponding positions with respect to the points of intersection. Their sides are parallel and extend in the same two directions. Rays in the same transversal are considered to be parallel. Two rays in parallel lines can extend in the same or opposite directions.

Thus, in Fig. 40, $\vec{BA}$ or $\vec{BC}$ is a ray and extends in the same direction as $\vec{AC}$. $\vec{BE}$ and $\vec{AD}$ are parallel rays extending in the same direction. $\vec{BE}$ and $\vec{AG}$ are rays extending in opposite directions.

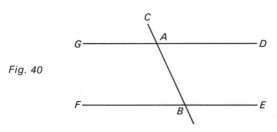

Fig. 40

THEOREM 24 **If the sides of two angles are parallel rays extending in the same or in opposite directions, then the angles are congruent.**

GIVEN: $\angle ABC$; $\overleftrightarrow{GD} \parallel \vec{BA}$; $\overleftrightarrow{EF} \parallel \vec{BC}$.

PROVE: $\angle DHF \cong \angle ABC$; $\angle GHE \cong \angle ABC$.

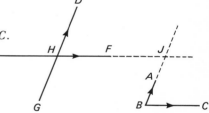

1. Extend $\vec{BA}$. Extend $\overleftrightarrow{EF}$ to intersect $\overleftrightarrow{BA}$ at J.	1. A line may be extended; 2 lines intersect in 1 point.
2. $\overleftrightarrow{GD} \parallel \vec{BA}$, $\overleftrightarrow{EF} \parallel \vec{BC}$.	2. Given.
3. $\angle DHF \cong \angle FJB$; $\angle ABC \cong \angle FJB$.	3. Trans $\parallel$, alt int $\angle$s $\cong$.
4. $\angle DHF \cong \angle ABC$.	4. First $\cong$ second $\cong$ third.
5. $\angle GHE \cong \angle DHF$.	5. Vertical $\angle$s $\cong$.
6. $\angle GHE \cong \angle ABC$.	6. Reason 4.

THEOREM 25 **The sum of the measures of the angles of a triangle equals the measure of one straight angle.**

GIVEN: $\triangle ABC$.

PROVE: $m\angle A + m\angle B + m\angle C = m$ st $\angle$.

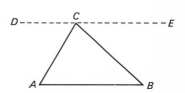

Through C draw $\overline{DE} \parallel \overline{AB}$; through a point 1 line $\parallel$ given line. Alternate interior $\measuredangle$: $\angle DCA \cong \angle A$ and $\angle ECB \cong \angle B$. $m\angle DCA + m\angle ACB + m\angle ECB$ = m st $\angle$; ray separates $\angle$ into parts, sum m = m whole. Substituting, $m\angle A + m\angle ACB + m\angle B =$ m st $\angle$.

COROLLARY 25.1   The sum of the measures of the angles of a triangle equals 180°.

COROLLARY 25.2   Only one angle of a triangle can be a right angle or an obtuse angle.

COROLLARY 25.3   The acute angles of a right triangle are complementary.

THEOREM 26   If two triangles have two angles of one congruent to the corresponding angles of the other, then the third angles are congruent. (AA $\cong$ AA, A $\cong$ A.)

GIVEN: $\triangle ABC$ and DEF;
       $\angle A \cong \angle D$;
       $\angle B \cong \angle E$.
PROVE: $\angle C \cong \angle F$.

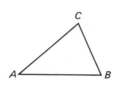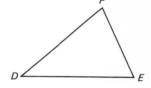

1. $m\angle A + m\angle B + m\angle C = 180°$; $m\angle D + m\angle E + m\angle F = 180°$.
2. $m\angle A + m\angle B + m\angle C = m\angle D + m\angle E + m\angle F$.
3. $\angle A \cong \angle D$; $\angle B \cong \angle E$.
4. $m\angle A + m\angle B = m\angle D + m\angle E$.
5. $m\angle C = m\angle F$; $\angle C \cong \angle F$.

1. Sum m $\measuredangle$ of $\triangle = 180°$.
2. First = second = third.
3. Given.
4. Equals + equals are equals.
5. Equals − equals are equals; $\measuredangle$ of same m $\cong$.

A convenient method of denoting corresponding angles of triangles is the plan of numbering angles known to correspond and then finding remaining angles. In $\triangle ABC$ (Fig. 41) D and E are points in the interior of

Fig. 41

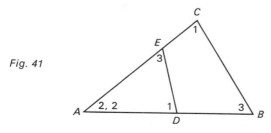

$\overline{AB}$ and $\overline{CA}$, respectively. GIVEN: $\angle ADE \cong \angle C$. Label each of these angles "1." Since $\angle A$ is a part of each triangle, label it "2, 2." Then the third angles are $\angle DEA$ and $\angle B$. Label each one "3."

THEOREM 27   The measure of an exterior angle of a triangle equals the sum of the measures of the two nonadjacent interior angles.

GIVEN: $\triangle ABC$; exterior $\angle CBD$ on
the same side of $\overline{AB}$ as C.

PROVE: $m\angle CBD = m\angle A + m\angle C$.

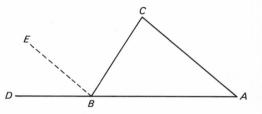

The proof is left to the student.

THEOREM 28   If two right triangles have the hypotenuse and a leg of one congruent to the corresponding parts of the other, then the triangles are congruent.   (hyp, leg $\cong$ hyp, leg)

GIVEN: Rt $\triangle ABC$ and rt $\triangle DEF$; $\angle A$ and $\angle D$ are rt $\angle$s; $\overline{BC} \cong \overline{EF}$; $\overline{AC} \cong \overline{DF}$.

PROVE: $\triangle ABC \cong \triangle DEF$.

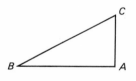 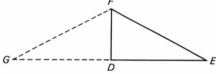

1. There is a point G of the ray opposite $\overrightarrow{DE}$ such that $\overline{DG} \cong \overline{AB}$. Construct it.
2. Draw $\overline{FG}$.
3. $\angle A$ and $\angle D$ are rt $\angle$s.
4. $\angle FDE \cong \angle FDG \cong \angle A$.

5. $\overline{BC} \cong \overline{EF}$; $\overline{AC} \cong \overline{DF}$.
6. $\triangle DGF \cong \triangle ABC$.
7. $\overline{GF} \cong \overline{BC}$.
8. $\overline{GF} \cong \overline{EF}$.
9. $\angle B \cong \angle G$.
10. $\angle G \cong \angle E$.
11. $\angle B \cong \angle E$.
12. $\angle C \cong \angle EFD$.
13. $\triangle ABC \cong \triangle DEF$.

1. To each coord corresp 1 point.

2. 2 points, 1 line.
3. Given.
4. Sides of rt $\angle$ $\perp$; $\perp$ lines form rt $\angle$s, $\cong$.
5. Given.
6. SAS $\cong$ SAS.
7. Corresp parts $\cong$ $\triangle$s $\cong$.
8. First $\cong$ second $\cong$ third.
9. Reason 7.
10. $\angle$s opp $\cong$ sides $\cong$.
11. Reason 8.
12. AA $\cong$ AA, A $\cong$ A.
13. ASA $\cong$ ASA.

Triangles and circles are among the strongest physical shapes. Circular tubing bolted or welded in triangular forms makes a structure such as a scaffold strong yet comparatively light in weight. The triangle is rigid, whereas a rectangle can be changed in shape, as illustrated by Fig. 42 on page 126. Photo by James Theologos.

THEOREM 29 **If two right triangles have the hypothenuse and an acute angle of one congruent to the corresponding parts of the other, then the triangles are congruent.**   (hyp, acute $\angle$ $\cong$ hyp, acute $\angle$)

The proof is left to the student.

EXERCISE 6.2

In equilateral $\triangle$ABC, $\overline{CD}$ *bisects* $\angle$BCA; $\overline{CD}$ $\perp$ $\overline{AB}$; $\overline{CD}$ *bisects* $\overline{AB}$.

1. What is the number of degrees in each angle of: **(a)** An equilateral triangle? **(b)** An equiangular triangle?

2. What is the number of degrees in each angle of $\triangle ADC$?

3. Compare the length of $\overline{AD}$ with the length of each side of $\triangle ABC$.

4. State a theorem about the comparative lengths of two sides of a triangle whose angles measure 30°, 60°, and 90°.

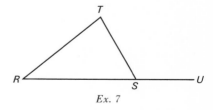

Exs. 1–5

5. **(a)** If $BC=18$, what is DB? **(b)** If $AD=20$, what is CA?

6. GIVEN: Line $\overleftrightarrow{AF}$; $\overline{BG} \parallel \overline{EH}$; $\overline{DG} \parallel \overline{CH}$. Name five pairs of congruent angles.

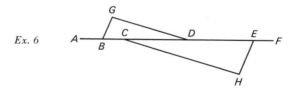

Ex. 6

7. The $\triangle RST$ has the exterior $\angle TSU$. m$\angle TSU = 120°$; m$\angle R = 40°$.

    (a) Find m$\angle RST$.
    (b) Find m$\angle T$.
    (c) Which is the longest side of the triangle and why?

Ex. 7

8. Copy the diagram of Exs. 13, 14. Label the angles proved congruent from the given of Ex. 14, 1 and 1; label other angles which can be

proved congruent 2 and 2; label the angles which then are shown to be congruent 3 and 3.

9. Find the number of degrees in the acute angles of an isosceles right triangle.

10.   GIVEN: Line $m \parallel n$; $m\angle w = 140°$; $m\angle x = 80°$.
FIND: $m\angle z$.

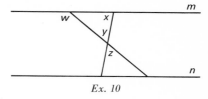

Ex. 10

Solution

1. $m\angle x + m\angle y = m\angle w$.
2. $m\angle y = m\angle w - m\angle x$.
3. $m\angle y = 140° - 80° = 60°$.
4. $m\angle z = m\angle y = 60°$.

1. m exterior $\angle$ = sum m nonadjacent interior $\angle$.
2. Equals − equals are equals.
3. Number sub for equal.
4. Vertical $\angle$ $\cong$, m =.

A less formal way of following the instruction FIND is to show the process used to find a number in place of a reason. Omitted steps of a formal proof are assumed. The solution of this exercise is written:

1. $m\angle y = 60°$.
2. $m\angle z = 60°$.

1. $140° - 80° = 60°$.
2. $m\angle z = m\angle y$.

11.   GIVEN: $\overline{AB} \cong \overline{BC}$; $m\angle CBD = 134°$.
FIND: $m\angle w$.

12.   GIVEN: $m\angle x = 70°$; $m\angle w = 60°$; $\overline{BE}$ bisects $\angle CBD$.
FIND: $m\angle z$.

Exs. 11, 12

13.   GIVEN: $\overline{DC} \perp \overline{AB}$; $\overline{EA} \perp \overline{BC}$; $m\angle B = 56°$.
FIND: $m\angle AFD$.

14.   GIVEN: $\overline{DC} \perp \overline{AB}$; $\overline{EA} \perp \overline{BC}$.
PROVE: $\angle A \cong \angle C$.

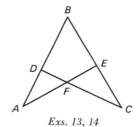

Exs. 13, 14

15. GIVEN: $\overline{QS} \perp \overline{QT}$; $\overline{US} \perp \overline{UT}$; $\overline{SQ} \cong$ $\overline{SU}$.
PROVE: $\triangle QTS \cong \triangle UTS$.

16. GIVEN: $\overline{QS} \perp \overline{QT}$; $\overline{US} \perp \overline{UT}$; $\overline{ST}$ bisects $\angle USQ$.
PROVE: $\triangle QTS \cong \triangle UTS$.

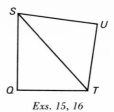

Exs. 15, 16

17. GIVEN: $\overline{DF} \parallel \overline{BC}$; $\overline{DE} \parallel \overline{AC}$; $\overline{AC} \cong \overline{BC}$.
PROVE: $\angle ADF \cong \angle BDE$.

18. GIVEN: $m\angle C = 80°$; $\overline{DF} \parallel \overline{BC}$; $\overline{DE} \parallel \overline{AC}$; $\overline{AC} \cong \overline{BC}$.
FIND: $m\angle BDE$.

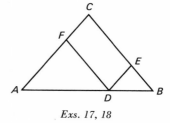

Exs. 17, 18

19. GIVEN: $\triangle RQT$; $\triangle RST$ is equilateral; $\overline{ST} \cong \overline{SQ}$.
FIND: $m\angle RTQ$.

20. GIVEN: $\overline{UW} \parallel \overline{RQ}$; $\overline{TR}$ bisects $\angle UTS$; $\overline{TQ}$ bisects $\angle WTS$.
PROVE: $\overline{RS} \cong \overline{SQ}$.

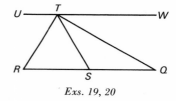

Exs. 19, 20

21. GIVEN: $\overline{AB} \parallel \overline{CD}$; $m\angle FEG = 0.6m\angle BEF$; $m\angle EFG = 0.4m\angle EFD$; $m\angle BEF = 115°$.
FIND: $m\angle EGF$.

22. GIVEN: $\overline{AB} \parallel \overline{CD}$; trans EF; $m\angle BEG = 44°$; $m\angle EGF = 82°$.
FIND: $m\angle GFD$.

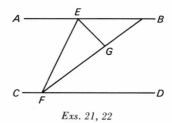

Exs. 21, 22

23. GIVEN: $m\angle y = 116°$; $\overline{AC}$ bisects $\angle DAB$; $\overline{BC}$ bisects $\angle ABD$.
FIND: $m\angle x$.

24. GIVEN: $m\angle x = 40°$; $\overline{AC}$ bisects $\angle DAB$; $\overline{BC}$ bisects $\angle ABD$.
FIND: $m\angle y$.

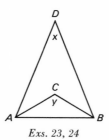

Exs. 23, 24

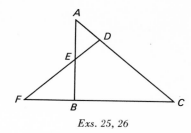

25. GIVEN: $\overline{CD} \cong \overline{DF}$; $\overline{ED} \cong \overline{DA}$.
   PROVE: $\overline{BA} \perp \overline{FC}$.

26. GIVEN: $\overline{BA} \perp \overline{FC}$; $\overline{CD} \cong \overline{DF}$.
   PROVE: $\angle DAE \cong \angle DEA$.

Exs. 25, 26

27. An isosceles triangle has a segment from the angle opposite the base to the base such that: **(a)** it bisects the base, or **(b)** it is perpendicular to the base, or **(c)** it bisects the angle. Given each one of these, prove the other two.

28 PROVE: If two triangles have two angles and a nonincluded side of one congruent to the corresponding parts of the other, then the triangles are congruent.

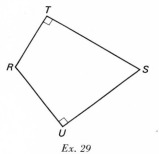

29. PROVE: If the sides of two angles are respectively perpendicular to each other, the angles are supplementary.

Ex. 29

30. Prove Theorem 27.

31. Prove Theorem 29.

6.3   Parallelograms

DEFINITIONS   A quadrilateral whose opposite sides are parallel is a **parallelogram**. A parallelogram all of whose sides are congruent is a **rhombus**. A parallelogram all of whose angles are right angles is a **rectangle**. A rectangle all of whose sides are congruent is a **square**. A quadrilateral which has exactly two sides parallel is a **trapezoid**. The parallel sides are **bases**. The other two sides are **legs**. If the legs are congruent, the trapezoid is an **isosceles trapezoid**. The symbol for parallelogram is $\square$.

DEFINITIONS   The sides and angles in consecutive order around a polygon are **consecutive sides** and **consecutive angles**. A segment joining vertices which are not consecutive is a **diagonal**.

THEOREM 30   The opposite sides and opposite angles of a parallelogram are congruent.

GIVEN: $\square$ *ABCD*.

PROVE: $\overline{AB} \cong \overline{CD}$; $\overline{DA} \cong \overline{BC}$; $\angle A \cong \angle C$;
    $\angle B \cong \angle D$.

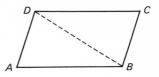

1. Draw diagonal $\overline{BD}$.
2. $\overline{BD} \cong \overline{DB}$.
3. $\overline{AD} \parallel \overline{BC}$; $\overline{AB} \parallel \overline{DC}$.
4. $\angle ABD \cong \angle CDB$; $\angle BDA \cong \angle DBC$.
5. $\triangle ABD \cong \triangle CDB$.
6. $AB \cong CD$; $DA \cong BC$; $\angle A \cong \angle C$.
7. $\angle ABC \cong \angle CDA$.

1. 2 points, 1 line.
2. Segment $\cong$ itself.
3. Opposite sides of $\square$ $\parallel$.
4. Trans $\parallel$, alt int $\angle$s $\cong$.
5. ASA $\cong$ ASA.
6. Corresp parts $\cong$ $\triangle$s $\cong$.
7. Equals + equals are equals.

COROLLARY 30.1   Either diagonal separates a parallelogram into two congruent triangles.

COROLLARY 30.2   Segments of parallel lines intercepted by parallel lines are congruent.

THEOREM 31   Two consecutive angles of a parallelogram are supplementary.

GIVEN: $\square$ *ABCD*.

PROVE: $\angle ABC$ supp $\angle BCD$.

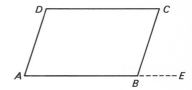

1. Extend $\overline{AB}$ through *B* to *E*.
2. $\overline{DC} \parallel \overline{AB}$.
3. $\angle C \cong \angle CBE$.
4. $\angle ABC$ supp $\angle CBE$.
5. $\angle ABC$ supp $\angle BCD$.

1. A line may be extended.
2. Opp sides of a $\square$ $\parallel$.
3. Trans $\parallel$, alt int $\angle$s $\cong$.
4. $\angle$s, sum m = m st $\angle$, are supp.
5. Name sub for name of $\cong$.

COROLLARY 31.1-   If a transversal intersects two parallel lines, interior angles on the same side of the transversal are supplementary.

THEOREM 32 **If two sides of a quadrilateral are congruent and parallel, the quadrilateral is a parallelogram.**

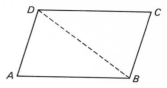

GIVEN: Quad $ABCD$; $\overline{AB} \cong \overline{CD}$; $\overline{AB} \parallel \overline{CD}$.

PROVE: $ABCD$ is $\square$.

1. $\overline{AB} \cong \overline{CD}$; $\overline{AB} \parallel \overline{CD}$.	1. Given.
2. Draw $\overline{BD}$.	2. 2 points, 1 line.
3. $\angle ABD \cong \angle CDB$.	3. Trans $\parallel$, alt int $\angle$s $\cong$.
4. $\overline{BD} \cong \overline{DB}$.	4. Segment $\cong$ itself.
5. $\triangle ABD \cong \triangle CDB$.	5. SAS $\cong$ SAS.
6. $\angle BDA \cong \angle DBC$.	6. Corresp parts $\cong$ $\angle$s $\cong$.
7. $\overline{AD} \parallel \overline{BC}$.	7. Alt int $\angle$s $\cong$, lines $\parallel$.
8. $ABCD$ is $\square$.	8. Opp sides $\parallel$, quad is $\square$.

THEOREM 33 **If the opposite sides of a quadrilateral are congruent, the quadrilateral is a parallelogram.**

The proof is left to the student.

Construction 5   *Divide a segment into congruent parts.*

GIVEN: Segment $\overline{AB}$.
Divide it into 5 parts of equal length.

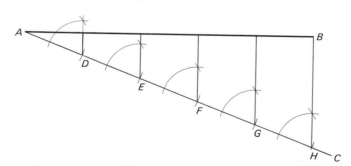

Through A draw any convenient ray $\overrightarrow{AC}$. Mark off 5 segments of equal length, AD, on $\overrightarrow{AC}$ at points D, E, F, G, and H. Draw $\overline{BH}$. Through each point on $\overrightarrow{AC}$ construct a line $\parallel \overline{BH}$; through a point 1 line $\parallel$ given line. These lines intercept congruent segments of $\overline{AB}$.

THEOREM 34 If three or more parallel lines intercept congruent segments of one transversal, they intercept congruent segments of every transversal.

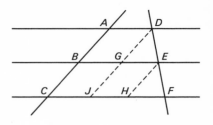

GIVEN: $\overleftrightarrow{AD} \parallel \overleftrightarrow{BE} \parallel \overleftrightarrow{CF}$; transversals $\overleftrightarrow{AC}$
and $\overleftrightarrow{DF}$; $\overline{AB} \cong \overline{BC}$.

PROVE: $\overline{DE} \cong \overline{EF}$.

1. Through D draw line $\parallel \overline{AC}$ and intersecting $\overline{BE}$ at G.
   Through E draw line $\parallel \overline{AC}$ and intersecting $\overline{CF}$ at H.
2. $\overline{DG} \cong \overline{AB}$; $\overline{EH} \cong \overline{BC}$.
3. $\overline{AB} \cong \overline{BC}$.
4. $\overline{DG} \cong \overline{EH}$.
5. $\overline{DG} \parallel \overline{EH}$.
6. $\angle EDG \cong \angle FEH$.
7. $\angle DGE \cong \angle EHF$.
8. $\triangle EDG \cong \triangle FEH$.
9. $\overline{DE} \cong \overline{EF}$.

1. Through point 1 line $\parallel$ given line.

2. $\parallel$ intercept $\cong$ segments of $\parallel$.
3. Given.
4. First $\cong$ second $\cong$ third.
5. First $\parallel$ second $\parallel$ third.
6. Trans $\parallel$ corresp $\angle$s $\cong$.
7. Sides $\parallel$, $\angle$s $\cong$.
8. ASA $\cong$ ASA.
9. Corresp parts $\cong$ $\triangle$s $\cong$.

COROLLARY 34.1   A line which bisects one side of a triangle and is parallel to the second side bisects the third side.   ($\overleftrightarrow{GE}$ bisects $\overline{DJ}$, $\overleftrightarrow{GE} \parallel \overleftrightarrow{JF}$; $\overline{GE}$ bisects $\overline{FD}$).

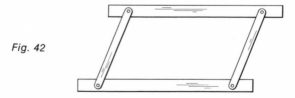

Fig. 42

   A very simple instrument used in mechanical drawing (Fig. 42) applies the principle of the parallelogram. With one side in a fixed position, the opposite side can be used to draw a number of parallel lines. The four intersections are flexible so that the two straight edges can assume any position from touching each other to maximum distance apart. How does the latter illustrate the definition of distance on page 130?

EXERCISE 6.3

1. The set of all _____ is a subset of the set of all _____.
   Give as many sentences as possible in which the two blanks are replaced with selections from the following names of figures: parallelograms, polygons, quadrilaterals, rectangles, rhombuses, squares,
   trapezoids, triangles.

2. Which of these figures contain all the others as subsets?

3. Which of these figures contain none of the others?

4. GIVEN: Trapezoid $ABCD$; $\overline{AB} \parallel \overline{DC}$;
   $\overline{AD} \perp \overline{AB}$; m∠$DAB$ ≠ m∠ABC;
   m∠v = 40°; m∠w = 30°.

   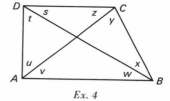

   (a) What angle, if any, is congruent
   to each: ∠w, ∠x, ∠y, ∠z?

   (b) Find, as far as possible from the
   given data, the measure of each
   of the other angles of the figure.

   Ex. 4

5. In Ex. 30 of this section we will find that the diagonals of a rhombus
   bisect the angles of the rhombus. The measure of one angle of a
   rhombus is 70°. Find the measures of the angles of the triangles formed
   by the rhombus and its diagonals.

6. State a theorem proved by each of the following in this section.

   (a) Ex. 14   (b) Ex. 16   (c) Ex. 19   (d) Ex. 24
   (e) Ex. 25   (f) Ex. 26

7. Divide a segment into three parts with the second twice the first and
   the third the sum of the first and the second.

8. The sum of the lengths of the sides of a polygon is the **perimeter** of
   the polygon. Given the segment $\overline{ST}$, construct the equilateral triangle
   whose perimeter is ST.

   Ex. 8   S _____ T

9. Given two sides and the included angle, construct a parallelogram:

   (a) By making opposite sides parallel
   (b) By making two sides parallel and congruent
   (c) By making opposite sides congruent

10. GIVEN: $\square$ *ABCD*; $\overline{AE} \cong \overline{CF}$.
 PROVE: *DEBF* is a $\square$.

11. GIVEN: $\square$ *ABCD*; m∠*ADE* = 0.7m∠*ADC*; m∠*CBF* = 0.7m∠*CBA*.
 PROVE: *DEBF* is a $\square$.

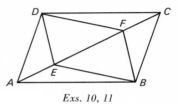

Exs. 10, 11

12. GIVEN: $\square$ *RSTU*; $\overline{VW}$ intersects $\overline{SU}$ at *X*, the midpoint of $\overline{SU}$
 PROVE: $\overline{XV} \cong \overline{XW}$.

13. GIVEN: $\square$ *RSTU*; $\overline{VW}$ intersects $\overline{SU}$ at *X*; $\overline{RV} \cong \overline{TW}$.
 PROVE: $\overline{VW}$ bisects $\overline{SU}$.

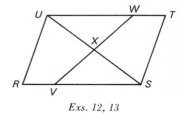

Exs. 12, 13

14. GIVEN: $\square$ *ABCD*; $\overline{DE}$ bisects ∠*CDA*; $\overline{BF}$ bisects ∠*ABC*.
 PROVE: $\overline{DE} \parallel \overline{BF}$.

15. GIVEN: $\square$ *ABCD*; $\overline{AE} \cong \overline{CF}$.
 PROVE: $\overline{DE} \parallel \overline{BF}$.

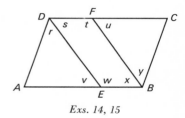

Exs. 14, 15

16. GIVEN: $\overline{AB} \perp \overline{AD}$; $\overline{DC} \perp \overline{AD}$; $\overline{AB} \cong \overline{DC}$.
 PROVE: $\overline{AC} \cong \overline{BD}$.

17. GIVEN: $\square$ *ABCD*; $\overline{AC} \cong \overline{BD}$.
 PROVE: ∠*ABC* is rt ∠.

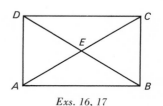

Exs. 16, 17

18. GIVEN: Rect *ABCD*; $\overline{HA} \cong \overline{FC}$; $\overline{GD} \cong \overline{EB}$.
 PROVE: *EFGH* is a $\square$.

19. GIVEN: Rect *ABCD*; *E*, *F*, *G*, *H* are midpoints of sides.
 PROVE: *EFGH* is a rhombus.

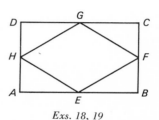

Exs. 18, 19

20. GIVEN: $\triangle QRS$; $\overline{TU}$ bisects $\overline{RS}$; $\overline{TU} \parallel$ $\overline{QR}$; $\overline{TW} \parallel \overline{RS}$.
    PROVE: $\overline{TU} \cong \overline{QW}$.

21. GIVEN: $\triangle QRS$; $\overline{TU}$ bisects $\overline{RS}$; $\overline{TU} \parallel$ $\overline{QR}$; $\overline{TW} \parallel \overline{RS}$.
    PROVE: W is midpoint of $\overline{QR}$.

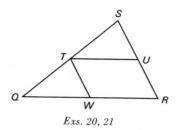

Exs. 20, 21

22. GIVEN: Trap $ABCD$; $\overline{DC} \parallel \overline{AB}$; $\overline{DC} \cong$ $\overline{BC}$.
    PROVE: $\overline{DB}$ bisects $\angle ABC$.

23. GIVEN: Trap $ABCD$; $\overline{DC} \parallel \overline{AB}$; $\overline{DC} \cong$ $\overline{BC}$; m$\angle BCD = 130°$.
    FIND: m$\angle CBA$.

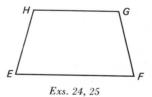

Exs. 22, 23

24. GIVEN: Trap $EFGH$; $\overline{HG} \parallel \overline{EF}$; $\overline{HE} \cong$ $\overline{GF}$.
    PROVE: $\angle E \cong \angle F$.

25. GIVEN: Trap $EFGH$; $\overline{HG} \parallel \overline{EF}$; $\angle E \cong$ $\angle F$.
    PROVE: $\overline{HE} \cong \overline{GF}$.

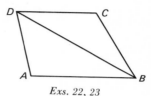

Exs. 24, 25

26. GIVEN: $\overline{QR} \parallel \overline{ST}$; $\overline{UW}$ bisects $\angle QUV$; $\overline{VW}$ bisects $\angle SVU$.
    PROVE: $\overline{UW} \perp \overline{VW}$.

27. GIVEN: $\overline{QR} \parallel \overline{ST}$; $\overline{UW}$ bisects $\angle QUV$; $\overline{VW}$ bisects $\angle SVU$.
    PROVE: $\angle VUW$ comp $\angle UVW$.

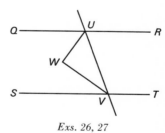

Exs. 26, 27

28. PROVE: The diagonals of a parallelogram bisect each other.

29. PROVE: The segment joining the midpoints of two opposite sides of a parallelogram bisects a diagonal.

30. PROVE: If a diagonal of a parallelogram bisects an angle of the parallelogram, then the parallelogram is a rhombus.

31. Prove Theorem 33.

6.4 Perpendiculars

Perpendiculars were introduced in Section 4.2 with these definitions: "Two lines which intersect forming right angles are perpendicular," and "The sides of a right angle are perpendicular." Then Theorem 8 gave other characteristics of perpendiculars. Lines, rays, and segments can be perpendicular. They intersect at exactly one point. The angles with their vertex at this point are right angles.

A theorem in Chapter 10 states: "For every line and every point not of the line, exactly one plane contains them." This will prove that any pair of lines perpendicular to each other is contained in one plane.

> DEFINITION   The length of the segment from a point and perpendicular to a line is the **distance** between the point and the line. The length of a segment perpendicular to two parallel lines and intercepted by them is the **distance** between the parallel lines.

Construction 6   *Through a point of a line construct a line perpendicular to the given line.*

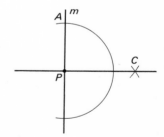

GIVEN: Line m; P a point of m.

CONSTRUCT: A line through $P \perp m$.

With P as a center and any convenient radius, construct an arc which intersects m at A and B. With A and B as centers and any convenient radius greater than half AB, construct arcs which intersect at C. Draw $\overline{PC}$. $\overline{PC} \perp m$.

THEOREM 35   Through a point of a line there is exactly one line in one plane perpendicular to the given line.

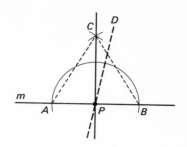

GIVEN: Line m; point P of m; $\overleftrightarrow{CP}$ from
Construction 6.

PROVE: $\overleftrightarrow{CP} \perp m$; $\overleftrightarrow{CP}$ the only line $\perp m$
in the plane.

1. Draw $\overline{AC}$ and $\overline{BC}$.
2. $\overline{PA} \cong \overline{PB}$.
3. $\overline{AC} \cong \overline{BC}$.
4. $\overline{CP} \cong \overline{CP}$.
5. $\triangle PAC \cong \triangle PBC$.
6. $\angle APC \cong \angle BPC$.
7. $\overleftrightarrow{CP} \perp \overline{AB}$.   (Existence)
8. Let $\overleftrightarrow{PD}$ be another line through P
   which may be $\perp m$; m$\angle BPD = 90°$.
9. m$\angle BPC = 90°$.
10. $\overleftrightarrow{PD}$ and $\overleftrightarrow{PC}$ coincide, and there is
   only 1 line $\perp m$ at P.   (Uniqueness)

1. 2 points, 1 line.
2. Radii of a ◯ $\cong$.
3. Radii of $\cong$ ⓢ $\cong$.
4. Segment $\cong$ itself.
5. SSS $\cong$ SSS.
6. Corresp parts $\cong$ ▲ $\cong$.
7. 2 lines forming $\cong$ adjacent ⩘ $\perp$.
8. $\perp$ lines form 90° ⩘.
9. Reason 8.
10. 1 ray, $\angle \cong \angle$.

Construction 7   *Through a point not of a line construct a line perpendicular
to the given line.*

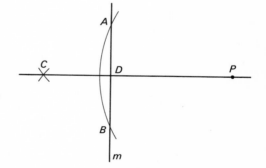

GIVEN: Line m; point P not of m.

CONSTRUCT: A line $\perp m$ through P.

With P as a center and any convenient radius, construct an arc which
intersects m at A and B. With A and B as centers and any convenient radius
greater than half AB, construct arcs which intersect at C. Construct $\overleftrightarrow{PC}$
intersecting $\overline{AB}$ at D. $\overleftrightarrow{PC} \perp \overline{AB}$ at D.

THEOREM 36 Through a point not of a line there is exactly one line in one plane perpendicular to the given line.

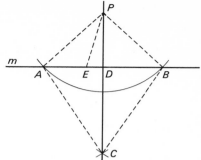

GIVEN: Line m; point P; $\overleftrightarrow{PC}$ from Construction 7.

PROVE: $\overleftrightarrow{PC} \perp m$; $\overleftrightarrow{PC}$ the only line $\perp m$ in the plane.

Draw $\overline{AP}$, $\overline{BP}$, $\overline{AC}$, $\overline{BC}$; radii of $\cong$ ⑤ $\cong$. $\overline{PC} \cong$ itself. $\triangle APC \cong \triangle BPC$ by SSS $\cong$ SSS. From these $\triangle$, $\angle APC \cong \angle BPC$. $\overline{PD} \cong$ itself. $\triangle APD \cong \triangle BPD$ by SAS $\cong$ SAS. Corresp $\angle ADP \cong \angle BDP$ and $\overline{PC} \perp m$.   (Existence)

Let $\overline{PE}$ be another line through P which may be $\perp m$. Then in $\triangle PED$, $\angle PDE$ is a rt $\angle$ and $\angle PED$ is a rt $\angle$: but only 1 $\angle$ of a $\triangle$ can be a rt $\angle$. Therefore, $\overline{PE}$ coincides with $\overline{PD}$ and through P there is only 1 line $\perp m$. (Uniqueness)

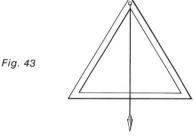

Fig. 43

An ancient form of level was an isosceles triangle with a plumb bob hanging down from the vertex (Fig 43). When the plumb line coincided exactly with its center, the base was horizontal.

Construction 8   *Construct the perpendicular bisector of a segment.*

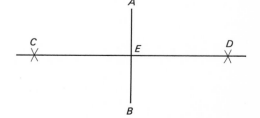

GIVEN: Segment $\overline{AB}$.

CONSTRUCT: The $\perp$ bisector of $\overline{AB}$.

With A and B as centers and any convenient radius $>$ half AB, construct arcs which intersect at C and D. Draw $\overleftrightarrow{CD}$ which intersects $\overline{AB}$ at E. $\overleftrightarrow{CD}$ is the $\perp$ bisector of $\overline{AB}$.

THEOREM 37   Every point equidistant from the ends of a segment is a point of its perpendicular bisector.

GIVEN: Segment $\overline{AB}$; $\overleftrightarrow{CD}$ from Construction 8.

PROVE: **(a)** $\overleftrightarrow{CD}$ is the $\perp$ bisector of $\overline{AB}$.
(b) Every point equidistant from A and B is of $\overleftrightarrow{CD}$.
(c) Every point of $\overleftrightarrow{CD}$ is equidistant from A and B.

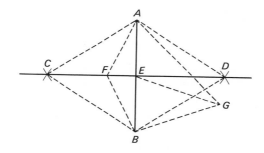

Part a: Draw $\overline{AC}$, $\overline{BC}$, $\overline{AD}$, $\overline{BD}$; $\cong$ radii. $\overleftrightarrow{CD} \cong$ itself; $\triangle ACD \cong \triangle BCD$ by SSS $\cong$ SSS. From these, $\angle ACE \cong \angle BCE$. With $CE \cong$ itself, $\triangle ACE \cong \triangle BCE$ by SAS $\cong$ SAS. Corresp parts $\overline{AE} \cong \overline{BE}$; $\overleftrightarrow{CD}$ bisects $\overline{AB}$ at E. With $\angle AEC \cong \angle BEC$, $\overleftrightarrow{CD} \perp \overline{AB}$; lines forming $\cong$ supp $\angle$s $\perp$.   (Existence)

Parts b and c: Let F be any point of $\overleftrightarrow{CD}$. Draw $\overline{AF}$ and $\overline{BF}$. In rt $\angle$s AEF and BEF, $\overline{EF} \cong$ itself. $\triangle AEF \cong \triangle BEF$; leg, leg $\cong$ leg, leg. $\overline{AF}$ and $\overline{BF}$ are corresp parts $\cong$. Let G be another point not of $\overleftrightarrow{CD}$ which may be equidistant from A and B. Then $\overline{AG} \cong \overline{BG}$. Draw $\overline{AG}$, $\overline{BG}$, and $\overline{EG}$. With $\overline{EG} \cong$ itself, $\triangle AEG \cong \triangle BEG$ by SAS $\cong$ SAS. $\angle AEG \cong$ corresp $\angle BEG$, and $\overline{GE} \perp \overline{AB}$. But there can be only 1 line $\perp \overline{AB}$ at E and $\overline{GE}$ coincides with $\overline{DE}$.   (Uniqueness)

COROLLARY 37.1   Every point of the perpendicular bisector of a segment is equidistant from the ends of the segment.

THEOREM 38   **Two lines perpendicular to the same line in one plane are parallel to each other.**

GIVEN: Lines m and $n \perp q$.

PROVE: $m \parallel n$.

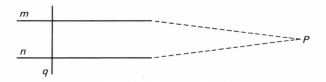

If m is not $\parallel n$, they intersect at a point P. Then there would be two lines through $P \perp q$; but through a point there is 1 line $\perp$ a given line. m and n do not intersect and are $\parallel$.

THEOREM 39   **In a plane a line perpendicular to one of two parallel lines is perpendicular to the other.**

The proof is left to the student.

6.5   More Complex Proofs

Theorems 35, 36, and 37 have introduced some new complexities into proofs. The first of these is the introduction of auxiliary lines as first discussed in Section 4.7. In addition to segments which just complete the triangles, other segments or rays are added. A constructed line complies with a minimum number of conditions — usually beginning with a point and satisfying one other condition. We cannot bisect an angle of a triangle and the opposite side with a single construction. The theorems or postulates which verify constructions contain the term *exactly one* or *every*. They are used as reasons for steps which call for construction. This is valid because every time a certain construction is made on a diagram the auxiliary line is the same, and there is exactly one resulting figure. All people using this definite construction have the same figure with which to proceed.

The second device is the proving of one congruence in order for it to contribute to another. In Theorem 36, we wanted to prove $\triangle APD \cong \triangle BPD$, but did not have the necessary corresponding parts until after we had proved $\triangle APC \cong \triangle BPC$. We prove the first triangles congruent as a prerequisite for the second congruence.

Thirdly, in Theorem 37 there are three facts to prove. Part (a) is existence. Part (c) is the converse of (b), and both together constitute uniqueness. In the past it has been required to prove a converse in a separate theorem. In the few cases in this text where the corollary is the converse of the theorem, as is Corollary 37.1, the relation is one of numerical measure.

This proof uses both an auxiliary line and the sequence of proving two pairs of triangles congruent.

PROVE: If a point of the base of an isosceles triangle is equidistant from the midpoints of the congruent sides, the point bisects the base.

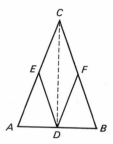

GIVEN: $\triangle ABC$, $\overline{AC} \cong \overline{BC}$; E is the midpoint of $\overline{AC}$; F is the midpoint of $\overline{BC}$; $\overline{DE} \cong \overline{DF}$.

PROVE: $\overline{AD} \cong \overline{BD}$.

Plan: There are not congruent parts sufficient to make $\triangle ADE \cong \triangle BDF$. Draw $\overline{CD}$ and prove $\triangle EDC \cong \triangle FDC$ so that from these triangles the necessary parts can be obtained to make $\triangle ADC \cong \triangle BDC$.

1. $\overline{AC} \cong \overline{BC}$; E and F are midpoints.
2. $EC = \frac{1}{2}AC$; $FC = \frac{1}{2}BC$.
3. $\overline{EC} \cong \overline{FC}$.
4. $\overline{DE} \cong \overline{DF}$.
5. Draw $\overline{CD}$.
6. $\overline{CD} \cong \overline{CD}$.
7. $\triangle EDC \cong \triangle FDC$.
8. $\angle DCE \cong \angle DCF$.
9. $\angle A \cong \angle B$.
10. $\triangle ADC \cong \triangle BDC$.
11. $\overline{AD} \cong \overline{BD}$.

1. Given.
2. Midpoint separates into halves.
3. Halves of $\cong$ segments $\cong$.
4. Given.
5. 2 points, 1 line.
6. Segment $\cong$ itself.
7. SSS $\cong$ SSS.
8. Corresp parts $\cong$ ⧌ $\cong$.
9. Sides of $\triangle \cong$, ⧌ opp $\cong$.
10. ASA $\cong$ ASA.
11. Reason 8.

EXERCISE 6.5

1. Given a straight angle, construct the following angles at the same vertex:

   (a) $90°$ **(b)** $45°$ **(c)** $135°$ **(d)** $67\frac{1}{2}°$

2. Construct a rectangle: **(a)** Given two consecutive sides. **(b)** Given one side and one diagonal.

3. (a) Show by construction: If two points are equidistant from the endpoints of a segment, any point of the line they determine is equidistant from the endpoints of the given segment. **(b)** Name the pairs of equal distances in the figure of (a).

4. State a theorem proved by Ex. 11 (below).

5. GIVEN: $\overleftrightarrow{AB} \parallel \overleftrightarrow{CD} \parallel \overleftrightarrow{EF}$; m$\angle RST = 112°$;
m$\angle ETS = 38°$.
FIND: m$\angle ARS$.

6. GIVEN: $\overleftrightarrow{AB} \parallel \overleftrightarrow{CD} \parallel \overleftrightarrow{EF}$; m$\angle ETS = 44°$;
m$\angle ARS = 72°$.
FIND: m$\angle RST$.

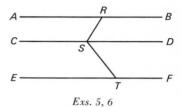

Exs. 5, 6

7. GIVEN: 30°–60°–90° $\triangle ABC$; D is the midpoint of hypotenuse $\overline{AB}$.
FIND: m$\angle y$ and m$\angle z$. (NOTE: Use Ex. 25.)

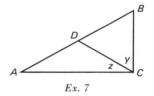

Ex. 7

8. GIVEN: Isosceles rt $\triangle EFG$; $\angle E$ is a rt $\angle$; $\overline{EG} \cong \overline{EF}$.
FIND: Measure of exterior $\angle z$.

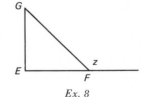

Ex. 8

9. GIVEN: $\angle EAB \cong \angle FBA$; $\overline{BE} \perp \overline{AE}$; $\overline{AF} \perp \overline{BF}$.
PROVE: $\overline{AD} \cong \overline{BD}$.

10. GIVEN: $\overline{AE} \cong \overline{BF}$; $\overline{BE} \perp \overline{AE}$; $\overline{AF} \perp \overline{BF}$.
PROVE: $\overline{DE} \cong \overline{DF}$.

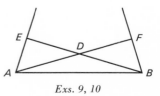

Exs. 9, 10

11. GIVEN: $\triangle UVW$; $\overline{YX} \perp$ bisector of $\overline{UV}$; $\overline{ZX} \perp$ bisector of $\overline{WU}$.
    PROVE: $\overline{UX} \cong \overline{VX} \cong \overline{WX}$.

12. GIVEN: $\overline{UX} \cong \overline{VX} \cong \overline{WX}$; $\overline{XY} \perp \overline{UV}$; $\overline{ZX} \perp \overline{WU}$.
    PROVE: $\overline{ZX}$ bisects $\overline{WU}$; $\overline{YX}$ bisects $\overline{UV}$.

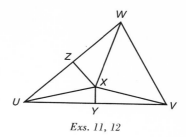

Exs. 11, 12

13. GIVEN: $\square ABCD$; $\overline{DE} \perp \overline{AC}$; $\overline{BF} \perp \overline{AC}$.
    PROVE: $\overline{DF} \cong \overline{BE}$.

14. GIVEN: $\square ABCD$; $\overline{DE} \perp \overline{AC}$; $\overline{BF} \perp \overline{AC}$.
    PROVE: $DEBF$ is a $\square$.

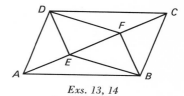

Exs. 13, 14

15. GIVEN: $\overline{SV} \parallel \overline{TW}$; $\overline{QR}$ and $\overline{ST}$ bisect each other at U.
    PROVE: $\overline{QV} \cong \overline{RW}$.

16. GIVEN: $\overline{SQ} \parallel \overline{TR}$; $\overline{SV} \parallel \overline{TW}$; $\overline{SQ} \cong \overline{TR}$.
    PROVE: $\overline{UV} \cong \overline{UW}$.

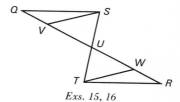

Exs. 15, 16

17. GIVEN: $\overline{AC} \parallel \overline{BD}$; $\overline{AC} \cong \overline{BD}$.
    PROVE: $\overline{GE} \cong \overline{GF}$.

18. GIVEN: $\overline{AB}$ and $\overline{CD}$ bisected at G.
    PROVE: $\overline{EF}$ bisected at G.

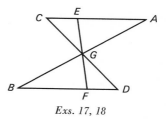

Exs. 17, 18

19. GIVEN: Trap $RSTU$; $\overline{RU} \cong \overline{ST}$; $\overline{UT} \parallel \overline{RS}$; $\angle STU \cong \angle RUT$.
    PROVE: $\triangle RVU \cong \triangle SVT$.

20. GIVEN: Trap $RSTU$; $\overline{RU} \cong \overline{ST}$; $\overline{UT} \parallel \overline{RS}$; $\angle STU \cong \angle RUT$.
    PROVE: $\triangle URS \cong \triangle TSR$.

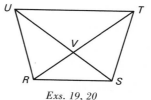

Exs. 19, 20

21. GIVEN: $\overline{AC} \cong \overline{BC}$; $\overline{AD} \cong \overline{BD}$.
PROVE: $\overline{AE} \cong \overline{BE}$.

22. GIVEN: $\overline{CF}$ bisects $\angle ACB$; $\overline{CF}$ bisects $\angle ADB$.
PROVE: $\overline{CF}$ bisects $\overline{AB}$.

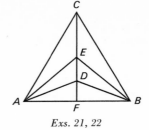

Exs. 21, 22

23. GIVEN: $\overline{AD} \perp \overline{AB}$; trapezoid $ABCD$; E is midpoint of $\overline{BC}$; $\overline{DC} \parallel \overline{AB}$.
PROVE: $\overline{AE} \cong \overline{DE}$.

24. GIVEN: $\overline{AD} \perp \overline{AB}$; trapezoid $ABCD$; $\overline{AE} \cong \overline{DE}$; $\overline{DC} \parallel \overline{AB}$.
PROVE: E is midpoint of $\overline{BC}$.

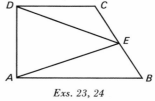

Exs. 23, 24

25. PROVE: The midpoint of the hypotenuse of a right triangle is equidistant from the three vertices.

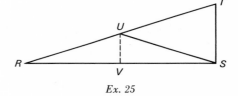

Ex. 25

26. PROVE: Every point of the bisector of an angle is equidistant from the sides of the angle.

27. PROVE: The diagonals of a rhombus are perpendicular to each other.

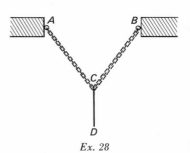

28. A sign $\overline{CD}$ hangs from the middle of a chain between two supports at the same height, A and B.
PROVE: $\angle ACD \cong \angle BCD$.

Ex. 28

29. Prove Theorem 39.

6.6 Summary Test

After each number (1–23) on answer sheet write the word(s) or symbol(s) which fill in the blank(s).

1. For every two parallel lines there is one _____ which contains them.
2. Two lines in a plane either _____ or are parallel.
3. Parallel lines _____ segments of a transversal.
4. When a transversal intersects parallel lines, if the measure of one pair of alternate interior angles is 65°, the other pair measure _____.
5. If the measure of one of two congruent angles of a triangle is 75°, the measure of the third angle is _____.
6. The largest base angle an isosceles triangle can have contains less than _____ degrees.
7. In an acute triangle the sum of the measures of two angles is _____ the measure of the third angle.
8. If the sum of the measures of two angles of a triangle equals the measure of the third, the triangle is _____.
9. In the quadrilateral $ABCD$, $\overline{CD}$ is named __(a)__, point D is a __(b)__, $\overline{BD}$ is a __(c)__, $\overline{AB}$ and $\overline{BC}$ are __(d)__ sides, $\overline{AB}$ and $\overline{CD}$ are __(e)__ sides, $\angle D$ and $\angle A$ are __(f)__ angles, $\angle A$ and $\angle C$ are __(g)__ angles, $\angle CDB$ and $\angle ABD$ are __(h)__ angles.
10. If the measure of one angle of a parallelogram is 70°, the measures of the other angles are _____.
11. If one pair of sides of a quadrilateral are __(a)__ and __(b)__, the quadrilateral is a parallelogram.
12. A parallelogram which has two consecutive angles congruent is _____.
13. The diagonals of a parallelogram _____ each other.
14. The distance between two parallel lines is the __(a)__ of the __(b)__ intercepted by the lines and __(c)__ them.
15. Two intersecting lines which form __(a)__ adjacent angles are __(b)__.
16. The distances from the center of a circle to any point of an arc of the circle are _____.
17. With a given base many isosceles triangles can be drawn; the third vertex of any of these triangles is a point of the _____ of the base.
18. In $\triangle ABC$ if $m\angle C = 30°$ and $m\angle B = 90°$, then $AB =$ _____ AC.
19. If line $q \perp m$ and $m \perp n$, then q _____ n.
20. If line $q \perp m$ and $m \parallel n$, then q _____ n.
21. When two transversals intersect parallel lines, the segments intercepted are congruent if _____.
22. The sum of the measures of the angles of a parallelogram is _____.
23. If three or more parallel lines intercept congruent segments of a transversal, then they _____ of a second transversal.

After each number (24–33) on answer sheet write *A* if the statement is always true, *S* if it is sometimes true, and *N* if it is never true.

24. When a transversal intersects parallel lines, corresponding angles are also alternate.

25. An exterior angle of a triangle is larger than any interior angle of the triangle.

26. A rectangle with all sides congruent is a rhombus.

27. In a trapezoid two sides are congruent.

28. The perpendicular bisectors of two sides of a triangle are parallel to each other.

29. The diagonals of a parallelogram are congruent.

30. If three or more parallel lines intercept congruent segments of a transversal, the parallel lines are equidistant.

31. Through any given point there is exactly one line perpendicular to any given line in one plane.

32. The bisector of a segment is also perpendicular to the segment.

33. The introduction of an auxiliary line does not change any of the facts of the original diagram.

CONDENSATIONS

Through a point 1 line ∥ given line.   (Post 13)

Opp sides ∥, quad is a ▱.   (Def)

Alt int (corresp, alt ext) ∡ ≅, lines ∥.   (Thm 22)

Trans ∥, alt int (corresp, alt ext) ∡ ≅.   (Thm 23)

Sides ∥ and in same directions, ∡ ≅.   (Thm 24)

Sum m ∡ of △ = 180° (m st ∠).   (Thm 25)

Acute ∡ of rt △ comp.   (Thm 25)

AA ≅ AA, A ≅ A.   (Thm 26)

m ext ∠ = sum m nonadjacent int ∡.   (Thm 27)

Hyp, leg ≅ hyp, leg.   (Thm 28)

Hyp, acute ∠ ≅ hyp, acute ∠.   (Thm 29)

Opp sides of ▱ ∥.   (Def)

Opp sides and opp ∠s of ▱ ≅.   (Thm 30)

Diagonal separates ▱ into ≅ △s.   (Thm 30)

Segments of ∥ intercepted by ∥ ≅.   (Thm 30)

Consecutive ∠s of ▱ supp.   (Thm 31)

Trans ∥, int ∠s on same side of trans supp.   (Thm 31)

2 sides ≅ and ∥, quad is ▱.   (Thm 32)

Opp sides ≅, quad is ▱.   (Thm 33)

∥ lines intercept ≅ segments of 1 trans, of every trans.   (Thm 34)

Line bisects 1 side of △, ∥ second, bisects third.   (Thm 34)

Through a point 1 line ⊥ given line.   (Thm 35)

2 lines ⊥ same line ∥.   (Thm 38)

Line ⊥ 1 of 2 ∥ lines, ⊥ other.   (Thm 39)

chapter **7**

Circles

7.1 Relation of Lines and Arcs

The circle as a mechanical device was discovered far back in antiquity. An understanding of the properties of the circle and lines related to it has grown through the centuries but was well developed by the early mathematicians.

DEFINITIONS The set of points of a plane a given distance from a given point is a **circle**. The given point is the **center** of the circle. A segment whose endpoints are the center and a point of the circle is a **radius** (plural **radii**). The length of a circle is the **circumference**. A subset of a circle with two distinct endpoints is an **arc**. The symbol for arc AB is $\overset{\frown}{AB}$.

DEFINITIONS The length of a radius is the **distance of the circle from the center**. The set of points of the plane whose distance from the center is less than the length of a radius is the **interior of the circle**. The set of points of its plane a greater distance from the center than the length of a radius is the **exterior of the circle**. The set of all points of an arc except its endpoints is the **interior of the arc**.

DEFINITIONS   A segment in the interior of a circle whose endpoints are points of the circle is a **chord**. A chord which contains the center of the circle is a **diameter**.

COROLLARIES   In each circle a diameter is the longest chord. The length of a diameter is twice the length of a radius. The length of a radius is half the length of a diameter.

When we name a circle, we label its center point with a letter. In this book when the letter O appears in a circle, it is always understood to locate the center. Circle O is written $\odot O$.

DEFINITIONS   A line in the plane of a circle which intersects the circle at exactly one point is a **tangent**. It is **tangent to** the circle. The one point is the **point of tangency**. A line which intersects a circle at exactly two points is a **secant**.

Except for the point of tangency, a tangent is in the exterior of the circle. A chord is a segment of a secant.

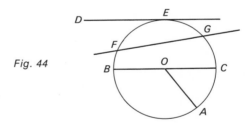

Fig. 44

In the circle, $\odot O$ (Fig. 44), with the center at O, a radius is $\overline{OA}$, a chord is $\overline{FG}$, and a diameter is $\overline{BC}$. The tangent $\overleftrightarrow{DE}$ is tangent to the circle at E. A secant is $\overleftrightarrow{FG}$. $\overline{OB}$ and $\overline{OC}$ are radii.

DEFINITION   When two lines intersect a circle such that an arc has one endpoint in each line and the points of the arc except the endpoints are contained in the interior of the lines, then the lines **intercept** the arc.

The sides of angles or parallel lines separate their plane into interior and exterior regions as formerly defined. Three cases of intercepted arcs are shown in Fig. 45. The interior regions are shaded.

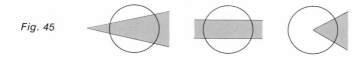

Fig. 45

DEFINITIONS   A diameter bisects a circle into two **semicircles**. The length of a semicircle is half the circumference. An arc which is less than a semicircle is a **minor arc**. An arc greater than a semicircle is a **major arc**.

DEFINITIONS   An angle whose vertex is the center of a circle is a **central angle**. An angle which intercepts an arc of a circle and whose vertex is a point of the circle is an **inscribed angle**.

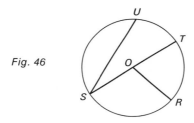

Fig. 46

In Fig. 46 the rays $\overrightarrow{OR}$ and $\overrightarrow{OS}$ form a central angle. They intercept the arc $\overset{\frown}{RS}$. An arc may be named by two or more letters. The diameter intercepts $\overset{\frown}{SRT}$ and $\overset{\frown}{SUT}$. A minor arc is $\overset{\frown}{TR}$ and the corresponding major arc is $\overset{\frown}{TSR}$. The angle $\angle TSU$ intercepts $\overset{\frown}{TU}$ and is inscribed in $\overset{\frown}{TSU}$. Its vertex is S. If the points of intersection of the sides of an inscribed angle with the circle are joined, an inscribed triangle is formed.

If each vertex of a polygon is a point of a circle, the polygon is **inscribed in** the circle, and the circle is **circumscribed about** the polygon. A side of the polygon is a chord of the circle. If each side of a polygon is tangent to a circle, the polygon is circumscribed about the circle and the

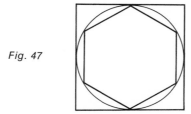

Fig. 47

circle is inscribed in the polygon. In Fig. 47 a square is circumscribed about the circle and the circle is inscribed in the square. A hexagon is inscribed in the circle and the circle is circumscribed about the hexagon.

EXERCISE 7.1

1. In the given figure name:

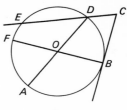

Ex. 1

(a) Two diameters
(b) Four radii
(c) Three chords
(d) One secant
(e) One tangent
(f) Four central angles
(g) One inscribed angle
(h) A semicircle
(i) The arc intercepted by central $\angle FOA$
(j) The arc intercepted by $\overrightarrow{DE}$ and $\overline{DA}$
(k) Two arcs intercepted by $\overleftrightarrow{EC}$ and $\overline{FB}$

2. Give the number of degrees in each angle of an equiangular triangle.

3. If there are vertices of equiangular triangles at a common point, how many triangles are located around the given point?

4. Let the common point be the center of a circle with sides of equilateral triangles as radii of the circle. What is the length of each segment which is both a side of a triangle and a chord of the circle?

5. Draw a circle and inscribe a regular hexagon in it.

6. As central angles of a circle draw angles of:
(a) 60°   (b) 30°   (c) 15°   (d) 75°

7.2   Congruence in Circles

A review of Section 4.7 reveals that circles which have congruent radii are congruent circles, and that all radii or diameters of a circle or of congruent circles are congruent. Comparison of circles to indicate congruence is a comparison of the lengths of their radii. Comparison of arcs of circles to indicate congruence is a comparison of their measures. The system of the measures of arcs is the same as the system for angles.

> DEFINITION   The ray-coordinate of a radius of a circle is the **coordinate of the point of the circle** which is the endpoint of the radius.

Corollary to Postulate 8   **To each point of a circle there corresponds exactly one coordinate and to each coordinate there corresponds exactly one point of the circle.**

The order of coordinates of points determines the order of their corresponding points.

> DEFINITION   The absolute value of the difference of the coordinates of its endpoints is the **measure of an arc**. The measure of arc AB is written m$\overset{\frown}{AB}$.

> COROLLARY   The measure of a central angle of a circle is the **measure of its intercepted arc**.

> DEFINITION   Arcs which have the same measure are **congruent arcs**.

THEOREM 40   On each side of a point of a circle there is exactly one point of the circle such that the measure of the arc determined by the two points is a constant.

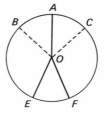

GIVEN: $\odot O$; radius $\overline{OA}$; central $\angle EOF$ intercepts $\overset{\frown}{EF}$ whose measure is k units.

PROVE: There is exactly one point on each side of A such that m arc $= k$.

There is exactly one radius $\overline{OB}$ such that m$\angle AOB = k$. There is exactly one radius $\overline{OC}$ on the other side of $\overline{OA}$ such that m$\angle AOC = k$; since there is exactly one ray such that m$\angle$ = a constant. Construct these radii. There is exactly one point of the circle which has the coordinate of each radius; the coordinate of the radius = the coordinate of the point. There is exactly one point, B, of the circle such that m$\overset{\frown}{AB} = k$ and one point C such that m$\overset{\frown}{AC} = k$; the difference of the coordinates = the measure of the arc.

COROLLARY 40.1   On each side of a point of a circle there is exactly one point of the circle such that the arc determined by the two points is congruent to the given arc.

COROLLARY 40.2   On each side of a point of a circle there is exactly one point of the circle such that the arc determined by the two points is a given multiple of a given measure.

COROLLARY 40.3   An arc has exactly one bisector.

COROLLARY 40.4   An arc is congruent to itself.   (R)

COROLLARY 40.5   **If an arc is congruent to a second arc, then the second is congruent to the first.** (S)

COROLLARY 40.6   **If an arc is congruent to a second arc and the second is congruent to a third arc, then the first is congruent to the third.** (T)

COROLLARY 40.7   **Doubles or halves of congruent arcs are congruent.**

COROLLARY 40.8   **A circle is congruent to itself.** (R)

COROLLARY 40.9   **If a circle is congruent to a second circle, then the second is congruent to the first.** (S)

COROLLARY 40.10   **If a circle is congruent to a second circle and the second is congruent to a third circle, then the first is congruent to the third.** (T)

COROLLARY 40.11   **In a circle or in congruent circles, congruent central angles intercept congruent arcs.**

COROLLARY 40.12   **In a circle or in congruent circles, central angles which intercept congruent arcs are congruent.**

THEOREM 41   **Points in the interior of an arc separate it into parts, the sum of whose measures equals the measure of the whole.**

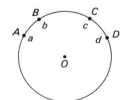

GIVEN: $\odot O$ with $\overparen{ABCD}$.

PROVE: $m\overparen{AB} + m\overparen{BC} + m\overparen{CD} = m\overparen{ABCD}$.

Let the ray coordinates of the points A, B, C, and D be a, b, c, and d, respectively. Then $m\overparen{AB} = |b - a|$, $m\overparen{BC} = |c - b|$, $m\overparen{CD} = |d - c|$, and $m\overparen{ABCD} = |d - a|$. Then $m\overparen{AB} + m\overparen{BC} + m\overparen{CD} = |(b - a) + (c - b) + (d - c)| = |(d - a)|$. Therefore, $m\overparen{AB} + m\overparen{BC} + m\overparen{CD} = m\overparen{ABCD}$.

COROLLARY 41.1   **The measure of part of an arc equals the measure of the whole minus the measure of the remainder of the arc.**

THEOREM 42   **In a circle or in congruent circles, arcs with the same endpoints as congruent chords are congruent.**

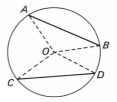

GIVEN: $\odot O$; chord $\overline{AB} \cong$ chord $\overline{CD}$.

PROVE: $\overset{\frown}{AB} \cong \overset{\frown}{CD}$.

1. Draw $\overline{AO}, \overline{BO}, \overline{CO}, \overline{DO}$.	1. 2 points, 1 line.
2. $\overline{AO} \cong \overline{BO} \cong \overline{CO} \cong \overline{DO}$.	2. Radii of $\odot \cong$.
3. $\overline{AB} \cong \overline{CD}$.	3. Given.
4. $\triangle ABO \cong \triangle CDO$.	4. SSS $\cong$ SSS.
5. $\angle AOB \cong \angle COD$.	5. Corresp parts $\cong$ ▲ $\cong$.
6. $\overset{\frown}{AB} \cong \overset{\frown}{CD}$.	6. In $\odot \cong$ central ▲ intercept $\cong$ arcs.

THEOREM 43 **In a circle or in congruent circles, chords with the same endpoints as congruent arcs are congruent.**

The proof is left to the student.

The above proofs include only minor arcs. Congruence of the corresponding major arcs can be proved if necessary.

THEOREM 44 **A line through the center of a circle and perpendicular to a chord bisects the chord and the arc with the same endpoints.**

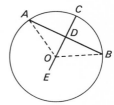

GIVEN: $\odot O$; segment of diameter $\overline{CE} \perp \overline{AB}$ at D.

PROVE: $\overline{CE}$ bisects $\overline{AB}$; $\overline{CE}$ bisects $\overset{\frown}{AB}$.

Draw $\overline{AO}$ and $\overline{BO}$ which are $\cong$ radii. $\overline{DO} \cong$ itself. Rt $\triangle ADO \cong$ rt $\triangle BDO$ by hyp, leg $\cong$ hyp, leg. Corresp parts $\overline{AD} \cong \overline{BD}$. Then $\overline{CE}$ bisects $\overline{AB}$. Corresp parts $\angle AOD \cong \angle BOD$. $\cong$ central ▲ $\cong$ make $\overset{\frown}{AC} \cong \overset{\frown}{BC}$, and $\overline{CE}$ bisects $\overset{\frown}{AB}$; a line which separates into 2 $\cong$ halves bisects.

THEOREM 45 **If a line through the center of a circle bisects a chord which is not a diameter, it is perpendicular to the chord.**

The proof is left to the student.

THEOREM 46 **In a circle or in congruent circles, chords equidistant from the center are congruent.**

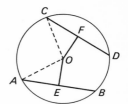

GIVEN: $\odot O$; chords $\overline{AB}$ and $\overline{CD}$; $\overline{OE} \perp \overline{AB}$; $\overline{OF} \perp \overline{CD}$; $\overline{OE} \cong \overline{OF}$.

PROVE: $\overline{AB} \cong \overline{CD}$.

1. Draw $\overline{OA}$ and $\overline{OC}$.	1. 2 points, 1 line.
2. $\overline{OA} \cong \overline{OC}$.	2. Radii of $\odot \cong$.
3. $\overline{OE} \cong \overline{OF}$; $\overline{OE} \perp \overline{AB}$; $\overline{OF} \perp \overline{CD}$	3. Given.
4. $\angle OEA$ and $\angle OFC$ are rt $\angle\!\!\!\angle$.	4. $\perp$ lines form rt $\angle\!\!\!\angle$.
5. $\triangle OEA \cong \triangle OFC$.	5. Hyp, leg $\cong$ hyp, leg.
6. $\overline{EA} \cong \overline{FC}$.	6. Corresp parts $\cong$ $\triangle\!\!\!\triangle$ $\cong$.
7. $\overline{OE}$ bisects $\overline{AB}$; $\overline{OF}$ bisects $\overline{CD}$.	7. Line through center of $\odot$ $\perp$ chord bisects chord.
8. $EA = \frac{1}{2}AB$; $FC = \frac{1}{2}CD$.	8. Bisector separates into $\cong$ halves.
9. $\overline{AB} \cong \overline{CD}$.	9. Doubles of $\cong$ segments $\cong$.

THEOREM 47 **In a circle or in congruent circles, congruent chords are equidistant from the center.**

The proof is left to the student.

EXERCISE 7.2

1. GIVEN: Chord $\overline{CD} \parallel$ diameter $\overline{AB}$ in $\odot O$.

(a) State a theorem proved by Ex. 13 below.
(b) Name two congruent arcs.
(c) Name two congruent chords.
(d) If m$\overset{\frown}{CD} = 70°$, give m$\overset{\frown}{BD}$ and m$\overset{\frown}{CA}$.
(e) If the coordinate of $\overline{OB}$ is 0°, give the coordinates of points D, C, and A.

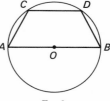

Ex. 1

2. State the definition or theorem (40–47) which is the reason for proving each statement in the right column from the corresponding one in the left column.

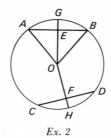

Ex. 2

(a) $\overline{OG}$ is a radius; $\overline{OH}$ is a radius. $\overline{OG} \cong \overline{OH}$.
(b) m$\angle AOG = 40°$.   m$\widehat{AG} = 40°$.
(c) The coordinate of $\overline{OB}$ is 50°; of $\overline{OG}$ is 90°.   m$\widehat{BG} = 40°$.
(d) m$\widehat{BG} = 40°$; m$\widehat{GA} = 40°$. $\widehat{BG} \cong \widehat{GA}$.
(e) $\widehat{BG} \cong \widehat{GA}$; $\widehat{GA} \cong \widehat{CH}$; $\widehat{CH} \cong \widehat{HD}$. $\widehat{BG} \cong \widehat{HD}$.
(f) $\overline{OG}$ is between $\overline{OA}$ and $\overline{OB}$.   m$\widehat{AG}$ + m$\widehat{GB}$ = m$\widehat{AB}$.
(g) $\widehat{AB} \cong \widehat{CD}$. $\overline{AB} \cong \overline{CD}$.
(h) $\widehat{AG} \cong \widehat{GB}$. $\angle AOG \cong \angle GOB$.
(i) $\overline{AB} \cong \overline{CD}$. $\widehat{AB} \cong \widehat{CD}$.
(j) $\overline{OH} \perp \overline{CD}$. $\overline{CF} \cong \overline{FD}$.
(k) $\overline{OG} \perp \overline{AB}$. $\overline{OG}$ bisects $\widehat{AGB}$.
(l) $\overline{OE} \cong \overline{OF}$. $\overline{AB} \cong \overline{CD}$.
(m) $\widehat{CH} \cong \widehat{HD}$. $\overline{CF} \cong \overline{FD}$.
(n) $\widehat{AE} \cong \widehat{EB}$. $\overline{OE} \perp \overline{AB}$.
(o) $\widehat{CD} \cong \widehat{AB}$. $\overline{OF} \cong \overline{OE}$.

3. GIVEN: m$\widehat{RS}$ > m$\widehat{TU}$.

(a) Compare the lengths of chords $\overline{RS}$ and $\overline{TU}$.
(b) Compare the measures of central angles $\angle ROS$ and $\angle TOU$.

4. Given point P in the interior of a circle, construct the chord of which P is the midpoint.

5. GIVEN: $\odot O$; $\overline{OC} \perp \overline{EF}$; $\overline{OD} \perp \overline{GH}$; $\angle EOF \cong \angle GOH$.
   PROVE: $\overline{OC} \cong \overline{OD}$.

6. GIVEN: $\odot O$; $\overline{OC} \perp \overline{EF}$; $\overline{OD} \perp \overline{GH}$; $\overline{OC} \cong \overline{OD}$.
   PROVE: $\angle EOF \cong \angle GOH$.

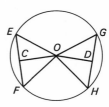

Exs. 5, 6

7. GIVEN: $\odot O$; $\overline{AB} \cong \overline{CD}$.
PROVE: $\angle AOC \cong \angle DOB$.

8. GIVEN: $\odot O$; $\overparen{AC} \cong \overparen{BD}$.
PROVE: $\overline{AB} \cong \overline{CD}$.

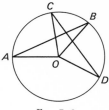

Exs. 7, 8

9. GIVEN: $\odot O$; $\overline{RY} \cong \overline{SU}$.
PROVE: $\overline{RU} \cong \overline{SY}$.

10. GIVEN: $\odot O$; $\overline{RU} \cong \overline{SY}$.
PROVE: $\triangle RSY \cong \triangle SRU$.

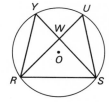

Exs. 9, 10

11. GIVEN: $\odot O$; chords $\overline{AB}, \overline{CD}$; $\angle OED \cong \angle OEA$; $\overline{OF} \perp \overline{CD}$; $\overline{OG} \perp \overline{AB}$.
PROVE: $\overline{AB} \cong \overline{CD}$.

12. GIVEN: $\odot O$; chord $\overline{AB} \cong \overline{CD}$; $\overline{OF} \perp \overline{CD}$; $\overline{OG} \perp \overline{AB}$.
PROVE: $\angle OED \cong \angle OEA$.

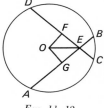

Exs. 11, 12

13. GIVEN: $\odot O$; chord $\overline{CD} \parallel$ diam $\overline{AB}$.
PROVE: $\overparen{AC} \cong \overparen{BD}$.

14. GIVEN: $\odot O$; chord $\overline{CD}$; diam $\overline{AB}$; $\overparen{AC} \cong \overparen{BD}$.
PROVE: $\overline{CD} \parallel \overline{AB}$.

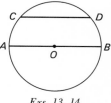

Exs. 13, 14

15. GIVEN: Chord $\overline{AB} \cong \overline{CD}$, extended to P; $\overline{OE} \perp \overline{AB}$; $\overline{OF} \perp \overline{CD}$.
PROVE: $\overline{AP} \cong \overline{CP}$.

16. GIVEN: Secants $\overline{AP}, \overline{CP}$; $\angle BPO \cong \angle DPO$; $\overline{OE} \perp \overline{AP}$, $\overline{OF} \perp \overline{CP}$.
PROVE: $\overline{AP} \cong \overline{CP}$.

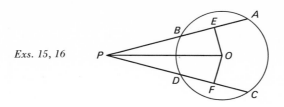

Exs. 15, 16

17. **GIVEN:** $\odot E \cong \odot F$; chords $\overline{AB}, \overline{CD}$; $\angle B \cong \angle D$.
    PROVE: $\overline{AB} \cong \overline{CD}$.

18. **GIVEN:** $\odot E \cong \odot F$; chord $\overline{AB} \cong \overline{CD}$.
    PROVE: $\angle A \cong \angle D$.

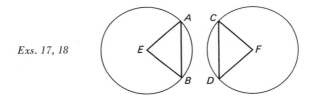

Exs. 17, 18

19. **GIVEN:** $\odot O$; diam $\overline{AB}$; chord $\overline{AC} \cong \overline{BD}$.
    PROVE: $\overline{AC} \parallel \overline{BD}$.

20. **GIVEN:** $\odot O$; diam $\overline{AB}$; chord $\overline{AC} \parallel \overline{BD}$.
    PROVE: $\overline{AC} \cong \overline{BD}$.

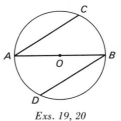

Exs. 19, 20

21. **GIVEN:** $\odot O$; chord $\overline{FH} \parallel \overline{OG}$; diam $\overline{EF}$.
    PROVE: $\overarc{EG} \cong \overarc{GH}$.

22. **GIVEN:** $\odot O$; chord $\overline{FH} \parallel \overline{OG}$; diam $\overline{EF}$.
    PROVE: $m\angle EOH = 2m\angle EOG$.

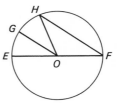

Exs. 21, 22

23. **PROVE:** A line through the center of a circle which bisects an arc bisects the chord with the same endpoints as the arc.

24. **PROVE:** A line which bisects a chord of a circle and the arc with the same endpoints is perpendicular to the chord.

25. PROVE: The midpoint of an arc is equidistant from the radii which intercept the arc.

26. Prove Theorem 43.

27. Prove Theorem 45.

28. Prove Theorem 47.

29. PROVE: If the sides of an inscribed angle in a circle are chords of unequal length, the longer chord is the shorter distance from the center.

30. PROVE: The length of half the chord of an arc of a circle is less than the length of the chord of half the arc.

31. PROVE: Parallel lines intercept congruent arcs of a circle. (NOTE: Draw a diameter parallel to the lines.)

32. Prove by the indirect method: The perpendicular bisector of a chord of a circle contains the center of the circle.

33. Draw a circle around a dish on paper. With two chords find the center of the circle. Use a third chord to check it. Given three noncollinear points of a plane, explain how to find the center of the circle containing the points.

7.3   Tangents to a Circle

THEOREM 48   A line tangent to a circle is perpendicular to the radius at the point of tangency.

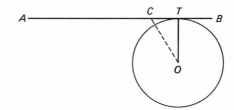

GIVEN: $\odot O$; radius $\overline{OT}$; $\overline{AB}$ tangent
        to $\odot O$ at T.

PROVE: $\overline{AB} \perp \overline{OT}$.

Let C be any other point of $\overleftrightarrow{AB}$ except T. Draw $\overline{OC}$. C is exterior to the circle. $OC > OT$ or $OT < OC$; distance of any exterior point from center > radius. Since the $\perp$ distance is the shortest from a point to a line, $\overline{AB} \perp \overline{OT}$.

THEOREM 49   A line perpendicular to a radius at its endpoint on a circle is tangent to the circle.

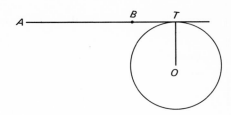

GIVEN: ⊙O; radius $\overline{OT}$; $\overleftrightarrow{AT} \perp \overline{OT}$
at T.

PROVE: $\overleftrightarrow{AT}$ tangent to ⊙O.

Let B be any point of $\overleftrightarrow{AT}$ except T. OB > OT, for a ⊥ is the shortest distance between a line and a point, and B is in the exterior of the circle. Thus, $\overleftrightarrow{AT}$ intersects the circle at exactly one point and is tangent to the circle.

THEOREM 50 Tangent segments joining an external point and a circle are congruent and make congruent angles with the segment joining the point and the center of the circle.

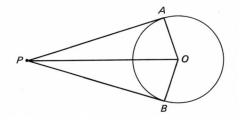

GIVEN: ⊙O; external point P; tangents $\overline{AP}$ and $\overline{BP}$; segment $\overline{OP}$.

PROVE: $\overline{AP} \cong \overline{BP}$; ∠APO ≅ ∠BPO.

The proof is left to the student.

One line can be tangent to two circles, and paired with another corresponding tangent. In Ex. 15 below there are common internal tangents, and in Ex. 16 there are common external tangents.

EXERCISE 7.3

1. If AB = 24 and ED = 14, find BD.

2. If m∠AOC = 118°, find m∠ABC.

3. Give a general rule for the comparison of OB and OA.

4. Compare:
   (a) BA and BC
   (b) m∠ABO and m∠CBO
   (c) m∠OCB and m∠OCD

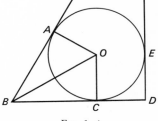

Exs. 1–4

5. Construct a tangent to a circle at a given point of tangency.

6. Draw a circle around a dish on paper. From points outside the circle draw tangents. Then construct three lines which intersect at the center of the circle.

7. GIVEN: ⊙O; radius $\overline{OT}$; chord $\overline{UW}$ ∥ tan $\overline{RS}$.
PROVE: $\overset{\frown}{UT} \cong \overset{\frown}{WT}$.

8. GIVEN: ⊙O; radius $\overline{OT}$ bisects $\overline{UW}$ at Y.
PROVE: $\overline{UT} \cong \overline{WT}$.

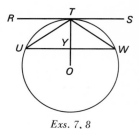

Exs. 7, 8

9. GIVEN: Concentric Ⓢ; chords of outer ⊙ are tangent to inner ⊙.
PROVE: $\overline{AE} \cong \overline{EB}$.

10. GIVEN: Concentric Ⓢ; chords of outer ⊙ are tangent to inner ⊙.
PROVE: $\overline{AB} \cong \overline{CD}$.

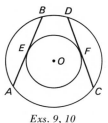

Exs. 9, 10

11. GIVEN: ⊙O; tan $\overline{PA}$; tan $\overline{PB}$.
PROVE: $\overline{AB} \perp \overline{PO}$.

12. GIVEN: ⊙O; tan $\overline{PA}$; tan $\overline{PB}$.
PROVE: $\angle OPB \cong \angle OBC$.

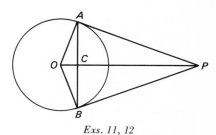

Exs. 11, 12

13. GIVEN: △ABC; $\overline{AC} \cong \overline{BC}$; sides of △ tan to ⊙ at D, E, and F.
PROVE: $\overline{AE} \cong \overline{BF}$.

14. GIVEN: △ABC; $\overline{AC} \cong \overline{BC}$; sides of △ tan to ⊙ at D, E, and F.
PROVE: $\overline{AD} \cong \overline{BD}$.

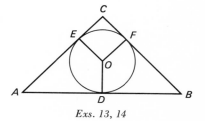

Exs. 13, 14

15. GIVEN: ⓢ E and F; tangents $\overline{AD}$ and $\overline{BC}$.
PROVE: $\overline{AD} \cong \overline{BC}$.

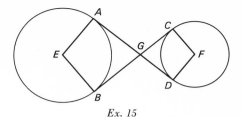

Ex. 15

16. GIVEN: ⓢ R and S; tangents $\overline{TU}$ and $\overline{VW}$.
PROVE: $\overline{TU} \cong \overline{VW}$. (NOTE: Draw $\overline{XS} \parallel \overline{TU}$ and $\overline{YS} \parallel \overline{VW}$.)

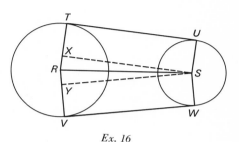

Ex. 16

17. PROVE: The sum of the lengths of the legs of a right triangle equals the sum of the lengths of the hypotenuse and the diameter of an inscribed circle.

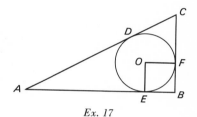

Ex. 17

18. PROVE: The segment joining the points of intersection of two circles is perpendicular to the segment joining their centers.

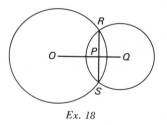

Ex. 18

19. Prove Theorem 50.

7.4   Measure Relations of Angles and Arcs

In Fig. 48 the arc $\overset{\frown}{BC}$ has the length of one diameter. There are nearly $3\frac{1}{7}$ of these in the circumference of the circle. If the circumference is measured, and that measure is divided by the measure of the diameter, for a circle of any size, the result is always the same within the limits of accuracy. The quotient is designated by the Greek letter **pi** (π). To the accuracy of seven digits this value is 3.141593. When we use pi, we take approximations of this depending on the precision required.

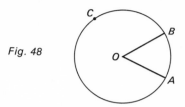

Fig. 48

The arc $\overset{\frown}{AB}$ in Fig. 48 has the length of one radius. The angle $\angle BOA$ and the arc $\overset{\frown}{AB}$ have the same measure, which is approximately $57\frac{1}{3}°$. There are 2π of these on one circle. This unit is one **radian**. It is the unit of measure most frequently used in advanced mathematics.

The degree is the measure employed for many practical uses, as in surveying and navigation. There are 360° around a point or in a circle.

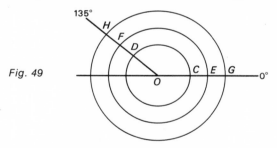

Fig. 49

The angle in Fig. 49 is measured with a protractor to have 135 *degrees of angular measure*. Then each arc which it intercepts has 135 *degrees of arc*. Each arc has a different *length of arc* because it is part of a circle of different size. Circles with the same center are **concentric circles**. The arcs $\overset{\frown}{CD}$, $\overset{\frown}{EF}$, and $\overset{\frown}{GH}$ have the same central angle, the same number of degrees, but different lengths.

We think of the radius or of the diameter sometimes as a length and sometimes as a segment. The distinction between the two uses is small enough so that we should be able to employ either one without serious ambiguity.

When lines intersect each other and a circle, there is a direct relation between the measure of the angle and the measure of the arc or arcs which the sides intercept on the circle. The theorems which follow indicate six of these relations.

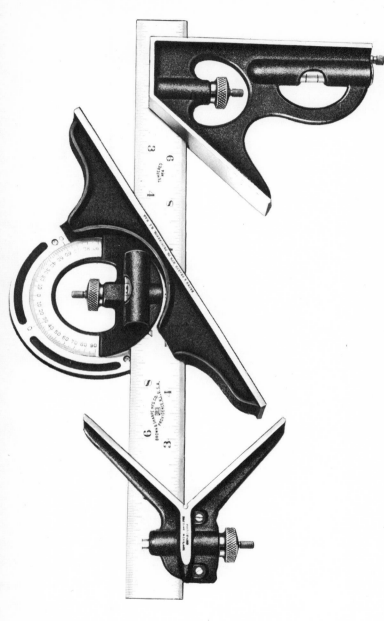

Simple tools apply the principles of geometry. On the left end of the rule is a "center head." The ruler bisects its angle; when its sides are placed tangent to a circle, the ruler edge is a diameter of the circle. Two diameters intersect at the center of the circle. The middle piece is an accurate protractor. The piece at the right end makes a perpendicular and a 45° angle with ruler. These two pieces are equipped with level glasses. Courtesy Brown and Sharpe Manufacturing Co.

THEOREM 51 **The measure of an angle inscribed in a circle is half the measure of its intercepted arc.**

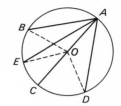

GIVEN: ⊙O.
　　　　Case 1: Chord $\overline{AB}$ and diameter $\overline{AC}$.

PROVE: m∠$BAC = \frac{1}{2}$m$\overset{\frown}{BC}$.

1. Draw $\overline{BO}, \overline{DO}, \overline{EO}$.	1. 2 points, 1 line.
2. $\overline{BO} \cong \overline{AO}$.	2. Radii of same ⊙ ≅.
3. m∠ABO = m∠BAO.	3. Sides ≅, ∠ opp ≅.
4. m∠BOC = m∠ABO + m∠BAO.	4. m ext ∠ = sum m nonadjacent int ∠.
5. m∠BOC = 2m∠BAC.	5. Number sub for equal.
6. m∠BOC = m$\overset{\frown}{BC}$.	6. m central ∠ = m arc.
7. 2m∠BAC = m$\overset{\frown}{BC}$.	7. First = second = third.
8. m∠$BAC = \frac{1}{2}$m$\overset{\frown}{BC}$.	8. Equals × equals are equals.

　　　　Case 2: Chord $\overline{AB}$ and chord $\overline{AD}$.

PROVE: m∠$BAD = \frac{1}{2}$m$\overset{\frown}{BCD}$.

1. m∠$DAC = \frac{1}{2}$m$\overset{\frown}{DC}$.	1. Case 1.
2. m∠$BAD = \frac{1}{2}$m$\overset{\frown}{BCD}$.	2. Equals + equals are equals.

　　　　Case 3: Chord $\overline{AB}$ and chord $\overline{AE}$.

PROVE: m∠$BAE = \frac{1}{2}$m$\overset{\frown}{BE}$.

1. m∠$EAC = \frac{1}{2}$m$\overset{\frown}{EC}$.	1. Case 1.
2. m∠$BAE = \frac{1}{2}$m$\overset{\frown}{BE}$.	2. Equals − equals are equals.

COROLLARY 51.1 **An angle inscribed in a semicircle is a right angle.** (It intercepts a semicircle.)

COROLLARY 51.2 **In a circle or in congruent circles, inscribed angles which intercept the same or congruent arcs are congruent angles.**

COROLLARY 51.3 **In a circle or in congruent circles, congruent inscribed angles intercept congruent arcs.**

COROLLARY 51.4   In a circle or in congruent circles, angles inscribed in the same or congruent arcs are congruent.

THEOREM 52   The measure of an angle formed by two chords intersecting in a circle is half the sum of the measures of the arcs intercepted by it and its vertical angle.

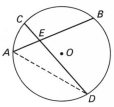

GIVEN: Chords $\overline{AB}$ and $\overline{CD}$ intersecting at E in $\odot O$.

PROVE: $m\angle AEC = \frac{1}{2}m(\overset{\frown}{AC} + \overset{\frown}{BD})$.

1. Draw $\overline{AD}$.	1. 2 points, 1 line.
2. $m\angle CDA = \frac{1}{2}m\overset{\frown}{AC}$; $m\angle BAD = \frac{1}{2}\overset{\frown}{BD}$.	2. m inscribed $\angle = \frac{1}{2}$m arc.
3. $m\angle AEC = m\angle CDA + m\angle BAD$.	3. m ext $\angle$ = sum m nonadjacent int $\angle$s.
4. $m\angle AEC = \frac{1}{2}m(\overset{\frown}{AC} + \overset{\frown}{BD})$.	4. Number sub for equal.

NOTE: The chords may be segments of secants.

THEOREM 53   The measure of the angle formed by a tangent and a chord of a circle intersecting at the point of tangency is half the measure of its intercepted arc.

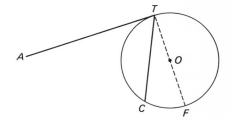

GIVEN: $\odot O$; tan $\overline{AT}$ and chord $\overline{TC}$ intersecting at T.

PROVE: $m\angle ATC = \frac{1}{2}m\overset{\frown}{TC}$.

1. Draw diam through T and O, intersecting $\odot$ at F.	1. 2 points, 1 line.
2. $m\overset{\frown}{TCF} = 180°$.	2. Diam bisects $\odot$.
3. $\frac{1}{2}m\overset{\frown}{TCF} = 90°$.	3. Equals $\times$ equals are equals.
4. $m\angle ATF = 90°$.	4. Tan $\perp$ radius, forms $90°$ $\angle$.
5. $m\angle ATF = \frac{1}{2}m\overset{\frown}{TCF}$.	5. First = second = third.
6. $m\angle CTF = \frac{1}{2}m\overset{\frown}{CF}$.	6. m inscribed $\angle = \frac{1}{2}$m intercepted arc.
7. $m\angle ATC = \frac{1}{2}m\overset{\frown}{TC}$.	7. Equals $-$ equals are equals.

THEOREM 54 The measure of the angle formed by two secants intersecting outside a circle is half the difference of the measures of the intercepted arcs.

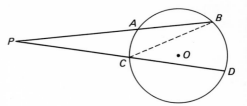

GIVEN: Secants $\overline{PB}$ and $\overline{PD}$ to $\odot O$.

PROVE: $m\angle P = \frac{1}{2}m(\overset{\frown}{BD} - \overset{\frown}{AC})$.

1. Draw $\overline{BC}$.
2. $m\angle BCD = m\angle P + m\angle PBC$.
3. $m\angle P = m\angle BCD - m\angle PBC$.
4. $m\angle BCD = \frac{1}{2}m\overset{\frown}{BD}$; $m\angle PBC = \frac{1}{2}m\overset{\frown}{AC}$.
5. $m\angle P = \frac{1}{2}m(\overset{\frown}{BD} - \overset{\frown}{AC})$.

1. 2 points, 1 line.
2. m ext $\angle$ = sum m nonadjacent int $\angle$s.
3. Equals − equals are equals.
4. m inscribed $\angle = \frac{1}{2}$m intercepted arc.
5. Number sub for equal.

COROLLARY 54.1 The measure of the angle formed by a secant and a tangent intersecting outside a circle is half the difference of the measures of the intercepted arcs.

COROLLARY 54.2 The measure of the angle formed by two tangents intersecting outside a circle is half the difference of the measures of the intercepted arcs.

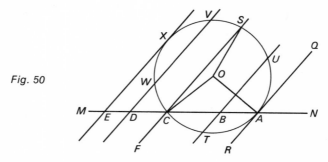

Fig. 50

All but one of these relationships are illustrated in Fig. 50. The measure of the acute angle between line $\overleftrightarrow{MN}$ and each of the parallel sloping secants is 50°. That is, $m\angle MAR = m\angle QAN = 50°$. Also $m\angle MAR = \frac{1}{2}m\overset{\frown}{AC}$, and $m\overset{\frown}{AC} = 100°$. The measure of the corresponding angle at B, $m\angle MBT = m\angle UBN = m(\overset{\frown}{AU} + \overset{\frown}{TC})$, and the sum of the measures of the arcs = 100°. When the sloping secant intersects $\overleftrightarrow{MN}$ at point C,

$m\angle MCF = m\angle SCN = \frac{1}{2}m\overset{\frown}{AS}$. The arc $\overset{\frown}{AC}$ has continued to decrease until it has become zero. The arc above $\overset{\leftrightarrow}{MN}$, such as $\overset{\frown}{AU}$, began at zero and has continued to increase until it has become 100° at S. In all cases the sum of the two arcs is 100°. As the line is moved over to D, the arc above $\overset{\leftrightarrow}{MN}$ has increased to greater than 100°. The measure of the angle is still half the sum of the measures of the arcs if we consider that the arc from A which decreased to zero at C has now decreased to a negative at W. Now $m\angle VDN = \frac{1}{2}m(\overset{\frown}{AV} + \overset{\frown}{CW})$ with $m\overset{\frown}{CW} <$ zero. When the secant becomes a tangent at X, $m\angle XEN = \frac{1}{2}m(\overset{\frown}{AX} + \overset{\frown}{CX})$ with $m\overset{\frown}{CX} <$ zero.

A central angle satisfies the same conditions. $m\overset{\frown}{AS} = 100°$, therefore $m\angle AOS = 100°$. If $\overline{AO}$ and $\overline{SO}$ were extended to become diameters, each arc intercepted by $\angle AOS$ and its vertical angle would be 100°, their sum would be 200°, and $m\angle AOS$ would be $\frac{1}{2}(200)$.

Therefore, a generalization may be formulated:

When intersecting lines intercept arcs of a circle, the measure of an angle equals half the sum of the measures of the intercepted arcs:
(a) When the intersection is in the interior of the circle, both arc measures are positive.
(b) When the intersection is on the circle, one arc is zero.
(c) When the intersection is in the exterior of the circle, the measure of the arc closer to the vertex in the angle is considered negative.

EXERCISE 7.4

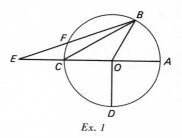

Ex. 1

1. **GIVEN:** $\odot O$ with diam $\overline{CA}$; $m\overset{\frown}{AB} = 60°$; $m\overset{\frown}{CF} = 20°$; $m\angle DOA = 90°$.
   FIND: (a) $m\overset{\frown}{DA}$. **(b)** $m\overset{\frown}{CD}$. **(c)** $m\overset{\frown}{FB}$.
   (d) $m\angle BOA$. **(e)** $m\angle BCA$. **(f)** $m\angle BEA$.

2. **GIVEN:** The measure of an inscribed angle $= 54°$.
   FIND: The measure of the central angle which intercepts the same arc.

3. In Theorem 52, if $m\overset{\frown}{BD} = 96°$ and $m\overset{\frown}{AC} = 52°$, find:

   (a) $m\angle BAD$ **(b)** $m\angle CDA$ **(c)** $m\angle AEC$

4. In Theorem 53, if $m\overset{\frown}{TC} = 132°$, find:

   (a) $m\overset{\frown}{CF}$ **(b)** $m\angle CTF$ **(c)** $m\angle ATC$

5. In Theorem 54, if m$\widehat{BD}$ = 80° and m$\widehat{AC}$ = 46°, find:

   (a) m∠BCD   **(b)** m∠PBC   **(c)** m∠P

6. In Fig. 50, the smaller angle formed by $\overleftrightarrow{MN}$ and each of the parallel lines is 50°.

   (a) GIVEN: m$\widehat{AU}$ = 58°.   **(b)** GIVEN: m$\widehat{AV}$ = 132°.
       FIND m$\widehat{TC}$.   FIND m$\widehat{CW}$.
   (c) GIVEN: m$\widehat{AX}$ = 180°.   **(d)** FIND m central ∠AOC.
       FIND m$\widehat{CX}$.

7. In Fig. 50, name a 50° angle which is:

   (a) An inscribed angle
   (b) Formed by two intersecting chords
   (c) Formed by a tangent and a chord
   (d) Formed by two secants
   (e) Formed by a secant and a tangent

8. Give a general rule for the size of an arc intercepted by an inscribed angle which is:

   (a) Acute   **(b)** Right   **(c)** Obtuse

9. GIVEN: ⊙O; △ABC; $\widehat{AE}$ ≅ $\widehat{BF}$.
    PROVE: $\overline{AC}$ ≅ $\overline{BC}$.

10. GIVEN: ⊙O; △ABC; $\overline{AC}$ ≅ $\overline{BC}$.
    PROVE: $\widehat{AE}$ ≅ $\widehat{BF}$.

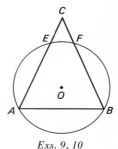

Exs. 9, 10

11. GIVEN: Inscribed △ RST and WUV; $\widehat{RS}$ ≅ $\widehat{WU}$; $\widehat{ST}$ ≅ $\widehat{UV}$.
    PROVE: ∠RST ≅ ∠WUV.

12. GIVEN: Inscribed △ RST and WUV; $\overline{RS}$ ≅ $\overline{WU}$; $\overline{ST}$ ≅ $\overline{UV}$.
    PROVE: $\overline{RT}$ ≅ $\overline{WV}$.

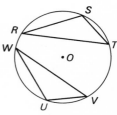

Exs. 11, 12

13. GIVEN: $\odot O$; diam $\overline{AB}$; $\angle ABC \cong \angle ABD$.
   PROVE: $\overline{BC} \cong \overline{BD}$.

14. GIVEN: $\odot O$; diam $\overline{AB}$; chord $\overline{BC} \cong \overline{BD}$.
   PROVE: $\angle AOC \cong \angle AOD$.

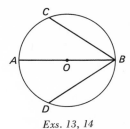

Exs. 13, 14

15. GIVEN: $\odot O$; diam $\overline{QR}$; secants $\overline{RT}$ and $\overline{QT}$;
   $\overset{\frown}{RS} \cong \overset{\frown}{SU}$.
   PROVE: $\overline{RS} \cong \overline{ST}$.

16. GIVEN: $\odot O$; diam $\overline{QR}$; secants $\overline{RT}$ and $\overline{QT}$;
   $\overline{RS} \cong \overline{ST}$.
   PROVE: $\overset{\frown}{RS} \cong \overset{\frown}{SU}$.

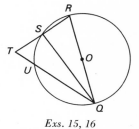

Exs. 15, 16

17. GIVEN: Square $RSTU$ inscribed in $\odot O$; V
   is a point of $\overset{\frown}{RS}$.
   PROVE: $\angle RVU \cong \angle UVT \cong \angle TVS$.

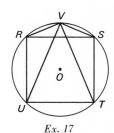

Ex. 17

18. GIVEN: $\odot O$; radius $\overline{OE} \perp$ chord $\overline{AB}$.
   PROVE: $\overline{CE}$ bisects $\angle ACB$.

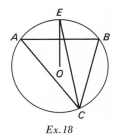

Ex.18

19. PROVE: The opposite angles of a quadrilateral inscribed in a circle are supplementary.

20. GIVEN: Quad *ABCD* inscribed in ⊙; m∠*B* = 130°.

   FIND: m∠*D*.

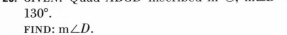

Exs. 19, 20

21. Give a general rule for the sum of the measures of the angles of a quadrilateral inscribed in a circle. Is it the same if there is a quadrilateral with no circle?

In Exs. 22–31, use the given figure, with number of degrees of angles and arcs as indicated and O the center of the circle, to find arcs labeled a *and* b *and angles* x *and* y.

22.

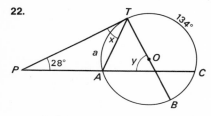

Solution

1. m$\widehat{a}$ = 78°.   1. 28° = $\frac{1}{2}$(134° − m$\widehat{a}$).

                          56° = 134° − ma.

2. m∠*x* = 39°.   2. $\frac{1}{2}$(78°) = m∠*x*.
3. m$\widehat{BC}$ = 46°.   3. 180° − 134° = m$\widehat{BC}$.
4. m∠*y* = 62°.   4. m∠*y* = $\frac{1}{2}$(78° + 46°).

23.

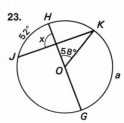

24.

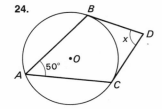

25.

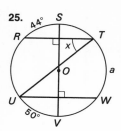

26.

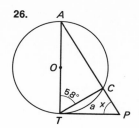

27.

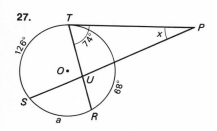

28.

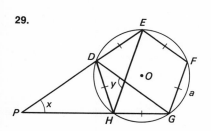

29.

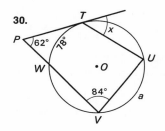

30.

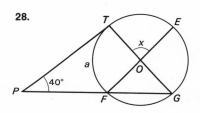

31.

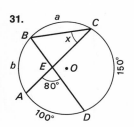

32.

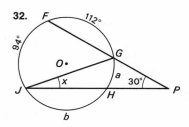

7.5 Summary Test

After each number (1–8) on answer sheet write the word(s) or symbol(s) which fill in the blank(s).

1. The endpoints of a _____ of a circle are points of the circle.
2. The set of points whose distance from __(a)__ is __(b)__ is the interior of the circle.
3. The __(a)__ is a chord which bisects a circle into two __(b)__.
4. The inscribed angle $\angle EGF$ is formed by sides __(a)__ and __(b)__; it is inscribed in the arc __(c)__; it intercepts the arc __(d)__; its measure equals __(e)__ the measure of the arc __(f)__.
5. If two chords of a circle are congruent, then also __(a)__ are congruent, and __(b)__ are equal.
6. If a diameter is perpendicular to a chord, it also __(a)__ and __(b)__.
7. In $\odot O$ the coordinate of point R is 60° and the coordinate of point S is 100°, and radius $\overline{OT}$ bisects $\angle ROS$; $\overset{\frown}{mRS} =$ __(a)__, $m\angle ROS =$ __(b)__, $m\angle SOT =$ __(c)__, $\overset{\frown}{mST} =$ __(d)__; chord $\overline{RT}$ __(e)__ chord $\overline{TS}$; $\overset{\frown}{mRT}$ __(f)__ $\overset{\frown}{mTS}$ __(g)__ $\overset{\frown}{mRS}$: $\overset{\frown}{RT}$ __(h)__ $\overset{\frown}{TS}$; radius $\overline{OT}$ __(i)__ $\overline{RS}$ and __(j)__ $\overline{RS}$ and __(k)__ $\overset{\frown}{RS}$; m inscribed $\angle RUT =$ __(l)__.
8. $\overset{\frown}{mAB} > \overset{\frown}{mCD}$; $m\angle AOB$ __(a)__ $m\angle COD$; CD __(b)__ AB.
9. Two secants intercept arcs of 80° and 30° in a circle; the measure of the angle formed by the secants is __(a)__.

After each number (10–22) on answer sheet write A if the statement is always true, S if it is sometimes true, and N if it is never true.

10. A given circle is the surface of the plane bounded by the circle.
11. If $\overline{AB}$ is a chord of a circle, $\overleftrightarrow{AB}$ is a secant.
12. A radius of a circle is a chord of the circle.
13. If a line intersects a circle, the intersection is two points.
14. A diameter $\overline{AB}$ and a tangent $\overrightarrow{BP}$ are perpendicular.
15. When an angle intersects a circle, the intercepted arc or arcs are on and in the interior of the angle.
16. The intersection of a line and a circle is the empty set.
17. The intersection of perpendicular bisectors of chords of a circle is the center of the circle.
18. A circle is in the exterior of a polygon circumscribed about it.
19. A triangle whose vertices are points of a circle is inscribed in the circle.
20. A tangent to a circle is contained in the plane of the circle.
21. If $\overline{AB}$ and $\overline{CD}$ are diameters of a circle, $ACBD$ is a rectangle.
22. The length of an arc whose measure is 10° is the same as the length of a second arc whose measure is 10°.

CONDENSATIONS

Radii of ⊙ (≅ Ⓢ) ≅. Ⓢ with ≅ radii ≅.   (Def)

In ⊙ (≅ Ⓢ) arcs with same m ≅. In ⊙ (≅ Ⓢ) ≅ arcs have same m.   (Def)

In ⊙ (≅ Ⓢ) ≅ central ∡ intercept ≅ arcs.   (Thm 40)

In ⊙ (≅ Ⓢ) central ∡ which intercept ≅ arcs ≅.   (Thm 40)

m central ∠ = m intercepted arc; m arc = m central ∠.   (Def)

Arc ≅ itself.   (Thm 40)

First ≅ second ≅ third.   (Thm 40)

Doubles (halves) of ≅ arcs ≅.   (Thm 40)

Points separate arc into parts, sum m = m whole.   (Thm 41)

Chords ≅, arcs with same endpoints ≅.   (Thm 42)

Arcs ≅, chords with same endpoints ≅.   (Thm 43)

Line through center of ⊙ ⊥ chord bisects chord and arc.   (Thm 44)

Line through center of ⊙ bisects chord, ⊥ chord.   (Thm 45)

Chords equidist from center ≅.   (Thm 46)

≅ chords equidist from center.   (Thm 47)

Tan ⊥ radius.   (Thm 48)

Tan segments from point ≅, make ≅ ∡ with line to center.   (Thm 50)

m inscribed ∠ = ½ m arc.   (Thm 51)

∠ inscribed in semicircle is a rt ∠.   (Thm 51)

Inscribed ∡ which intercept ≅ arcs ≅.   (Thm 51)

≅ inscribed ∡ intercept ≅ arcs.   (Thm 51)

m∠ formed by chords = ½ sum m arcs.   (Thm 52)

m∠ formed by tan and chord = ½ m arc.   (Thm 53)

m∠ formed by tan and sec (2 tan, 2 sec) = ½ diff m arcs.   (Thm 54)

chapter **8**

Similar Triangles and Proportion

8.1 Basic Proportions

There are many geometric figures congruent to each other. There are others which have corresponding angles but not corresponding sides congruent. They may be placed so that their corresponding sides are parallel, and it becomes apparent that they have the same shape. Their sides have another kind of correspondence. Its characteristics are numerical. The sides of the triangles in Fig. 51 have this relationship. The lengths

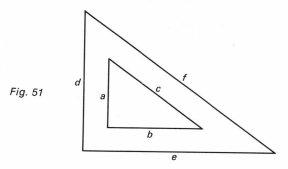

Fig. 51

of the lettered segments are: $a = 3$ units, $b = 4$ units, $c = 5$ units, $d = 3$ units, $e = 4$ units, $f = 5$ units. In the smaller triangle each unit is $\frac{1}{4}$ inch. In the larger triangle each unit is $\frac{1}{2}$ inch. Each side of the larger triangle is exactly twice as long as the corresponding side of the smaller triangle.

DEFINITION   If there is a one-to-one correspondence between the numbers of two sets such that the numbers of one set multiplied by a constant result in the corresponding numbers of the second set, then the corresponding numbers are **proportional**, or **in proportion**. The multiplier is the **constant of proportionality**. The relation between two corresponding numbers, one of each set, is a **ratio**. The equality of two ratios is a **proportion**.

The mathematical process by which two numbers of a ratio are compared is division. In the triangles in Fig. 51, the sets of lengths to be compared are: $\{a, b, c\}$ and $\{d, e, f\}$. Now,

$$d = 2a \qquad e = 2b \qquad f = 2c$$

and 2 is the constant of proportionality. In general if $d = ka$, then k is the constant. The relation between d and a is

$$\frac{d}{a} = 2$$

and d/a is a ratio. Likewise,

$$\frac{e}{b} = 2 \qquad \text{and} \qquad \frac{f}{c} = 2$$

Since

$$2 = \frac{d}{a} \quad \text{or} \quad \frac{e}{b} \quad \text{or} \quad \frac{f}{c}$$

then

$$\frac{d}{a} = \frac{e}{b}$$

and this equality is a proportion. Other proportions are

$$\frac{d}{a} = \frac{f}{c} \qquad \text{and} \qquad \frac{e}{b} = \frac{f}{c}$$

A traditional way of writing the first proportion is $d : a = e : b$. Either form is read: "d is to a as e is to b." In the traditional form, the numbers on the ends of the expression are the **extremes** and the numbers between the ends are the **means**. When the means are multiplied the product is ae; when the extremes are multiplied the product is db.

Other proportions can be written from difference correspondence. The sets of numbers to be compared can also be $\{a, d\}$, $\{b, e\}$, and $\{c, f\}$.

Since $b = \frac{4}{3}a$ and $e = \frac{4}{3}d$,

$$\frac{4}{3} = \frac{b}{a} \quad \text{and} \quad \frac{e}{d}$$

Then

$$\frac{b}{a} = \frac{e}{d}$$

is a proportion. In all the proportions derived from the same pairs of corresponding sides, one product is ae, and the other product is db.

THEOREM 55 In every proportion the product of the means equals the product of the extremes.

GIVEN: $d : a = e : b \quad or \quad \dfrac{d}{a} = \dfrac{e}{b}$.

PROVE: $db = ae$.

The common denominator of the fraction is ab. Multiplying both members by ab gives $db = ea$ or $bd = ae$.

This proof is the source of the technique called *cross multiplying* in algebra.

COROLLARY 55.1 Given the equation of two products, any arrangement of the factors can be made which allows the product of the means to equal the product of the extremes.

Any three numbers of a proportion can be given and the **fourth proportional** can be found.

Example:

$$\frac{6}{14} = \frac{9}{x}$$

Then

$$6x = 126$$
$$x = 21$$

This solution can be checked by using the constant of proportionality 1.5. If $6 \cdot 1.5 = 9$, then $14 \cdot 1.5 = 21$.

Two equations for the same relationship are here expressed. The one:

$$\frac{6}{14} = \frac{9}{x}$$

is the **proportional equation**. The result of multiplying is

$$6x = 126$$

which is the **product equation**. Theorem 55 indicates that the two equations can be interchanged at will.

The corollary of the theorem means that x can be placed in any of the four parts of a proportion and the other three numbers so placed that the proportion equation is a true expression of the product equation: $6x = 126$. When x is used as any one of the four numbers of the proportion, the location of the 6 is then determined—in a position such that it will be multiplied by x. Then the 9 and the 14 can be placed in either of the two remaining positions. Thus:

$$\frac{x}{-} = \frac{-}{6} \qquad \frac{-}{x} = \frac{6}{-} \qquad \frac{-}{6} = \frac{x}{-} \qquad \frac{6}{-} = \frac{-}{x}$$

The choice for the location of the 9 and the 14 in each of these gives eight different proportions which can be written with the same four numbers. Multiplying in all cases gives the same product equation numerically.

Sometimes a proportion is such that the same number appears twice. When it is in the means, the number is the **mean proportional** or the **geometric mean**. Knowing the two extremes, we solve for the mean. The mean proportional between 4 and 9 is found by the proportion

$$\frac{4}{x} = \frac{x}{9}$$

Then

$$x^2 = 36$$
$$x = 6$$

We are concerned only with cases in which numbers are positive.

A proportion can be made from any ratio using any constant of proportionality. In some cases the constant is deliberately chosen so as to make one number of the proportion exactly 1. Specific gravity as a property of matter is found by dividing the weight of a certain volume of a material by the weight of the same volume of pure water. This ratio for aluminum is 8 to 3. A block of aluminum which weighs 8 grams has the same volume as water weighing 3 grams. All specific gravity fractions are reduced to decimal quantities with 1 as the denominator. When both numerator and denominator of 8/3 are divided by 3, the proportion is $8 : 3 = 2.7 : 1$, and the specific gravity of aluminum is 2.7.

Another volume of aluminum weighs 40 grams and that volume of water weighs 15 grams. We write a proportion by equating two ratios:

$$\frac{8}{3} = \frac{40}{15}$$

The second volume is exactly 5 times the first volume, the specific gravity of each sample of aluminum is 2.7. Multiplying the numerator and denominator of any ratio by a constant is one method of finding an unknown number of a proportion.

Example: What will be the weight of aluminum if the same volume of water weighs 21 grams? The equality of two ratios gives $8/3 = x/21$. Since the constant of proportionality for the denominator is 7, it is the same for the numerator, and $x = 8 \cdot 7 = 56$ grams.

When a proportion is established, new ratios can be developed from it by addition and subtraction. When we add or subtract numerators and also denominators, the results form a new ratio equal to the given ratios. Thus, by addition:

$$\frac{8}{3} = \frac{40}{15} \text{ gives the equal ratio } \frac{48}{18}$$

or by subtraction:

$$\frac{8}{3} = \frac{40}{15} = \frac{32}{12} = \frac{24}{9}, \text{ etc.}$$

THEOREM 56   In a series of equal ratios the sum of the numerators is to the sum of the denominators as the numerator is to the denominator of one of the ratios.

GIVEN: $\dfrac{a}{b} = \dfrac{c}{d} = \dfrac{e}{f}$.

PROVE: $\dfrac{a + c + e}{b + d + f} = \dfrac{a}{b}$.

Let $c = ka$, $d = kb$, $e = ja$, $f = jb$. Then $\dfrac{a}{b} = \dfrac{ka}{kb} = \dfrac{ja}{jb}$. With the common denominator kjb, $\dfrac{kja}{kjb} = \dfrac{kja}{kjb} = \dfrac{kja}{kjb}$. Then $a + c + e = 3kja$ and $b + d + f = 3kjb$. Dividing, $\dfrac{3kja}{3kjb} = \dfrac{a}{b}$ and $\dfrac{a + c + e}{b + d + f} = \dfrac{a}{b}$.

COROLLARY 56.1   In a series of equal ratios the difference of the numerators is to the difference of the denominators as the numerator is to the denominator of one of the ratios.

We can add or subtract numbers of each ratio to make another set of proportions. The sums and differences are new ratios.

THEOREM 57   The sum of the numbers of one ratio is to one of the numbers as the sum of the numbers of an equal ratio is to the corresponding number of the second ratio.

GIVEN: $\dfrac{b}{c} = \dfrac{d}{e}$.

PROVE: $\dfrac{b+c}{c} = \dfrac{d+e}{e}$.

Add 1 to each of the ratios: $\dfrac{b}{c} + 1 = \dfrac{d}{e} + 1$, and $\dfrac{b+c}{c} = \dfrac{d+e}{e}$.

COROLLARY 57.1   The difference of the numbers of one ratio is to one of the numbers as the difference of the numbers of an equal ratio is to the corresponding number of the second ratio.

With $8/3 = 40/15$ two proportions made by addition are $11/8 = 55/40$ and $11/3 = 55/15$. The process for the difference gives $5/8 = 25/40$ or $5/3 = 25/15$. New ratios are formed which are not equal to the original ratios, but are equal to each other.

EXERCISE 8.1

1. Given the fraction 30/54:
   (a) Reduce to lowest terms.
   (b) What is the constant of proportionality?
   (c) Write this proportion in seven more expressions.
   (d) Write the product equation.
   (e) Write two proportions following Theorems 56 and 57.

2. Give the ratio which equals x/y in each of the following:

   (a) $\dfrac{y}{x} = \dfrac{3}{14}$ (b) $\dfrac{y}{9} = \dfrac{x}{11}$ (c) $\dfrac{x}{r} = \dfrac{y}{s}$ (d) $5x = 12y$

   (e) $cx = dy$

3. Solve for x in each of the following:

   (a) $6x = 42$ (b) $\dfrac{4}{x} = \dfrac{18}{45}$ (c) $\dfrac{12}{9} = \dfrac{x}{6}$ (d) $\dfrac{4}{x} = \dfrac{x}{25}$

   (e) $\dfrac{x}{a} = \dfrac{64}{4}$ (f) $\dfrac{g}{h} = \dfrac{x}{f}$

4. One angle measures 3 times its supplement. Find the number of degrees in each.

5. One angle measures twice its complement. Find the number of degrees in each.

6. The measure of an exterior angle of a triangle is 130°. The nonadjacent interior angles have measures in the ratio of 2 to 3. Find the measures of these angles.

7. Find the measures of the angles of a triangle in the ratio of 2 to 3 to 5.

8. Find the measures of the angles of a triangle in the ratio of 2 to 3 to 4.

9. Find the measures of the acute angles of a right triangle in the ratio of 7 to 11.

8.2   Similar Polygons

DEFINITION   If two polygons have a one-to-one correspondence between their vertices such that their corresponding angles are congruent and the lengths of their corresponding sides are proportional, the polygons are **similar polygons**. One polygon is **similar to** the other. The symbol is ~.

COROLLARY   All congruent polygons are similar.

DEFINITION   The sum of the lengths of the sides of a polygon is its **perimeter**.

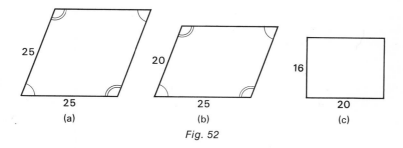

Fig. 52

Two parallelograms can have corresponding angles congruent and sides not proportional. In Fig. 52, (a) and (b) are not similar. One can be a rhombus, for instance. A rectangle (c) can have sides proportional to those of a parallelogram (b) and the two are not similar.

The properties of numbers called reflexive, symmetric, and transitive are also relations of proportion between similar polygons. They are proved here for triangles.

THEOREM 58   Of three triangles, if the first is similar to the second and the second is similar to the third, then the first is similar to the third. (T)

GIVEN: $\triangle ABC \sim \triangle DEF$; $\triangle DEF \sim \triangle GHJ$.

PROVE: $\triangle ABC \sim \triangle GHJ$.

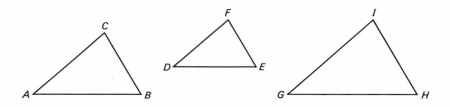

In similar △ corresp ∡ ≅: $\angle A \cong \angle D \cong \angle G$; $\angle B \cong \angle E \cong \angle H$; $\angle C \cong \angle F \cong \angle J$. Corresp sides are prop: $\dfrac{AB}{BC} = \dfrac{DE}{EF}$ and $\dfrac{AB}{CA} = \dfrac{DE}{FD}$ and $\dfrac{DE}{EF} = \dfrac{GH}{HJ}$ and $\dfrac{DE}{FD} = \dfrac{GH}{JG}$. Then $\dfrac{AB}{BC} = \dfrac{GH}{HJ}$ and $\dfrac{AB}{CA} = \dfrac{GH}{JG}$; first = second = third. With corresp ∡ ≅ and corresp lengths of sides prop, $\triangle ABC \sim \triangle GHJ$.

COROLLARY 58.1   A triangle is similar to itself.   (R)

COROLLARY 58.2   If a triangle is similar to a second triangle, then the second is similar to the first.   (S)

Irregular shapes can also be similar. Maps, mechanical drawings, and models of many kinds compare proportionally with real objects. Their corresponding angles are congruent; their corresponding lengths are proportional. Photo enlargements are similar to the original negatives.

DEFINITION   The ratio of corresponding lengths in similar figures is the constant of proportionality, commonly called the **scale** of the proportion.

The scale may be stated in many ways. A drawing may show a scale of 1 : 120, or it may have the notation: "1 inch = 10 feet." The scale equals the ratio of a given length on the model to the corresponding length on the object.

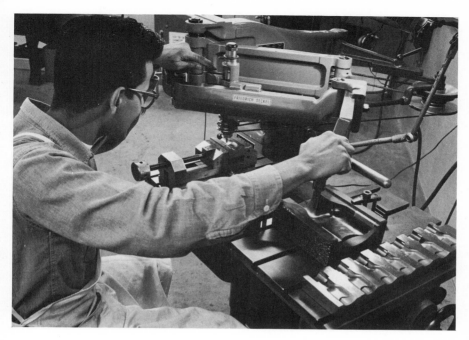

A pantograph is an instrument for copying a figure accurately. Above is a commercial pantograph cutting a shape out of metal. A cutter, revolving at 16,000 rpm, follows the movement of the stylus in the pattern and cuts out a form exactly one quarter the size of the pattern. Photo courtesy Caco Pacific. Below is a home-made pantograph. The stylus traces lines on a map, and the pen copies the lines at double the size. Photo by Haven Bishop.

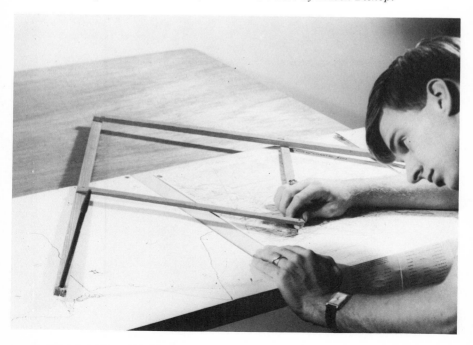

Example: If a drawing has a scale of 1 inch = 8 feet (or $\frac{1}{8}$ inch = 1 foot), what is the length on a building corresponding to a length on the drawing of $2\frac{3}{4}$ inches? The proportion is the equality of the scale ratio to the length ratio:

$$\frac{1}{8} = \frac{2\frac{3}{4}}{x}$$
$$x = 22 \text{ feet}$$

Similar figures are congruent when their constant of proportionality is 1.

EXERCISE 8.2

1. What is the specific gravity of a sample of alcohol which weighs 72 grams if the same volume of water weighs 90 grams?

2. The distance between two towns on a map is $4\frac{1}{2}$ inches. The towns are 90 miles apart. What is the scale of the map?

3. What is the ratio of the circumference of a circle to its diameter?

4. What is the ratio of: **(a)** The number of inches to the number of feet in any distance? **(b)** The length of 1 inch to the length of 1 foot?

5. A certain segment has the length of 20 inches and 50.8 cm. What is the ratio of: **(a)** The number of centimeters to the number of inches in the segment? **(b)** The length of 1 cm to the length of 1 inch?

6. A photographic negative has the length of 35 mm. The enlarged print has a length of 210 mm.

  (a) A line on the print is 12 mm. long; how long is it in the negative?
  (b) A line in the negative is 1 mm. long; how long is it on the print?

7. A blueprint has a scale: $\frac{1}{4}$ inch = 1 foot.

  (a) What measure on a building corresponds to $6\frac{1}{4}$ inches on the drawing?
  (b) What measure on the drawing corresponds to 14 feet on the building?

8. A model boat has a length of 38 inches. The original boat has a length of 190 feet.

  (a) What is the height on the model of a mast which on the original is 40 feet high?
  (b) What is the length of a rail on the original whose model is 7 inches long?

8.3   Similar Triangles

Postulate 14   **Corresponding segments of transversals intercepted by parallel lines are proportional.**

THEOREM 59   **A line parallel to one side of a triangle and intersecting the other two sides divides these sides such that one side is to one of its segments as the other side is to its corresponding segment.**

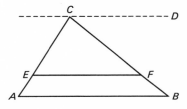

GIVEN: $\triangle ABC$; $\overline{EF} \parallel \overline{AB}$; $\overline{EF}$ intersects $\overline{AC}$
at E and $\overline{BC}$ at F.

PROVE: $\dfrac{CA}{CE} = \dfrac{CF}{FB}$.

Through C draw $\overleftrightarrow{CD} \parallel \overline{AB}$; one line $\parallel$ given line. Then $\overleftrightarrow{CD} \parallel \overline{EF}$; first $\parallel$ second $\parallel$ third. Then $\dfrac{CE}{EA} = \dfrac{CF}{FB}$, for corresp segments of trans intercepted by $\parallel$ are prop. Then $\dfrac{CE + EA}{CE} = \dfrac{CF + FB}{CF}$; sum : one = sum : one; or $\dfrac{CA}{CE} = \dfrac{CB}{CF}$; number sub for equal.

COROLLARY 59.1   **A line parallel to one side of a triangle and intersecting the other two sides divides these sides proportionally.**

THEOREM 60   **A line which intersects two sides of a triangle and divides them proportionally is parallel to the third side.**

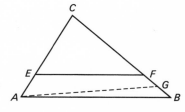

GIVEN: $\triangle ABC$; $\overline{EF}$ intersects $\overline{AC}$ at E
and $\overline{BC}$ at F; $\dfrac{CE}{EA} = \dfrac{CF}{FB}$.

PROVE: $\overline{EF} \parallel \overline{AB}$.

Through A construct a line which may be $\parallel \overline{EF}$ and intersects $\overline{BC}$ at G. Then $\dfrac{CE}{EA} = \dfrac{CF}{FG}$; line $\parallel$ one side divides other sides prop. Then $\dfrac{CA}{CE} = \dfrac{CG}{CF}$, for sum : one = sum : corresp one. But $\dfrac{CE}{EA} = \dfrac{CF}{FB}$ and so $\dfrac{CA}{CE} = \dfrac{CB}{CF}$. Two numbers, both = same: $\dfrac{CG}{CF} = \dfrac{CB}{CF}$. Multiply both members by CF, $CG = CB$; G coincides with B and $\overline{EF} \parallel \overline{AB}$.

COROLLARY 60.1   A line which bisects two sides of a triangle is parallel to the third side.

THEOREM 61   If two triangles have two angles of one congruent to the corresponding angles of the other, then the triangles are similar.   (AA ~ AA)

GIVEN: $\triangle$ ABC and DEF; $\angle A \cong \angle D$; $\angle B \cong \angle E$.

PROVE: $\triangle ABC \sim \triangle DEF$.

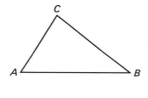 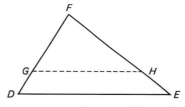

1. There is a point G of $\overline{DF}$ such that $\overline{GF} \cong \overline{AC}$. There is a point H of $\overline{FE}$ such that $\overline{HF} \cong \overline{BC}$. Construct them.
2. Draw $\overline{GH}$.
3. $\angle A \cong \angle D$; $\angle B \cong \angle E$.
4. $\angle C \cong \angle F$.
5. $\triangle GHF \cong \triangle ABC$.
6. $\angle FGH \cong \angle A$; $\angle FHG \cong \angle B$.
7. $\angle FGH \cong \angle D$; $\angle FHG \cong \angle E$.
8. $\overline{GH} \parallel \overline{DE}$.
9. $\dfrac{DF}{GF} = \dfrac{EF}{HF}$.
10. $\overline{AC} \cong \overline{GF}$; $\overline{BC} \cong \overline{HF}$.
11. $\dfrac{DF}{AC} = \dfrac{HF}{BC}$.
12. In like manner $\dfrac{DF}{AC} = \dfrac{DE}{AB}$.
13. $\triangle ABC \sim \triangle DEF$.

1. To each coord corresp 1 point.

2. 2 points, 1 line.
3. Given.
4. AA $\cong$ AA; A $\cong$ A.
5. SAS $\cong$ SAS.
6. Corresp parts $\cong$ $\triangle$ $\cong$.
7. First $\cong$ second $\cong$ third.
8. Corresp $\triangle$ $\cong$, lines $\parallel$.
9. Line $\parallel$ side of $\triangle$ divides 2 sides, side : segment = side : segment.
10. Reason 6.
11. Number sub for equal.

12. Steps 1–11.
13. $\triangle$ $\cong$, sides prop, $\triangle$ $\sim$.

COROLLARY 61.1 **If two right triangles have an acute angle of one congruent to a corresponding angle of the other, then the triangles are similar.**

COROLLARY 61.2 **A line parallel to one side of a triangle and intersecting the other two sides forms a triangle similar to the given triangle.**

COROLLARY 61.3 **If a segment joins the midpoints of two sides of a triangle, its length is half the length of the third side.**

THEOREM 62 **If two triangles have their corresponding sides proportional, then the triangles are similar.**   (SSS ~ SSS.)

GIVEN: △ *ABC* and *DEF*; $\dfrac{AC}{DF} = \dfrac{BC}{EF} = \dfrac{BA}{ED}$.

PROVE: $\triangle ABC \sim \triangle DEF$.

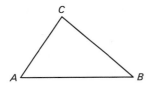 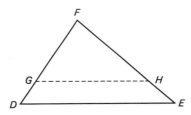

There is a point *G* of $\overline{DF}$ such that *GF = AC*. There is a point *H* of $\overline{FE}$ such that *HF = BC*. Construct them. Draw $\overline{GH}$. By substitution in $\dfrac{AC}{DF} = \dfrac{BC}{EF}$, $\dfrac{GF}{DF} = \dfrac{HF}{EF}$. $\overline{GH} \parallel \overline{DE}$; line divides 2 sides of △ prop $\parallel$ third side. $\triangle DEF \sim \triangle GHF$; line $\parallel$ 1 side of △ forms ~ △. Corresp sides $\dfrac{HG}{ED} = \dfrac{GF}{DF}$. Substituting, $\dfrac{GF}{DF} = \dfrac{AC}{DF}$. Given $\dfrac{AC}{DF} = \dfrac{BA}{ED}$, then $\dfrac{HG}{ED} = \dfrac{BA}{ED}$ and $\overline{HG} \cong \overline{BA}$. $\triangle ABC \cong \triangle GHF$ by SSS $\cong$ SSS and $\triangle ABC \sim \triangle DEF$; first ~ second ~ third.

COROLLARY 62.1 **If two triangles have two sides of one proportional to the corresponding sides of the other and the included angles congruent, then the triangles are similar.**   (SAS ~ SAS)

COROLLARY 62.2 Perimeters of similar triangles are to each other as the lengths of a pair of corresponding sides.

8.4 Corresponding Parts of Similar Triangles

By definition all similar triangles have corresponding angles congruent and sides proportional. The corresponding pairs of angles and sides may be ascertained by means of a visual method. Given $\overline{AF} \perp \overline{BC}$ and $\overline{CE} \perp \overline{AB}$ (Fig. 53), find congruent angles and give the proportions of corresponding sides. In two triangles the most obvious pair of congruent angles are labeled "1." If an angle is an identity in two triangles, it is marked twice. The next pair to be found are labeled "2." Then the remaining pair, which we can now prove to be congruent, are labeled "3." Their location becomes apparent from the other two.

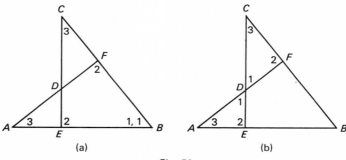

Fig. 53

The corresponding sides are now evident. The three letters of the vertices are written in 1–2–3 order. The corresponding sides are discovered by taking the letters which correspond from these names. The first and second letters in the names of the two triangles name a pair of corresponding sides (a and a'). The second and third letters designate a second pair of corresponding sides (b and b'). The third and first letters name the third pair (c and c'). Thus in Fig. 53(a):

$$\overset{\overset{a\;\;\;b}{\frown\frown}}{\triangle\ B\ E\ C}\underset{\underset{c}{\smile}}{} \sim \overset{\overset{a'\;\;b'}{\frown\frown}}{\triangle\ B\ F\ A}\underset{\underset{c'}{\smile}}{}$$

In any pair of similar triangles one set of relations is

$$\frac{a}{a'} = \frac{b}{b'} = \frac{c}{c'}.$$

Useful proportions found from this are

$$\frac{a}{c} = \frac{a'}{c'} \quad \text{and} \quad \frac{b}{c} = \frac{b'}{c'}$$

Fig 53(b) shows $\triangle DFC \sim \triangle DEA$. We can go on to find all four of these triangles similar: $\triangle BEC \sim \triangle BFA \sim \triangle DFC \sim \triangle DEA$.

EXERCISE 8.4

1. GIVEN: Transversals intersect parallel lines giving segments of lengths a, b, c, d, e, and f. Complete the proportions:

(a) $\dfrac{a}{c} = \dfrac{d}{\_}$

(b) $\dfrac{\quad}{\quad} = \dfrac{f - e}{f}$

(c) $\dfrac{a + b}{b} = \underline{\quad\quad}$

(d) $\dfrac{c}{f} = \dfrac{\_}{d}$

(e) $\dfrac{f}{c} = \dfrac{\_}{a}$

(f) $\dfrac{a + b + c}{a} = \underline{\quad\quad\quad}$

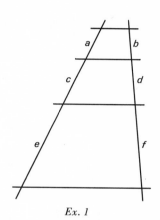

Ex. 1

2. GIVEN: Trapezoid $RSTU$; $\overline{UT} \parallel \overline{VW} \parallel \overline{RS}$. Complete each of the following:

	Left leg	*Diagonal*	*Right leg*
(a)	$\dfrac{UV}{VR} =$	$\dfrac{?}{?} =$	$\dfrac{?}{?}$
(b)	$\dfrac{?}{?} =$	$\dfrac{UX}{US} =$	$\dfrac{?}{?}$
(c)	$\dfrac{?}{?} =$	$\dfrac{?}{?} =$	$\dfrac{WS}{TS}$

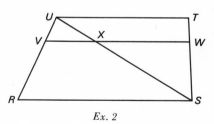

Ex. 2

3. GIVEN: Trapezoid $ABCD$; $\overline{DC} \parallel \overline{AB}$; $\overline{EF} \parallel \overline{AD}$; $\overline{AC}$, $\overline{BD}$, and $\overline{EF}$ intersect at G. Name the pairs of similar triangles.

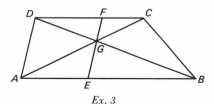

Ex. 3

4. GIVEN: $\triangle ABC$; $\overline{GF} \parallel \overline{AB}$.

(a) If $CA = 36$, $BC = 32$, and $FC = 24$, find CG.

(b) If $AB = 24$, $BC = 32$, and $FC = 24$, find GF.

(c) If $GA = 9$, $CG = 18$, and $BC = 24$, find FB.

(d) If $GA = 9$, $CG = 18$, and $GF = 12$, find AB.

(e) If perimeter of $\triangle ABC = 27$, $GF = 4$, and $AB = 6$, find perimeter of $\triangle GFC$.

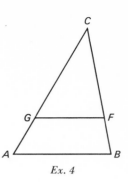

Ex. 4

5. GIVEN: $\angle CDE \cong \angle A$.

(a) If $CD = 18$, $BC = 24$, and $EC = 16$, find CA.

(b) If $AB = 9$, $BC = 12$, and $EC = 8$, find DE.

(c) If $CD = 36$, $AE = 22$, and $EC = 32$, find BD.

(d) If $m\angle A = 60°$ and $m\angle C = 40°$, find $m\angle DEC$.

(e) If perimeter of $\triangle CDE = 46$, $EC = 16$, and $BC = 24$, find perimeter of $\triangle ABC$.

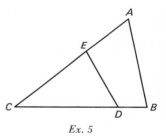

Ex. 5

6. GIVEN: $\overline{RS} \parallel \overline{UW} \parallel \overline{XY}$; $\overline{RU} \cong \overline{UX}$.

(a) If $RT = 12$, $RY = 40$, and $ST = 15$, find SX.

(b) If $TX = 20$, $TY = 15$, and $SX = 28$, find RY.

(c) If $RS = 10$, find UV.

(d) If $UW = 11$, find XY.

(e) If $RY = 30$, find WY.

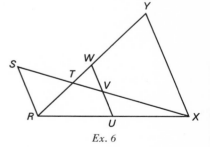

Ex. 6

7. A quadrilateral has sides of lengths 8, 10, 12, and 14. A similar figure has a perimeter of 56. Find the lengths of the sides of the second quadrilateral.

8. The sides of a triangle have lengths 16, 20, and 28. Find the perimeter of the triangle formed by joining the midpoints of the sides.

9. GIVEN: $\triangle ABC$; $\overline{DE} \parallel \overline{BC}$; $\overline{AC} \cong \overline{AB}$;
$\overline{DE} \cong \overline{DF}$.
PROVE: $\triangle EDA \sim \triangle EFD$.

10. GIVEN: $\triangle ABC$; $\overline{DE} \parallel \overline{BC}$; $\overline{AC} \cong \overline{AB}$;
$\overline{DE} \cong \overline{DF}$.
PROVE: $\dfrac{AB}{BC} = \dfrac{DF}{FE}$.

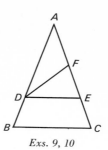

Exs. 9, 10

11. GIVEN: Chord $\overline{AC}$ bisects $\angle DAB$.
PROVE: $\dfrac{AD}{EA} = \dfrac{AC}{BA}$.

12. GIVEN: $m\overset{\frown}{DC} = m\overset{\frown}{CB}$.
PROVE: $\triangle ACB \sim \triangle BCE$.

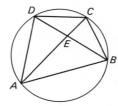

Exs. 11, 12

13. GIVEN: $\odot O$; tangent $\overline{PT}$; secant $\overline{AP}$.
PROVE: $AP \cdot TB = AT \cdot TP$.

14. GIVEN: $\odot O$; tangent $\overline{PT}$; secant $\overline{AP}$.
PROVE: $AP \cdot PB = PT^2$.

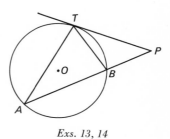

Exs. 13, 14

15. GIVEN: $\triangle ABC$; $\overline{FE} \parallel \overline{AB}$; $\overline{ED} \parallel \overline{CA}$.
PROVE: $\dfrac{CF}{FA} = \dfrac{AD}{DB}$.

16. GIVEN: $\triangle ABC$; $\overline{FE} \parallel \overline{AB}$; $\overline{ED} \parallel \overline{CA}$.
PROVE: $\dfrac{CF}{FE} = \dfrac{ED}{DB}$.

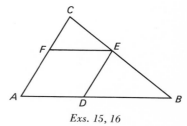

Exs. 15, 16

17. GIVEN: $\triangle ABC$; $\overline{AC} \parallel \overline{PR} \parallel \overline{QT}$; $AP = PR = QT$.
PROVE: $PR + QT = AC$.

18. GIVEN: $\triangle ABC$; $\overline{AC} \parallel \overline{PR} \parallel \overline{QT}$; $AP = PR = QT$.
PROVE: $QT : PR = 1 : 2$.

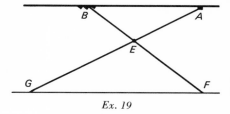

Exs. 17, 18

19. If the legs of an ironing board are attached so that $AE = 0.4AG$, and $BE = 0.4BF$, prove that the board is parallel to the floor.

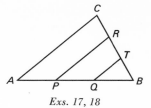

Ex. 19

20. When two chords intersect in a circle, prove that the product of the lengths of the segments of one chord equals the product of the lengths of the segments of the other chord.

21. PROVE: The segments joining the midpoints of the sides of a triangle form another triangle which is similar to the given triangle.

22. PROVE: The segments joining the midpoints of consecutive sides of any quadrilateral form a parallelogram.

23. PROVE: If a tangent and a secant to a circle intersect, the length of the tangent segment is the mean proportional between the lengths of the secant segment and its exterior segment. (See figure for Exs. 13, 14.)

24. A surveyor wishes to find the radius of the circle of which a certain street curb is an arc. He draws a tape to find a chord of the arc, which is 200 feet long. Perpendicular to the chord at its midpoint he measures to the curb, which is 50 feet. Find the radius of the circle.

8.5 Right Triangles

DEFINITION   When one side of a triangle is taken as a **base**, the segment extending from the opposite vertex and perpendicular to the base is the **altitude** to the given base.

THEOREM 63   **The altitude to the hypotenuse of a right triangle forms two right triangles which are similar to the given triangle and to each other.**

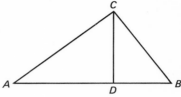

GIVEN: Rt $\triangle ABC$; $\angle ACB$ is a rt $\angle$; $\overline{CD} \perp \overline{AB}$.

PROVE: $\triangle ADC \sim \triangle ACB$; $\triangle CDB \sim \triangle ACB$;
$\triangle ADC \sim \triangle CDB$.

1. $\angle ACB$ is a rt $\angle$; $\overline{CD} \perp \overline{AB}$.	1. Given.
2. $\angle ADC$ is a rt $\angle$; $\angle CDB$ is a rt $\angle$.	2. $\perp$ lines form rt $\angle$s.
3. $\angle A \cong \angle A$; $\angle B \cong \angle B$.	3. $\angle \cong$ itself.
4. $\triangle ADC \sim \triangle ACB$; $\triangle CDB \sim \triangle ACB$.	4. Acute $\angle \cong \angle$, rt $\triangle \sim \triangle$.
5. $\triangle ADC \sim \triangle CDB$.	5. First $\sim$ second $\sim$ third.

COROLLARY 63.1   **The altitude to the hypotenuse of a right triangle is the mean proportional between the segments of the hypotenuse which it intercepts.**

THEOREM 64   **The square of the length of the hypotenuse of a right triangle equals the sum of the squares of the lengths of the legs.**   (Pythagorean Theorem)

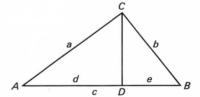

GIVEN: Rt $\triangle ABC$; $\angle ACB$ is a rt $\angle$;
length of side $\overline{AC} = a$, of side $\overline{CB} = b$, of side $\overline{BA} = c$.

PROVE: $a^2 + b^2 = c^2$.

From C draw $\overline{CD} \perp \overline{AB}$; through a point 1 $\perp$. Let length of $\overline{AD} = d$ and length of $\overline{BD} = e$. $\triangle ADC \sim \triangle ACB \sim \triangle CDB$, for alt to hyp forms rt $\angle$s $\sim$. In $\triangle ADC$ and $\triangle ACB$, $\dfrac{d}{a} = \dfrac{a}{c}$ and $d = \dfrac{a^2}{c}$. In $\triangle CDB$ and $\triangle ACB$, $\dfrac{e}{b} = \dfrac{b}{c}$ and $e = \dfrac{b^2}{c}$. But $d + e = c$; point separates segment into parts, sum = whole. Substituting, $\dfrac{a^2}{c} + \dfrac{b^2}{c} = c$. Multiplying by c, $a^2 + b^2 = c^2$.

COROLLARY 64.1   The square of the length of a leg of a right triangle equals the square of the length of the hypotenuse minus the square of the length of the other leg.

Using the square root symbol, the lengths of sides of right triangles are shown thus:

$$c = \sqrt{a^2 + b^2} \quad \text{and} \quad a = \sqrt{c^2 - b^2}$$

Example: Find the length of the short leg of a right triangle whose hypotenuse is 17 units long and whose long leg is 15.

$$a = \sqrt{17^2 - 15^2} = \sqrt{289 - 225} = \sqrt{64} = 8$$

EXERCISE 8.5

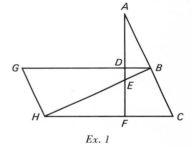

1. GIVEN: $\overline{FA} \perp \overline{CH}$; $\overline{BH} \perp \overline{AC}$; $\overline{BG} \perp \overline{AF}$; $\overline{HG} \perp \overline{BH}$.

   (a) Name all angles congruent to $\angle A$.
   (b) Name six similar triangles with corresponding vertices in order.

Ex. 1

2. Lay the 3-inch end of a 3 by 5 card on a sheet of ruled paper at an angle such that the corners have a one-to-one correspondence with line 1 and line 7 on the paper. There is exactly one angle between card and lines at which this is true. Mark off points on the card which correspond to lines 2 through 6. At the same angle mark off points on the 5-inch side of the card. Consecutive points are exactly $\frac{1}{2}$ inch apart, whatever the distance between lines on the ruled paper.

3. Using Construction 5 (Section 6.3), construct the fourth proportional, x, of $4 : 7 = 5 : x$.

4. Draw a segment of unknown length. Separate it into parts whose lengths are in the ratio 5 to 2.

5. Using Corollary 63.1, construct the mean proportional between 3 and 8. (NOTE: Let the segment of 11 units length be the diameter of a semicircle.)

6. GIVEN: $\odot O$, $\overline{OE} \perp \overline{AB}$; $\overline{OF} \perp \overline{CD}$.

   (a) If $AB = 24$, and $OE = 9$, find radius of $\odot$.
   (b) If radius $= 10$, and $OF = 8$, find CD.

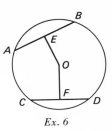

Ex. 6

7. Find the hypotenuse of a right triangle whose legs measure 24 and 32.

8. The diagonals of a rhombus have lengths of 18 and 24. Find the perimeter of the rhombus.

9. GIVEN: $\triangle ABC$; $\angle ACB$ is a rt $\angle$; $\overline{CD} \perp \overline{AB}$; $\overline{DE} \parallel \overline{AC}$.
   PROVE: $\triangle ACD \sim \triangle CDE$.

10. GIVEN: $\triangle ABC$; $\overline{CD} \perp \overline{AB}$; $\overline{CA} \perp \overline{CB}$; $\overline{ED} \perp \overline{CB}$.
   PROVE: $\triangle EDC \sim \triangle CBA$.

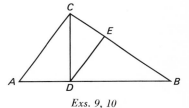

Exs. 9, 10

11. GIVEN: $\overline{BF} \perp \overline{BA}$; $\overline{BE} \perp \overline{AC}$; $\overline{FE} \perp \overline{FB}$.
   PROVE: $\dfrac{BC}{CD} = \dfrac{BE}{EF}$.

12. GIVEN: $\overline{BF} \perp \overline{BA}$; $\overline{BE} \perp \overline{AC}$; $\overline{FE} \perp \overline{FB}$.
   PROVE: $\dfrac{FE}{BE} = \dfrac{DB}{AB}$.

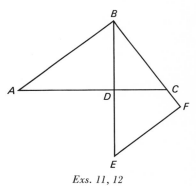

Exs. 11, 12

13. GIVEN: $\square QRST$; $\overline{UQ} \perp \overline{RT}$; $\overline{VW} \perp \overline{RT}$.
   PROVE: $\dfrac{WV}{QU} = \dfrac{TV}{RU}$.

14. GIVEN: $\square QRST$; $\overline{UQ} \perp \overline{RT}$; $\overline{XY} \perp \overline{RT}$.
   PROVE: $\dfrac{RX}{TU} = \dfrac{RY}{TQ}$.

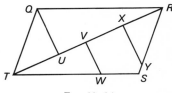

Exs. 13, 14

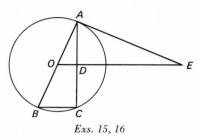

15. GIVEN: $\odot O$; diam $\overline{AB}$; tan $\overline{AE}$;
$\overline{OE} \perp \overline{AC}$.

PROVE: $\dfrac{EA}{AB} = \dfrac{ED}{AC}$.

16. GIVEN: $\odot O$; diam $\overline{AB}$; tan $\overline{AE}$;
$\overline{OE} \perp \overline{AC}$.

PROVE: $\dfrac{EA}{OA} = \dfrac{AD}{OD}$.

Exs. 15, 16

17. A person can estimate the length of a distant object by holding a ruler at arm's length, if he knows two horizontal distances. He finds that from his eye to the ruler is 28 inches and he is 280 feet from the tree. If $3\frac{1}{2}$ inches of the ruler just cover his view of the tree, find the height of the tree.

18. A tennis ball is struck at a height of 7 feet from a point 32 feet behind a net. It just clears the net 3 feet above the ground. If it travels in a straight line, how far behind the net is the point where it hits the ground.

19. A boy casts a shadow of 15 feet at the same time that a tree casts a shadow of 330 feet. If the boy is 6 feet tall, find the height of the tree.

20. Boy Scouts find the height of Washington Monument. At a point 500 feet from the foot of the Monument they place a pan of water. They set up a vertical stick 5 feet beyond the pan. At a point $5\frac{1}{2}$ feet up the stick the reflection of the top of the Monument is seen. How high is the Monument? (See Exs. 23, 24 of Section 5.4.)

21. If the top of a 13-foot ladder touches the side of a house 12 feet from the ground, how far is the bottom of the ladder from the house?

22. When surveyors wish to find the distance to a point across a stream, they may use a method of *triangulation*. They lay down a baseline $\overleftrightarrow{DE}$ and any segments $\overline{DF} \perp \overline{DE}$ and $\overline{EG} \perp \overline{DE}$. Sighting to locate the lines $\overleftrightarrow{FP}$ and $\overleftrightarrow{GP}$, they find A such that $\overleftrightarrow{AP} \perp \overleftrightarrow{DE}$ and measure the segments of $\overleftrightarrow{DE}$.
If $DF = 78$, $DB = 30$, $BA = 70$, $EG = 63$, $CE = 14$, and $AC = 40$, find AP from two sets of data and state by how much the two distances differ.

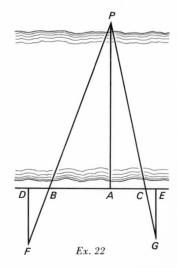

Ex. 22

In Exs. 23–28, with the lengths as given, find the unknown length with a proportion or the Pythagorean Theorem.

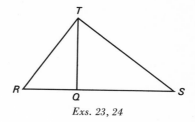

23. GIVEN: Rt $\triangle RST$; $\angle STR$ is a rt $\angle$; $\overline{TQ}$ is the altitude on the hypotenuse. If $RT = 15$ and $RS = 25$, find QR.

Exs. 23, 24

Solution: The triangles with congruent angles, written in corresponding order, are: $\triangle TRS \sim \triangle QRT \sim \triangle QTS$. In the chart the corresponding sides are given in order. Some of them appear twice. Under each of these we place a number, if one is given for it, and write x for the number to be found. A rectangle of these numbers forms a proportion. In this example RT appears twice and is used twice in the proportion. The proportion—the corners of the rectangle—is

$\triangle TRS$	$\triangle QRT$	$\triangle QTS$
TR	QR	QT
15	x	
RS	RT	TS
25	15	
TS	QT	QS

$$\frac{15}{25} = \frac{x}{15}$$
$$x = 9$$

In the chart of nine segments those which are common sides of two triangles appear twice. When one of these sides is used in a case and its length is written into the chart twice, perhaps two rectangles of numbers will be formed. In Ex. 24(a) each length given is included twice. The x is contained in two rectangles. We solve each proportion to find that both give the same product equation.

24. GIVEN: Rt $\triangle RST$; $\angle STR$ is a rt $\angle$; $\overline{TQ}$ is the altitude on the hypotenuse.

(a) If $RT = 30$, $QT = 24$, and $TS = 40$, find RS.
(b) If $RT = 30$, $QT = 24$, and $TS = 40$, find QR.
(c) If $RT = 45$, $QT = 36$, and $TS = 60$, find QS.
(d) If $QR = 9$, and $QS = 16$, find QT.
(e) If $QR = 9$, and $RT = 15$, find RS.
(f) If $RS = 50$, and $QS = 32$, find TS.

25. GIVEN: $\overline{AF} \perp \overline{BC}$; $\overline{CE} \perp \overline{AB}$.

(a) If $EC = 24$, $BE = 32$, and $BF = 28$, find FA.

(b) If $BC = 40$, $DC = 20$, and $EC = 24$, find FC.

(c) If $DA = 5$, $EA = 3$, and $FA = 21$, find BA.

(d) If $ED = 8$, $DA = 10$, and $EB = 64$, find BC.

(e) If $CD = 40$, $FA = 42$, and $FC = 24$, find AB.

(f) If $CD = 20$ and $DF = 16$, find FC.

(g) If $EC = 24$ and $EB = 32$, find BC.

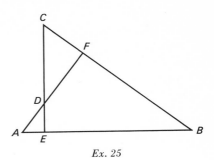

Ex. 25

26. GIVEN: Secants $\overline{AP}$ and $\overline{CP}$; chords $\overline{AD}$ and $\overline{CB}$.

(a) If $AP = 48$, $CP = 54$, and $BP = 27$, find DP.

(b) If $AP = 48$, $CP = 54$, and $DA = 24$, find BC.

(c) If $AP = 16$, $DP = 8$, and $CD = 10$, find AB.

(d) If $CE = 20$, $AE = 16$, and $EB = 8$, find ED.

(e) If $CE = 20$, $AE = 16$, and $AB = 20$, find CD.

(f) If $CE = 30$, $CB = 42$, and $AE = 24$, find AD.

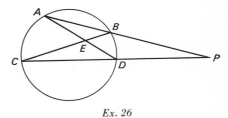

Ex. 26

27. GIVEN: Secant $\overline{FP}$; tangent $\overline{PT}$.

(a) If $FT = 24$, $TG = 18$, and $PT = 36$, find PG.

(b) If $FT = 12$, $TG = 9$, and $PT = 18$, find PF.

(c) If $PF = 16$ and $PG = 9$, find PT.

(d) If $PF = 32$ and $PT = 24$, find PG.

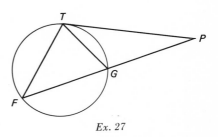

Ex. 27

28. GIVEN: Diameter $\overline{TR}$; chord $\overline{TS}$; tangent $\overline{PT}$; secant $\overline{PR}$.

  (a) If $OT = 5$ and $OP = 13$, find TP.

  (b) If $TR = 10$ and $RS = 6$, find ST.

  (c) If $TR = 12$ and $TP = 16$, find RP.

  (d) If $TS = 15$ and $TP = 25$, find SP.

  (e) If $TR = 9$ and $RP = 15$, find TP.

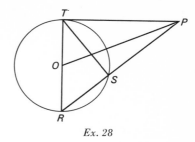

Ex. 28

8.6 Applications of Proportion

Radiations of all kinds are emissions of energy from a source into space in all directions along straight rays. As diagramed in Fig. 54, light from a point source S is stopped by a square I at a distance d_1 from the source.

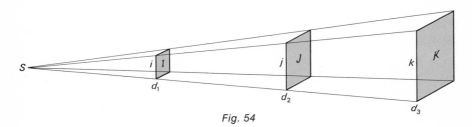

Fig. 54

The shadow behind I is made by straight lines from S through each point on the edge of I and is cast on a surface at any distance from S. The length i, j, or k of a side of each square is proportional to the distance of the square from point S. Thus, the ratios of areas of squares is

$$\frac{i^2}{d_1{}^2} = \frac{j^2}{d_2{}^2} = \frac{k^2}{d_3{}^2}$$

The energy received by each of these squares, when it is not in a shadow, is the same. The energy on a unit area of each square is inversely proportional to the area of the square. And so the energy on a unit area follows the **inverse square law**: it is inversely proportional to the square of the distance from the source.

Fig. 54 also illustrates a method of making a copy of a drawing which is proportionally larger or smaller than the original. Lines from a point through the ends of the side j will give the side i half the length of j at half the distance from S, and will give the side k $\frac{3}{2}$ the length of j at $\frac{3}{2}$ the distance from S.

8.7   Summary Test

After each number on answer sheet write the word(s) or symbol(s) which fill in the blank(s).

1. If $a : b = c : d$, the product form of the equation is _____.
2. If $r : s = t : u$, then $u : s =$ _____.
3. If $c : d = e : f$, then $c :$ _____ $= e : 5f$.
4. If $5 : 2 = x : 6$, then $x =$ _____.
5. If $7a = 8b$, than $a : b =$ _____.
6. If $e : f = g : h$, then $e + f : f =$ _____.
7. If $a : b = c : d$ and $y : z = c : d$, then _____.
8. If x is the mean proportional between s and t, the proportion is written _____.
9. The ratio of the length of a yard to the length of an inch is _____.
10. The ratio of the number of yards in a piece of rope to the number of inches in the rope is _____.
11. A scale on a mechanical drawing reads "3 inches = 1 foot"; the ratio of the length of the drawing to the length of the object is _____.
12. If a map has the scale $\frac{1}{2}$ inch = 1 mile, _____ on the map corresponds to 10 miles on the ground.
13. If two triangles have the same _____, they are similar.
14. If two triangles have corresponding angles congruent, then they have corresponding __(a)__ __(b)__.
15. The set of congruent polygons is a subset of the set of _____ polygons.
16. The perimeters of two similar triangles have the same ratio as _____.
17. If two similar triangles have the ratio of corresponding sides = 1, then the triangles are _____.
18. If two similar triangles have the proportionality constant = 8, and the sides of the smaller have lengths 3, 6, and 5, then the sides of the larger have lengths __(a)__, __(b)__, and __(c)__.
19. If a segment divides two sides of a given triangle proportionally, it completes a second triangle which is _____ the given triangle.
20. A line which bisects two sides of a triangle is _____.

21. If _____ pairs of corresponding sides of two triangles are proportional, the triangles are similar.

22. If two sides of a triangle are proportional to the corresponding sides of a second triangle, the triangles are similar if also _____ are congruent.

23. GIVEN: $\triangle RST \sim \triangle XYZ$ with corresponding vertices in order. If $RS > ST$, then m∠___(a)___ > m∠___(b)___.

24. Three or more parallel lines intercept _____ segments of transversals.

25. A triangle, the lengths of whose sides are proportional to 3:4:5, is _____ triangle.

26. The ___(a)___ of the hypotenuse of a right triangle equals the ___(b)___ of the legs.

27. A 1-foot upright stick 3 feet from a light bulb casts a shadow _____ feet high 15 feet from the bulb.

CONDENSATIONS

Corresp sides $\sim$ ◬ prop. Corresp ∡ $\sim$ ◬ $\cong$.　　(Def)

Prod means = prod extremes.　　(Thm 55)

Any prop which allows prod means = prod extremes.　　(Thm 55)

Sum (diff) : one = sum (diff) : corresp one.　　(Thms 56, 57)

First $\triangle \sim$ second $\sim$ third.　　(Thm 58)

Corresp segments of trans intercepted by ∥ prop.　　(Post 14)

Line ∥ one side of $\triangle$ divides 2 sides prop.　　(Thm 59)

Line divides prop (bisects) 2 sides of $\triangle$, ∥ third side.　　(Thm 60)

AA $\sim$ AA.　　(Thm 61)

SSS $\sim$ SSS; SAS $\sim$ SAS.　　(Thm 62)

Alt to hyp of rt $\triangle$ forms $\sim$ ◬.　　(Thm 63)

$hyp^2 = leg^2 + leg^2$. $leg^2 = hyp^2 - leg^2$.　　(Thm 64)

chapter 9

Loci

9.1 The Location of a Path

When we constructed geometric figures in previous chapters, we carefully required each line or arc to satisfy a small number of specific conditions. Concerning these constructions we ask the question: "What is the location of all the points which satisfy these conditions?" The answer to this question for each of many simple conditions is the description of a **locus**, which is a Latin word meaning *place*. The plural is **loci**.

> DEFINITION The set of all the points and only those points which satisfy a given condition or conditions is the **locus of the points**.

It is possible to think of a locus as the path through which a point moves under the required conditions. We know the locus of an airplane at night by watching one of its lights move through a path. When a ball is started rolling on a smooth level floor, its center travels a straight line at the distance from the floor equal to its radius. This is the locus of the center. A point on its surface travels through a more complex path.

In establishing a locus we fulfill these requirements:

1. Take the steps to construct the required lines and/or curves.

199

2. Prove (a) that all points of the lines or curves satisfy the conditions and (b) that all points which satisfy the conditions are points of the constructed lines or curves. The second is the converse of the first.

One theorem which has already been proved, in association with a construction, is a typical locus proposition. It is reworded here in locus terminology:

THEOREM 37 **The locus of points equidistant from two points is the perpendicular bisector of the segment joining the points.**

Postulate 9 (Section 4.6) can be worded in locus terms which we shall accept and use:

The locus of points a given distance from a given point is a circle with the center at the given point and the radius equal to the given distance.

Construction 9   *Construct a line a given distance from a given line.*

GIVEN: Line k; distance d.

CONSTRUCT: Lines distance d from k.

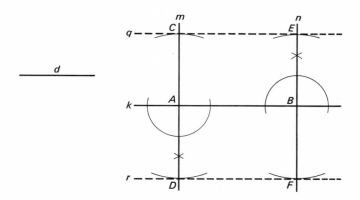

Through two points, A and B, of line k construct lines m and n perpendicular to k. With A and B as centers and with radius $= d$, draw arcs intersecting m and n on both sides of k at points C, D, E, and F. Draw line q through C and E and line r through D and F. Lines q and r are two lines $\parallel k$ and distance d from k.

THEOREM 65 **The locus of points a given distance from a given line is a pair of lines parallel to the given line and the given distance from it.**

GIVEN: Construction 9.

PROVE: Every point of q and r is distance d from k; every point distance d from k is a point of q and r.

$AC = BE = AD = BF = d$; radii of $\cong$ ⑤ $\cong$. All points of q and r are distance d from k, for distance from point to line = length of segment from point $\perp$ line. Another point, G, which is not of q or r cannot be distance d from k; to every coord corresp 1 point. Every point distance d from k is a point of q and r.

THEOREM 66 **The locus of points equidistant from two parallel lines is a line parallel to the given lines and midway between them.**

GIVEN: Line $m \parallel$ line n; $\overline{CD} \perp m$ and n; $\overline{AB} \perp m$ and n; $CR = RD$; $AS = SB$.

PROVE: $\overleftrightarrow{RS} \parallel m$ and n; every point of $\overleftrightarrow{RS}$ is midway between m and n; every point midway between m and n is a point of $\overleftrightarrow{RS}$.

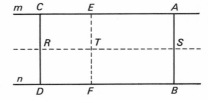

$\overleftrightarrow{RS} \parallel m$ and n; lines everywhere equidist $\parallel$. Let $\overline{EF}$ be another segment intercepted by and $\perp m$ and n, intersecting $\overleftrightarrow{RS}$ at T. $\overline{CD} \parallel \overline{AB} \parallel \overline{EF}$; lines $\perp$ same line $\parallel$. $ET = CR = AS = FT = DR = BS$; segments of $\parallel$ intercepted by $\parallel \cong$. R, S, and T are midpoints; point which separates segment into $2 =$ halves is midpoint. Every point of $\overleftrightarrow{RS}$ is midway between m and n, and every point midway between m and n is a point of $\overleftrightarrow{RS}$.

THEOREM 67 **The locus of points equidistant from two intersecting lines is the pair of perpendicular lines which bisect the angles formed by the given lines.**

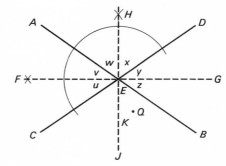

GIVEN: Lines $\overleftrightarrow{AB}$ and $\overleftrightarrow{CD}$ intersecting at E.

PROVE: Every point of the bisectors is equidistant from $\overleftrightarrow{AB}$ and $\overleftrightarrow{CD}$; every point equidistant from $\overleftrightarrow{AB}$ and $\overleftrightarrow{CD}$ is a point of the bisectors; bisectors $\perp$.

Construct $\overleftrightarrow{HJ}$, the bisector of $\angle AED$, and $\overleftrightarrow{FG}$, the bisector of $\angle AEC$. Prove $\overleftrightarrow{FG}$ bisects $\angle DEB$ and $\overleftrightarrow{HJ}$ bisects $\angle CEB$ (see Ex. 10, Section 4.5). Prove point K is equidistant from $\overleftrightarrow{EC}$ and $\overleftrightarrow{EB}$ (see Ex. 26, Section 6.5).

Prove point Q is not equidistant from $\overrightarrow{EC}$ and $\overrightarrow{EB}$. Prove $\overleftrightarrow{HJ} \perp \overleftrightarrow{FG}$ (see Ex. 3, Section 4.5).

A locus condition may be an inequality. The locus of points less than 4 inches from a given point is the interior of the circle with the given point as its center and a radius of 4 inches. The locus of points greater than 2 inches from a given line is the exterior of the lines parallel to the given line and 2 inches from it.

The answer to a locus question is a precise statement of the location of all points which satisfy the condition, using the wording of a locus theorem or definition applied to the case.

EXERCISE 9.1

State the locus of points which satisfy the conditions in Exs. 1–13.

1. The centers of circles of given radius r which pass through a common point P.

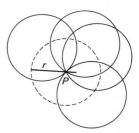

> *Solution:* The locus is a circle whose center is P and whose radius is r.
> We show this by drawing a few circles of radius r which pass through P. The aggregation of all the centers is a circle whose center is P and whose radius is r.
> All points not of $\odot P$ are at a distance $< r$ or $> r$ from P.

2. The midpoints of chords in a circle parallel to a given diameter.
3. The midpoints of chords of a given length in a circle.
4. The centers of all circles tangent to a given line at a given point.
5. The centers of circles such that the sides of a given angle are tangent to the circles.
6. The points in the interior of a circle equidistant from the endpoints of a chord.
7. The midpoints of all radii of a circle of radius 6 inches.
8. The points 2 inches from a circle of radius 5 inches.
9. The points less than 2 inches from a circle of radius 5 inches.
10. The points $\frac{1}{2}$ inch from a segment 2 inches long.
11. The points less than 1 inch from a given line.
12. The points distance d from a circle of radius r when $d > r$.
13. The points equal to or less than 3 inches from a given point.

Phantom drawing showing how the observer gets on and off the tube

Crane track

Telescope cage

Prime focus
f 3.3

me focus
tform

me, 137 ft
meter

me shutter

ght
ension
ve

ssenger
vator

me
conies

udé focus
f 30

nstant
mperature
om

servatory
ll

r
nditioning
cts

uth
lar axis
aring

60 ton crane

Coudé and
Cassegrain
mirrors

Horse shoe
north polar
axis bearing

Declination
axis

North
pressure
bearings

200 inch
mirror

North pier

Cassegrain
focus *f* 16

Control desk

Dome
drive

Dome
trucks

Electrical
control
panels

South pier   Ground floor   Base frame supports   Mezzanine floor   Offices   Observation floor 5598 ft above sea level

THE TWO HVNDRED INCH TELESCOPE

A great telescope has a "polar axis" parallel to the axis of the earth, located here by the north and south bearings. The mirror mount is elevated up from the horizon on the declination axis to sight on a distant point. Then, as the Earth rotates eastward, the right ascension drive rotates the polar axis westward. The locus of the telescope is such that it continues to sight on the same area in the sky for several hours. Photograph from the Mount Wilson and Palomar Observatories.

9.2   Intersection of Loci

The intersections of loci are important in the world's structures. An airplane wing must have a certain shape to provide maximum lift. Both wing and body must be shaped to produce minimum drag. How can the wing and body be joined so that strength of the structure can be at a maximum and the other effects are retained? An *optimum*, a compromise to satisfy as much more than the minimum of each as possible, is designed.

We have already used the intersections and unions of loci. An angle is the union of two rays extending from a common endpoint. It is the locus of the points of the two rays. The locus of points common to two lines is their intersection, which from Theorem 3 is exactly one point.

The procedure in a problem of locus intersection is to describe in a separate step the locus of each independent condition. Then the last step names the intersecting points. The points which satisfy both conditions at once are the **points of intersection** of the separate loci.

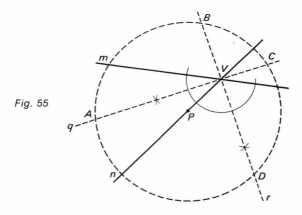

Fig. 55

Example (Fig. 55): Find the locus of points equidistant from two intersecting lines *m* and *n* *and* 1 inch from a point *P* of one of them which is $\frac{1}{2}$ inch from the intersection.

1. The locus of points equidistant from *m* and *n* is the lines *q* and *r*, bisectors of the vertical angles.
2. The locus of points 1 inch from point *P* is the circle with *P* as a center and radius of 1 inch.
3. The points which satisfy both conditions are *A*, *B*, *C*, and *D*, the intersections of $\odot P$ and lines *q* and *r*.

It is possible that two loci do not intersect, and then the set of points of the intersection is the empty set.

9.3   Concurrent Lines in Triangles

Some loci are sets of three lines satisfying specific conditions with respect to triangles. These sets have the characteristic of intersecting at exactly one point. We shall consider four cases.

DEFINITION   Lines which intersect at one point are **concurrent**.

1. The intersection of loci each equidistant from two sides of a triangle. In $\triangle ABC$ (Fig. 56) the points equidistant from the sides of $\angle A$ are elements of the angle bisector. Any point of the bisector can be taken as the center of one circle to which the sides of the angle are tangent. Each of these circles is inscribed in the angle. Likewise the bisector of $\angle B$ contains all the centers of circles inscribed in the angle. The intersection of the two bisectors is the center of the circle to which $\overline{AB}$, $\overline{AC}$, and $\overline{BC}$ are all tangent. The bisector of $\angle C$ passes through this point also. Thus these bisectors are concurrent and establish the point which is the center of the circle **inscribed** in the triangle, equidistant from the three sides of the triangle. Also the triangle is **circumscribed** about the circle.

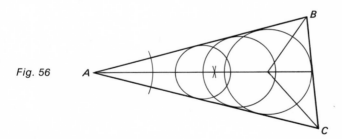

Fig. 56

2. The intersection of loci each equidistant from two vertices of a triangle. The locus of points equidistant from two points is the perpendicular bisector of the segment between them. Any point of this line is the center of a circle which passes through the vertices. These three loci are concurrent at the center of the circle which is **circumscribed** around the triangle. Also the triangle is **inscribed** in the circle. (See Ex. 11, Section 6.5.)

3. The intersection of the medians to the three sides. A **median** is a segment extending from a vertex to the midpoint of the opposite side. The midpoint of the side is the intersection of the side and its perpendicular bisector. The intersection of the medians is an important point in physics, the center of gravity. If a triangle, cut out of a card, is supported by a thread at this point, it hangs horizontally. This is the point around which the weight of the card material is balanced. In Fig. 57, D, E, and F are midpoints of the three sides of $\triangle ABC$, and G is the point of intersection of the three medians.

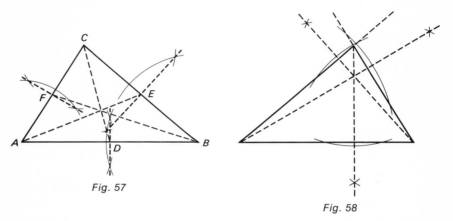

Fig. 57

Fig. 58

4. The altitudes of a triangle are concurrent (Fig. 58). An altitude extends from a vertex of a triangle perpendicular to the opposite side. In an obtuse triangle two altitudes intersect sides outside the triangle, but the altitudes extended intersect at one point.

EXERCISE 9.3

Describe each of the loci in Exs. 1–7.

1. The midpoints of segments in a triangle parallel to one side.

2. The midpoints of all chords with one of their endpoints the same point.

3. The third vertices of all triangles with the same base and medians to the given base all congruent.

4. The vertices included between the congruent sides of all isosceles triangles having a given segment as base.

5. The vertices of all right angles of right triangles having a given segment as their hypotenuse.

6. The third vertices of the triangles with the same base and altitudes to the given base all congruent.

7. All points equidistant from the points of intersection of two circles.

By construction find the intersection of the loci in Exs. 8–15. Write a step describing each locus and a step describing the points which satisfy both conditions.

8. Points equidistant from two parallel lines *and* a given distance from a point of one of them.

9. Points in the interior of an angle equidistant from the sides of the angle and 1 inch from the vertex.

10. Points in the interior of an angle equidistant from the sides of the angle and $\frac{1}{2}$ inch from one of the sides.

11. Points equidistant from two intersecting lines and a given distance from one of them.

12. Points 1 inch from each of two intersecting lines.

13. In the interior of an irregular quadrilateral, points equidistant from two consecutive sides and from two consecutive vertices.

14. Points distance $s/2$ from the midpoint of a segment of length s and equidistant from the midpoint and one end of the segment.

15. Points 2 inches from A and 3 inches from B of a segment $\overline{AB}$ 4 inches long.

16. Given acute scalene $\triangle ABC$, find and describe each locus.
    (a) Points equidistant from $\overline{AC}$ and $\overline{BC}$ on the altitude from B
    (b) Points on the median from A and equidistant from A and C
    (c) Points distance d from vertex C and distance e from $\overline{AC}$

17. Inscribe a circle: (a) In an acute triangle. (b) In an obtuse triangle.

18. Circumscribe a circle about a right triangle. Does this satisfy the proposition that the midpoint of the hypotenuse is equidistant from the three vertices? Does this satisfy the proposition that an angle inscribed in a semicircle is a right angle?

19. Circumscribe a circle about an obtuse triangle.

20. On card material construct a triangle and its medians. Cut out the triangle and hang it by a thread at the intersection of its three medians.

21. Construct the three altitudes of an obtuse triangle. Are they concurrent?

22. In equilateral triangle ABC construct: **(a)** The bisector of $\angle C$. **(b)** The altitude to $\overline{AB}$. **(c)** The median to $\overline{AB}$. How do these segments intersect?

23. Draw $\triangle ABC$ with $AB = 3$ inches, $BC = 2$ inches, $CA = 2\frac{1}{2}$ inches. Draw and describe the loci of points equidistant from the sides of $\angle CAB$ *and*:

(a) Equidistant from the vertices B and C
(b) 1 inch from B
(c) 1 inch from side $\overline{BC}$ (two points)

24. By construction show the intersection of $\odot G$ and $\odot H$, with radii g and h, respectively, with $g > h$, when the distance between the centers of the circles is:

(a) Greater than $g + h$
(b) Equal to $g + h$
(c) Less than $g + h$ and greater than $g - h$
(d) Equal to $g - h$
(e) Less than $g - h$

25. There are two points of $\triangle RST$ equidistant from R and S. Give a general rule comparing the lengths of $\overline{ST}$ and $\overline{RT}$ in determining which one is intersected by the perpendicular bisector of $\overline{RS}$.

26. In $\triangle DEF$ there is a point of the side $\overline{EF}$ which intersects the bisector of $\angle D$. Give a general rule for the condition under which the intersection is the midpoint of $\overline{EF}$.

27. Draw an irregular quadrilateral inscribed in a circle. Are the perpendicular bisectors of the four sides concurrent? What point is this point of concurrence? (Compare this with Ex. 33, Section 7.2.)

28. Draw an irregular quadrilateral not related to a circle. Are the perpendicular bisectors of the sides concurrent?

29. Draw an irregular quadrilateral circumscribed around a circle. Are the bisectors of the angles concurrent? What point is this point of concurrence? (Compare this with Ex. 6, Section 7.3.)

30. Draw an irregular quadrilateral not related to a circle. Are the bisectors of the angles concurrent?

31. Draw an isosceles right triangle given the radius of the circumscribed circle.

9.4   Loci in Space

The loci considered thus far have been in one plane, but many loci are of three dimensions. Their theorems are somewhat difficult to prove. For our purposes it will suffice to state a few of these theorems without proving them. They illustrate the process of development from plane to solid geometry.

THEOREM   The locus of points in space equidistant from two points is a plane perpendicular to the segment joining the given points at its midpoint.

THEOREM   The locus of points in space a given distance from a plane is a pair of planes parallel to the given plane and at the given distance from it.

THEOREM   The locus of points in space equidistant from two parallel planes is a plane parallel to the given planes and midway between them.

The definition of a circle is modified to become the definition of a sphere:

DEFINITION   The locus of points in space a given distance from a point is a **sphere** with the given point as center and the given distance as radius.

chapter **10**

Lines and Planes in Space

10.1 Basic Relations

Throughout this study we have considered figures which are contained in a plane, recognizing the existence of a third dimension. The principles which applied to plane figures apply also to solid objects with some modifications. Section 9.4 contains examples of loci whose characteristics in a plane are readily adaptable to corresponding loci in space. At the beginning we had postulates which denote the orientation of points, lines, and planes in space. They are repeated here for review.

Postulate 3 **For every three noncollinear points, there is exactly one plane containing them.**

Postulate 4 **Every plane is a set of points and contains at least three noncollinear points.**

Postulate 5 **A plane which contains two points of a line contains the entire line.**

The Incas of South America patiently chipped away two stones until the edges fit smoothly, forming remarkably precise planes and dihedral angles. The largest number of angles found in any one stone is twelve; this stone (above) is built into a wall in Cuzco, Peru. The two stones below, from a structure in process of restoration, show details of front and side surfaces. A pencil gives an indication of their size. Photos by the author.

Postulate 6   **Space contains at least four noncoplanar points.**

These postulates state the case that through any three points in space exactly one plane can pass. The bottoms of the three wheels of an airplane determine a plane even when they are up in the air. This plane continually changes its location as the airplane flies, and becomes a tangible plane when the wheels touch down on the ground. The airplane has three points on which to land rather than more, since a fourth point can be noncoplanar with the other three.

THEOREM 68   For every line and every point not of the line, exactly one plane contains them.

GIVEN: Line *m* and point *A* not of the line.

PROVE: One and only one plane contains them.

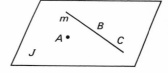

Let *B* and *C* be two points of *m*. One plane, *J*, contains *A*, *B*, and *C*; a plane contains three noncollinear points. Then *J* contains *m*; a plane which contains two points of a line contains the entire line.   (Existence)

Let *K* be another plane which may contain *m*. It contains *B* and *C*. If *K* also contains *A*, it concides with *J*; for three points one plane. Then only one plane contains *m* and *A*.   (Uniqueness)

COROLLARY 68.1   If two lines intersect, exactly one plane contains them.

10.2   Separation

A line separates a plane into two **half-planes**. In Fig. 59, the line $\overleftrightarrow{PQ}$ separates the plane *J* into half-planes J_1 and J_2, but it is a part of neither. It is the **edge** of each. Each half-plane is a set of points. No point of one is an element of the other. If the points *R* and *T* are elements of one set, they are both on the same side of the edge, and a segment joining *R* and *T* is contained in the half-plane. If points *R* and *U* are elements of opposite half-planes, they are on opposite sides of the edge, and a segment joining them intersects the line $\overleftrightarrow{PQ}$.

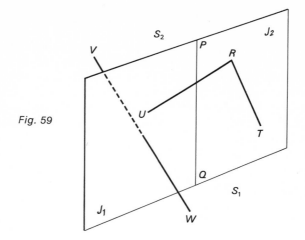

Fig. 59

This separation was introduced in Section 5.3. Its postulates are repeated here:

Postulate 11   **A line separates a plane into two convex sets of points such that every segment joining a point of one set to a point of the other intersects the line at exactly one point.**

Postulate 12   **A convex geometric figure separates a plane into two regions, interior and exterior, such that a segment joining a point of one region to a point of the other intersects the figure at exactly one point.**

A plane separates space into two **half-spaces**. The plane J in Fig. 59 separates space into S_1 and S_2. The plane is the **face** of each half-space and is contained in neither. Points V and W are elements, each of one half-space. A segment joining V and W intersects the plane J. Points of one half-space are joined by segments which are contained in the half-space and do not intersect the face.

Postulate 15   **A plane separates space into two sets of points such that every segment joining a point of one set to a point of the other intersects the given plane at exactly one point.**

We state many propositions in geometry. Each one which is proved can be a theorem, used as the basis for making other proofs. The answers to the questions below can be stated as propositions. We will prove only those which we need for exercises.

1. How many planes can pass through a line? When a point not of the

line is located in space, how many planes passing through the given line can pass through the given point?

2. Through four points in space how many planes can pass?

3. Given three distinct noncoplanar lines, how many planes can they determine: When they are parallel? When they are mutually perpendicular? When they are neither parallel nor perpendicular?

4. Three noncollinear points determine a plane. If lines pass through these points, must every point of the lines be contained in the given plane?

5. A mason builds forms for a concrete floor. He makes one side of the form sloping to allow for water drainage. His helper makes the opposite side of the rectangle level. Can a plane surface fit between the sides? How can he tell by sighting with his eye that the top edges of the two forms are not parallel? Are the vertical sides of the two forms parallel planes? How can they find with a string if the surface of the concrete is a plane?

10.3   Parallel Lines and Planes

THEOREM 69   **Two parallel lines are contained in exactly one plane.**

GIVEN: Line $m \parallel n$.

PROVE: Exactly one plane contains them.

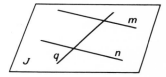

There is at least one plane J which contains m and n, since two parallel lines are contained in one plane.   (Existence)

Draw q, a transversal intersecting m and n. Let K be a second plane which may contain m and q, since one plane contains intersecting lines. But the intersection of n and q is contained in q and both are contained in J. Therefore, n and q are contained in J, plane $K =$ plane J, and the lines are contained in at most one plane.   (Uniqueness)

COROLLARY 69.1   **Two lines in space parallel to the same line are parallel to each other.**

In space two lines can be not parallel and can also not intersect. A bridge and a road beneath it are a common example. And there is no plane in space which can contain both of them.

DEFINITION   Two lines in space which are not contained in one plane are **skew lines**.

DEFINITIONS   Planes which do not intersect are **parallel** planes. A line and a plane which do not intersect are **parallel to each other**.

Postulate 16   **If two planes intersect, their intersection is exactly one line.**

THEOREM 70   The intersections of two parallel planes with a third plane are parallel lines.

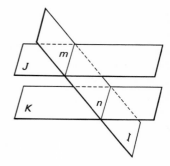

GIVEN: Plane $J \parallel K$ intersected by I at lines
$\quad\quad\quad$ m and n.

PROVE: $m \parallel n$.

m and n are contained in planes which do not intersect and also in I. $m \parallel n$, for lines in one plane which do not intersect are parallel.

EXERCISE 10.3

1. Complete each of the following sentences.

   (a) When a line is parallel to a plane, the intersection is _____.
   (b) When a line is contained in a plane, the intersection is _____.
   (c) When a line is neither of these, the intersection is _____.

2. Given three planes no two of which are parallel, how are they arranged if their intersections are: **(a)** One line? **(b)** Three concurrent lines? **(c)** Three parallel lines?

3. A line intersects one of three parallel planes.

   (a) Must it intersect the others?
   (b) The intersection is how many points in each plane?

4. Two planes are each parallel to a third plane. How are they oriented with respect to each other?

5. **(a)** How many planes are determined by four points, not coplanar, no three of which are collinear?
   (b) Name a common solid figure made by such an arrangement.

6. **(a)** Are the four vertices of every parallelogram coplanar?

(b) Are the four vertices of every quadrilateral coplanar?
(NOTE: Draw a quadrilateral on a piece of paper and try to fold it.)

7. Can three planes have: **(a)** Exactly one line of intersection? **(b)** Two lines? **(c)** Three lines? **(d)** Four lines?

8. Three parallel noncoplanar lines can determine how many planes?

9. Through a point 3 feet above a floor, how many planes can pass which are parallel to the floor?

10. Given two parallel planes. One line can be drawn in each. Can these two lines: **(a)** Be parallel? **(b)** Be skew? **(c)** Intersect?

11. Under what conditions can two lines joining points of skew lines: **(a)** Be parallel? **(b)** Be contained in one plane?

12. **(a)** If a line l, not in plane J, is parallel to a line in J, under what conditions will it be parallel to plane J?
(b) What lines in plane J are parallel to l?

10.4   Perpendicular Lines and Planes

DEFINITIONS   If a line is perpendicular to a plane, the point of intersection of the line and the plane is the **foot of the line**. A line perpendicular to every line of a plane containing its foot is **perpendicular to the plane**. The length of the segment from a point perpendicular to a plane is the **distance** from the point to the plane.

THEOREM 71   A line perpendicular to two intersecting lines is perpendicular to the plane containing the lines.

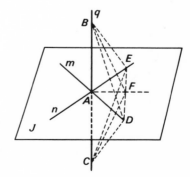

GIVEN: Lines m and n intersecting at A in plane J; line $q \perp m$ and n at A.

PROVE: $q \perp J$.

Let B and C be points of q such that $\overline{AB} \cong \overline{AC}$. Let D and E be points of m and n, respectively. $\overline{BD} \cong \overline{CD}$; $\overline{BE} \cong \overline{CE}$; points of $\perp$ bisector of segment are equidistant from endpoints. $\overline{DE} \cong$ itself. $\triangle BDE \cong \triangle CDE$ by SSS $\cong$ SSS. Then $\angle BDE \cong \angle CDE$. Let F be a point of $\overline{DE}$; it is a point of J, since every point of a line in a plane is a point of the plane. $\overline{DF} \cong \overline{DF}$. $\triangle BDF \cong \triangle CDF$ by SAS $\cong$ SAS, and $\overline{BF} \cong \overline{CF}$. Then $\overline{AF}$ is a $\perp$ bisector of $\overline{BC}$, for every point equidistant from 2 points is a point of the $\perp$ bisector. Every line through A intersecting $\overline{DE} \perp \overline{BC}$.

COROLLARY 71.1   If a line is perpendicular to a plane, the plane is perpendicular to the line.

COROLLARY 71.2   Exactly one plane is perpendicular to a line at a point of the line.

EXERCISE 10.4

Discover the possibilities of the many perpendiculars in space by answering the following questions. Show the relationships with cards and pencils.

1. Through a point in space near a line how many planes can pass which are perpendicular to the given line?

2. Through a point in space near a plane how many lines can pass which perpendicular to the given plane?

3. Through a point of a plane how many lines can pass which are perpendicular to the given plane?

4. Through a point of a line how many lines in space can pass which are perpendicular to the given line?

5. A line is perpendicular to one line of a plane. Is the given line perpendicular to the plane?

6. A line is perpendicular to a plane. How is every plane containing the line related to the given plane?

7. Two lines are perpendicular to a line in a plane.

   (a) Can the given lines both lie in the plane?
   (b) Can they both lie in a plane other than the given plane?
   (c) Can they be skew lines?

8. Two lines are perpendicular to a plane. How many planes can contain both these lines?

9. If one of two parallel lines is perpendicular to a plane, must the second line be perpendicular to the plane?

10. If three lines are perpendicular to a plane, how are the lines related to each other?

11. If three planes are perpendicular to a line at three points of the line, how are the planes related to each other?

12. Each of three concurrent lines is perpendicular to the other two.

  (a) How many planes do these lines determine?
  (b) Is each line perpendicular to the plane determined by the other two?
  (c) Is each plane perpendicular to the plane determined by the other two?
  (d) Give a classroom illustration of this condition.

13. A segment may have a perpendicular bisector in space. What kind of a figure is such a perpendicular bisector?

14. On a plane perpendicular to a line what is the figure which is a constant distance from a point of the line?

15. Draw a figure showing two transversals intersecting three parallel planes. Write proportions relating the lengths of the segments of the transversals.

10.5   Angles in Space

When two planes intersect, they form angles.

DEFINITION   The union of two half-planes and their line of intersection is a **dihedral angle**. The line of intersection is the **edge** of each half-plane. The union of the line of intersection and either half-plane is a **face** of the dihedral angle.

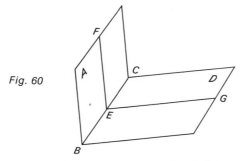

Fig. 60

The half-planes A and D in Fig. 60 have the edge $\overleftrightarrow{BC}$. The dihedral angle is named A–BC–D.

The measure of the dihedral angle is the measure of a certain plane angle. At any point of the line of intersection, such as E, there is exactly one ray perpendicular to $\overleftrightarrow{BC}$ in each plane, namely $\overrightarrow{EF}$ and $\overrightarrow{EG}$. These intersecting rays determine a plane perpendicular to $\overleftrightarrow{BC}$ at E. The angle $\angle FEG$ intercepted in this plane by the two half-planes is the angle whose measure $= m\angle A\text{–}BC\text{–}D$. The vertex of the plane angle is the point of intersection of the three planes.

> **DEFINITION** The intersection of the faces of a dihedral angle and a plane perpendicular to the edge is the **plane angle** of the dihedral angle.

> **DEFINITION** The measure of the plane angle of a dihedral angle is the **measure of the dihedral angle**.

The plane angle is formed by two rays perpendicular to the edge of the half-planes, one ray contained in each half-plane. Every plane angle of a given dihedral has the same measure. Dihedral angles between planes can be vertical, alternate, interior, and exterior the same as angles between lines in a plane.

> **DEFINITION** Two planes located so that the sides of their plane angles are perpendicular are **perpendicular planes**.

THEOREM 72 **If two parallel planes intersect a dihedral angle, then the angles in the given planes intercepted by the dihedral angle are congruent.**

GIVEN: Dihedral angle $A\text{–}BC\text{–}D$; plane J intersecting plane A in $\overline{EQ}$ and plane D in $\overline{ES}$; plane K intersecting A in $\overline{FR}$ and D in $\overline{FT}$.

PROVE: $\angle QES \cong \angle RFT$.

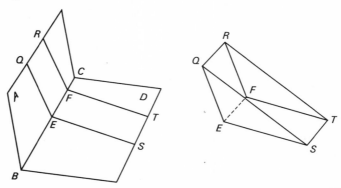

Let Q, R, S, and T be found in their respective rays such that $\overline{EQ} \cong \overline{FR}$ and $\overline{ES} \cong \overline{FT}$. $\overline{EQ} \parallel \overline{FR}$; $\overline{ES} \parallel \overline{FT}$; the intersections of two $\parallel$ planes with a third plane are $\parallel$. $EQRF$ and $ESTF$ are parallelograms with two sides $\cong$

and ∥. $\overline{QR} \parallel \overline{EF}$; $\overline{ST} \parallel \overline{EF}$; $\overline{QR} \cong \overline{EF}$; $\overline{ST} \cong \overline{EF}$, since opp sides of ▱ are ∥ and ≅. $\overline{QR} \parallel \overline{ST}$; $\overline{QR} \cong \overline{ST}$, and QRTS is ▱. Opp sides $\overline{QS}$ and $\overline{RT}$ are ≅; △QES ≅ △RFT by SSS and ∠QES ≅ ∠RFT.

EXERCISE 10.5

1. Two parallel planes are intersected by a third plane. **(a)** Are the plane angles of the dihedral comparable to alternate interior, alternate exterior, and corresponding angles in a plane? **(b)** Do the theorems of plane geometry concerning such angles apply as well to angles between planes?

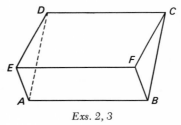

2. GIVEN: ▱ *ABCD* and ▱ *EFCD*.
   PROVE: *ABFE* is ▱.

3. GIVEN: ▱ *ABCD* and ▱ *EFCD*.
   PROVE: △*ADE* ≅ △*BCF*.

Exs. 2, 3

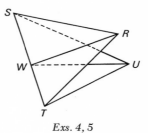

4. GIVEN: △*RST* ≅ △*UST* (on a paper folded at $\overline{ST}$).
   PROVE: $\overline{RW} \cong \overline{UW}$.

5. GIVEN: $RS \cong US$; $\overline{RT} \cong \overline{UT}$ (on a paper folded at $\overline{ST}$).
   PROVE: ∠*RST* ≅ ∠*UST*.

Exs. 4, 5

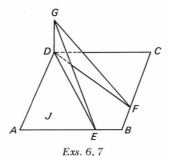

6. GIVEN: Square *ABCD*; $\overline{BE} \cong \overline{BF}$; $\overline{DG} \perp$ plane *J*.
   PROVE: $\overline{DE} \cong \overline{DF}$.

7. GIVEN: Square *ABCD*; $\overline{GE} \cong \overline{GF}$; $\overline{DG} \perp$ plane *J*.
   PROVE: $\overline{DE} \cong \overline{DF}$.

Exs. 6, 7

8. GIVEN: $ST \perp$ plane J; T, U, and V in J; $US > VS$.
PROVE: $TU > TV$. (NOTE: Extend TV to $TW = TU$.)

9. GIVEN: $ST \perp$ plane J; T, U, and V in J; $TU > TV$.
PROVE: $US > VS$. (NOTE: Extend TV to $TW = TU$.)

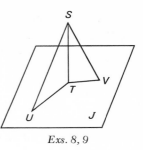

Exs. 8, 9

10. GIVEN: C midpoint of $\overline{DE}$; A, B, C, F in plane J; $\overline{AD} \cong \overline{AE}$; $\overline{BD} \cong \overline{BE}$.
PROVE: $\overline{FD} \cong \overline{FE}$.

11. GIVEN: C midpoint of $\overline{DE}$; A, B, C, F in plane J; $\overline{BD} \cong \overline{BE}$; $\angle DBA \cong \angle EBA$.
PROVE: $\overline{AC} \perp \overline{DE}$.

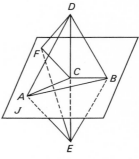

Exs. 10, 11

12. PROVE: Segments of parallel lines intercepted by two parallel planes are congruent.

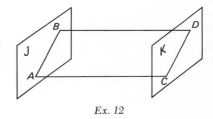

Ex. 12

Describe the locus in space of each set in Exs. 13–25.

13. The points less than 10 inches from a given point.

14. The points equidistant from two points 8 inches apart.

15. The points 1 foot from a flat table top.

16. The points equidistant from two parallel shelves 14 inches apart.

17. The points a given distance from a given line.

18. The points less than 2 feet from a given line.

19. The points 9 inches from a sphere of radius r and outside of it.

20. The points equidistant from all points of a circle.

21. The points equidistant from the vertices of a triangle.

22. The points 2 inches from the side of a cylinder of 4-inch radius.

23. The circles which have one common diameter.

24. The points equidistant from two intersecting lines.

25. The points equidistant from two parallel lines.

10.6 Summary Test

For each number write A if it is always true, S if it is sometimes true, and N if it is never true.

1. If three points are not collinear, they are coplanar.
2. Two straight lines determine a plane.
3. Three concurrent lines are coplanar.
4. Three parallel lines are coplanar.
5. Two intersecting lines are coplanar.
6. Two lines perpendicular to a plane can intersect in one point.
7. Planes perpendicular to a line are parallel.
8. A line perpendicular to a line in a plane is perpendicular to the given plane.
9. Two lines parallel to the same plane are parallel to each other.
10. Two lines perpendicular to a plane are perpendicular to each other.
11. If a line is parallel to a plane, then a plane containing the given line is parallel to the given plane.
12. Two lines parallel to a third line are coplanar.
13. If a plane contains one of two skew lines, then it intersects the other line.
14. If two planes are each perpendicular to a third plane, the intersection of the two planes lies in the third plane.
15. Two lines perpendicular to a line at a point are parallel.
16. If a plane and a line not in it are both perpendicular to the same line, then they are parallel to each other.
17. A plane perpendicular to one of two intersecting planes intersects the other.
18. Two planes perpendicular to the same line intersect.
19. A line perpendicular to a plane is perpendicular to any line in the plane passing through the foot of the perpendicular.
20. If three points of a plane are equidistant from two points of a line which intersects the plane, then every point of the plane is equidistant from the two points of the line.
21. A line parallel to a plane is parallel to lines in the plane.
22. If two planes are parallel to the same line, they are parallel to each other.

CONDENSATIONS

Lines ‖ same line ‖.   (Thm 69)

Intersections of ‖ planes with third plane are ‖ lines.   (Thm 70)

Line ⊥ intersecting lines, ⊥ plane containing them.   (Thm 71)

m dihedral ∠ = m its plane ∠.   (Def)

Sides of their plane ∠ ⊥, 2 planes ⊥.   (Def)

⊿ in ‖ planes intercepted by dihedral, ≅.   (Thm 72)

chapter **11**

Polygons, Areas, and Volumes

11.1 Polygons

We have been using polygons of three or four sides. We now increase the number of sides.

DEFINITIONS   The union of n consecutive segments in a plane intersecting at and only at n points which are their common endpoints, with no two consecutive segments colinear, is a **polygon**. A polygon of n sides may be called an n-gon. Each segment is a **side** of the polygon; each point of intersection is a **vertex**; each angle formed by sides at a vertex is an **angle** of the polygon. The sides in order around the polygon are **consecutive sides**; the angles in order are **consecutive angles**. A segment which joins any two vertices which are not consecutive is a **diagonal**.

DEFINITIONS   Polygons with a one-to-one correspondence between their vertices, such that their corresponding parts are congruent, are **congruent polygons**. When the corresponding angles are congruent and the lengths of the corresponding sides are proportional, they are **similar polygons**.

227

DEFINITION   A polygon all of whose sides and all of whose angles are congruent is a **regular polygon**. It is equilateral and equiangular.

A square is a regular quadrilateral. The end of a new wooden pencil
is a regular hexagon of six congruent sides and six congruent angles. All
regular polygons of the same number of sides are similar.

Some examples of figures which are not polygons are given in Fig. 61.

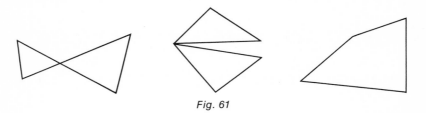

Fig. 61

Segments must intersect only at their endpoints. The number of points of
intersection is the same as the number of segments. No consecutive segments may be collinear.

Extend each side of a polygon to form a line. Each line separates the
plane of the figure into two half-planes. If the polygon is fully contained
in only one of each pair of half-planes, the polygon is **convex**, and a
segment joining any two points of the polygonal region does not intersect
the figure (see Section 5.3).

A regular polygon, like an equilateral triangle, has one center, the
center of both the inscribed circle and the circumscribed circle. Segments
joining the center and the vertices of the polygon are the radii of the
circumscribed circle. These segments separate the polygon into congruent
isosceles triangles. Each side of the polygon is the base of one of these triangles. A radius of the inscribed circle is a segment from the center perpendicular to a side at its midpoint. This segment is the **apothem** of the
polygon. In the regular hexagon in Fig. 62, $\overline{OA}$ is the radius of the circumscribed circle and $\overline{OB}$ is the apothem.

Fig. 62

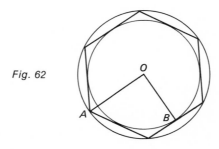

A polygon may have exterior angles as a triangle has. Extend a side through a vertex. The union of the extension and the second side with the same vertex is an **exterior angle**.

DEFINITION   The union of a polygon and its interior is a **polygonal region**.

All polygonal regions can be separated into triangular regions using necessary segments. The triangles must not overlap. Their intersections are segments and points. The method of dividing up the polygon is dependent upon the purpose of the separation. One purpose is to find the sum of the measures of the angles. Another is to find the area of the polygonal region which is the sum of the areas of the separate triangles. Two useful arrangements are shown in Fig. 63.

Fig. 63

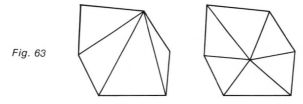

EXERCISE 11.1

NOTE: Symbols and formulas for lengths, areas, and volumes are listed in Section 11.5.

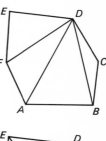

1. (a) PROVE (by two methods): The sum of the measures of interior angles of a hexagon is four straight angles.
   (b) Apply the principle of adding the measures of angles of a triangle to a decagon (ten sides).
   (c) State a general rule for the sum of the angles of an *n*-gon.
   (d) State a rule for the measure of each angle of a regular *n*-gon.

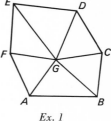

Ex. 1

2. **(a)** PROVE: The sum of the measures of exterior angles formed by extending each side of a pentagon consecutively in one direction is two straight angles. (NOTE: The sides of the numbered angles in the figure are parallel to the sides of the pentagon.)

   (b) From this proof, state a general rule for the sum of the measures of exterior angles formed in like manner on an n-gon.

   (c) State a rule for the measure of each exterior angle of a regular n-gon.

Ex. 2

3. Make a table of the measures of the parts of regular n-gons, from $n = 3$ to $n = 12$. GIVEN: The perimeter is 100 inches.

n	m interior $\angle$	m exterior $\angle$	length of side
3	60	120	$33\frac{1}{3}$
4			

4. PROVE: Any two diagonals of a regular pentagon are congruent.

11.2   Areas of Polygons

Areas are computed from linear measures made on segments perpendicular to each other in a plane. The area of a geometric figure is the number of unit squares in the interior of the figure. Take a card which is 5 inches long and 3 inches wide. Mark off segments parallel to the sides 1 inch from the sides and from each other. Two segments will separate the card into three regions. Mark off segments parallel to the ends which separate the sides into inches and there are five regions. Fifteen square inches is the sum of three rows of five squares each or five rows of three squares each.

Postulate 17   **The area of a rectangle whose consecutive sides are length and width is the product of length and width. The area is measured in square units.**

The sides of a rectangle are commonly called either length and width or base and altitude. Thus the area of a rectangle is either lw or ba. Other area formulas are derived from this postulate. We have determined a correct formula when it declares that the area of the figure is the number of unit squares which the figure is actually found to contain by experiment. In these relationships, when we mention a segment, we are referring to its length; when we mention an angle, we refer to its measure.

NOTE: See the system of letter symbols in Section 11.5.

THEOREM 73   The area of a parallelogram is the product of one side as base and the altitude perpendicular to it.

GIVEN: $\square ABCD$.

PROVE: Area = base × altitude.

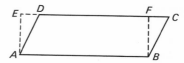

Through B draw $\overline{BF} \perp \overline{CD}$ intersecting $\overline{CD}$ at F. Through A draw $\overline{AE} \perp$ $\overline{CD}$ intersecting $\overline{CD}$ extended at E. These segments $\perp \overline{CD}$ are $\perp \overline{AB}$ which is $\parallel \overline{CD}$. Also $\overline{AE} \cong \overline{BF}$; segments of $\parallel$ intercepted by $\parallel \cong$. Opp sides of $\square$, $\overline{AD} \cong \overline{BC}$. Rt $\triangle ADE \cong$ rt $\triangle BCF$ by hyp and leg. Area $ABFD +$ area $\triangle BCF$ = area $\square ABCD$. Area $ABFD$ + area $\triangle ADE$ = area rect $ABFE$. These sums of = areas =. Area rect = $AB \times BF$ and area $\square ABCD$ = $AB \times BF$.

COROLLARY 73.1   The area of a square is the square of a side.

COROLLARY 73.2   Two parallelograms with equal bases and altitudes have equal areas.

COROLLARY 73.3   Two parallelograms with equal bases have areas proportional to the altitudes. Two parallelograms with equal altitudes have areas proportional to the bases.

THEOREM 74   The area of a triangle is one half the product of one side as base and the altitude to the given base.

GIVEN: $\triangle ABC$; base $\overline{AB}$; altitude $\overline{CE} \perp$ $\overline{AB}$.

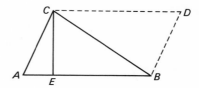

PROVE: Area $\triangle ABC = \frac{1}{2}(AB \times CE)$.

Through B draw $\overline{BD} \parallel \overline{AC}$. Through C draw $\overline{CD} \parallel \overline{AB}$ and intersecting $\overline{BD}$ at D. Area $\square ABDC = AB \times EC$. Area $\triangle ABC = \frac{1}{2}$ area $ABCD$; a diagonal separates a $\square$ into 2 $\cong \triangle$. Area $\triangle ABC = \frac{1}{2}(AB \times EC)$.

COROLLARY 74.1   The area of a right triangle equals one half the product of its legs.

COROLLARY 74.2   Two triangles with equal bases and altitudes have equal areas.

COROLLARY 74.3   Two triangles with equal bases have areas proportional to the altitudes. Two triangles with equal altitudes have areas proportional to the bases.

COROLLARY 74.4   Areas of congruent polygons are equal. (NOTE: Separate the polygons into triangles as in Section 11.1.)

THEOREM 75   The areas of two similar triangles are proportional to the squares of two corresponding sides.

GIVEN: $\triangle ABC \sim \triangle DEF$; corresp sides b, e; bases c, f; altitudes g, h.

PROVE: $\dfrac{\text{area } \triangle ABC}{\text{area } \triangle DEF} = \dfrac{c^2}{f^2}.$

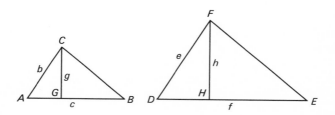

$\angle A \cong \angle D$; corresp $\measuredangle \sim \measuredangle \cong$. Rt $\angle AGC \cong$ rt $\angle DHF$, making $\triangle AGC \sim \triangle DHF$ by AA $\sim$ AA. In $\triangle ABC$ and $\triangle DEF$ corresp sides $\dfrac{b}{e} = \dfrac{c}{f}$. In $\triangle AGC$ and $\triangle DHF$ $\dfrac{b}{e} = \dfrac{g}{h}$. Hence, $\dfrac{g}{h} = \dfrac{c}{f}$ and $g = \dfrac{ch}{f}$. Dividing area $\triangle ABC$ by area $\triangle DEF$, $\dfrac{cg}{fh} = \dfrac{c}{fh} \times \dfrac{ch}{f} = \dfrac{c^2}{f^2}.$

COROLLARY 75.1   Areas of similar polygons are proportional to the squares of corresponding sides. (NOTE: Separate similar polygons into similar triangles.)

EXERCISE 11.2

The area of the same figure is to be found in different ways in Exs. 1 and 2:

1. GIVEN: $\triangle ABC$; $AB = 30$; $CE = 12$; $EA = 6$.

(a) Find area $\square\,ABDC$ and then area $\triangle ABC$.

(b) Find area rect $EFDC$ and then area $\triangle ABC$.

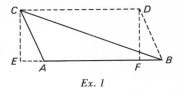

Ex. 1

2. GIVEN: Trapezoid $ABCD$; $AB = 15$; $CD = 5$; $EK = 6$; $AE = 2$; $FB = 3$; MN is median.

(a) Find area $\triangle ABD$ and $\triangle BCD$ and then area $ABCD$.

(b) Find area rectangle $EFHK$ and then area $ABCD$.

(c) Find area $AJGD$ and then area $ABCD$.

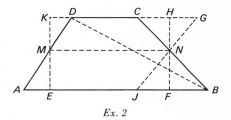

Ex. 2

3. GIVEN: $\triangle ABC$; $\overline{AD}$ and $\overline{BE}$ are medians. Compare the areas of: **(a)** $\triangle BAE$ and $\triangle ABD$. **(b)** $\triangle AEB$ and $\triangle CEB$.

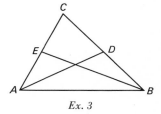

Ex. 3

The area of a polygon can be found by using different sides as bases with altitudes corresponding. From the equation of two products an unknown length can be found. Solve Exs. 4–6.

4. GIVEN: $\triangle QRS$; $\overline{UQ} \perp \overline{RS}$; $\overline{TS} \perp \overline{QR}$; $QR = 15$; $TS = 8$; $UQ = 12$. Find: **(a)** Area of $\triangle QRS$. **(b)** Length of base RS.

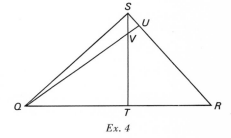

Ex. 4

5. GIVEN: $\square ABCD$; $\overline{ED} \perp \overline{AB}$; $\overline{FD} \perp$ $\overline{BC}$; $AB = 40$; $DA = 24$; $ED = 21$. Find: **(a)** Area of $\square ABCD$. **(b)** Length of altitude FD.

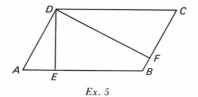

Ex. 5

6. GIVEN: Quad $RSTU$; V is midpoint of $\overline{RT}$; $\overline{RW} \perp \overline{SU}$; $\overline{TX} \perp \overline{SU}$. PROVE: Area $\triangle RSU$ = area $\triangle TSU$.

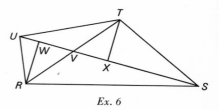

Ex. 6

7. The areas of two similar triangles are 100 and 64 square centimeters, respectively. If a side of the second is 16 centimeters, find the corresponding side of the first.

8. Find the ratio of the area of figure 2 to the area of figure 1 in each of the following:

	figure 1	base, in.	altitude, in.	figure 2	base, in.	altitude, in.
(a)	$\triangle 1$	14	10	$\triangle 2$	14	15
(b)	$\square 1$	20	16	$\square 2$	40	16
(c)	rect 1	12	8	rect 2	24	16
(d)	rect 1	b	a	rect 2	$\dfrac{b}{2}$	$2a$
(e)	$\triangle$	6	5	$\square$	6	5

(f) Reg hexagon 1: side 3 inches; reg hexagon 2: side 6 inches.

9. One right triangle has legs of 12 and 18 inches. A similar right triangle has the shorter leg of 8 inches.

(a) Find the longer leg of the second triangle.
(b) Find the ratio of the areas of the first to the second.
(c) Find the area of each.

10. The cross section of a piece of metal has the shape and dimensions given. Separate it into appropriate rectangles and find the area of the figure.

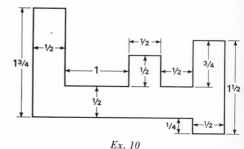

Ex. 10

11. GIVEN: $\square ABCD$; $DE = 2EC$. Find the ratio of the areas $\triangle AED$: $\triangle ABE$: $\triangle BCE$.

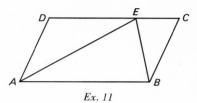

Ex. 11

12. The diagonals of a parallelogram form four triangles. Prove that all triangles have the same area.

13. (a) Determine the area of a regular octagon in terms of its apothem and its perimeter.
(b) From this, state a general rule for the area of a regular n-gon.

14. The hypotenuse as a base of a right triangle is divided into parts of 4 and 9 inches by the altitude.

(a) Find the altitude.
(b) Find the areas of the three triangles.

15. The diagonals of a rhombus are 9 centimeters and 14 centimeters long. (NOTE: Diagonals are perpendicular.)

(a) Find the lengths of the sides.
(b) Find the area of the rhombus.
(c) Show that the area of a rhombus is one half the product of the lengths of the diagonals.

16. A method for proving the Pythagorean Theorem uses a square within a square. The outside square has each side $= a + b$. The inside square has each side $= c$. Each right triangle has hypotenuse c and legs a and b.
PROVE: $c^2 = a^2 + b^2$.

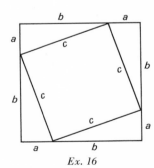

Ex. 16

17. To approximate the area of a curved figure, a base line is divided into equal segments s, and distances are recorded perpendicular to

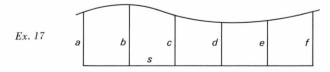

Ex. 17

the base line. The area of each part is the average of its two sides multiplied by s. Each distance except the first and last is used twice. The formula for area is

$$A = \left(\frac{a}{2} + b + c + d + e + \frac{f}{2}\right)s$$

Find the area of the surface when $a = 9.2$ feet, $b = 10.6$ feet, $c = 8.8$ feet, $d = 7.6$ feet, $e = 7.8$ feet, $f = 9.4$ feet and $s = 8.0$ feet.

11.3 Polyhedrons

DEFINITIONS   The union of polygonal regions whose intersections are exactly the sides of the polygons is a **polyhedron**. Each region is a **face**. The intersections are **edges**. The edges intersect at points which are **vertices** of angles. If the figure is convex, and all faces are congruent regular polygons, it is a regular **polyhedron**.

DEFINITIONS   A polyhedron with two faces in parallel planes and all lateral edges parallel is a **prism**. The parallel faces are **bases**. The faces joining the bases are **lateral faces**. They intersect in **lateral edges**. If the lateral edges are perpendicular to the bases, the prism is a **right prism**.

DEFINITIONS   A prism whose bases are parallelograms is a **parallelepiped**. A parallelepiped all of whose faces are rectangles is a **rectangular solid**. A rectangular solid all of whose faces are squares is a **cube**. A polyhedron whose base is a polygon and whose edges from the base intersect in exactly one point is a **pyramid**. The one point is a **vertex**. If the base is a regular polygon and the altitude from the vertex intersects the base at its center, the pyramid is a **regular** or **right pyramid**.

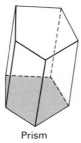
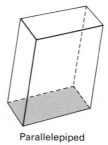
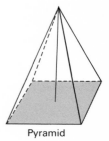

Fig. 64

Prism   Parallelepiped   Pyramid

A great many of the articles of industry have the characteristics of prisms. The intersections of lateral surfaces are all parallel lines. The surfaces may be either plane or curved. The word *lateral* applies to the sides as contrasted with the ends. Often long pieces of these materials are cut up into parts. The intersection of the plane of the cut and the piece of material is a **cross section**. If all cross sections made by parallel planes are congruent, the piece has a **uniform cross section**. If the plane of the cut is perpendicular to the lateral edges, the section is a **right section**.

THEOREM 76 **The bases of a prism are congruent polygons.**

GIVEN: Prism with bases $ABCDE$ and
        $RSTUV$.

PROVE: $ABCDE \cong RSTUV$.

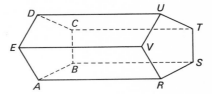

$\overline{AB} \parallel \overline{RS}$; intersections of $\parallel$ planes with a third plane $\parallel$. $\overline{AR} \parallel \overline{BS}$; lateral edges $\parallel$. $ARSB$ is a $\square$; quad with opp sides $\parallel$ is a $\square$. $\overline{AB} \cong \overline{RS}$; opp sides of $\square \cong$. In like manner all corresp sides $\cong$. $\angle VRS \cong \angle EAB$; $\angle$ of $\parallel$ planes intercepted by dihedral $\angle \cong$. In like manner all corresp $\angle \cong$. Then $ABCDE \cong RSTUV$; polygons, corresp $\angle \cong$ and sides $\cong$, are $\cong$ polygons.

COROLLARY 76.1   **Lateral faces of a prism are parallelograms.**

COROLLARY 76.2   **Opposite faces of a parallelepiped are congruent parallelograms.**

COROLLARY 76.3   **Parallel sections of a prism are congruent polygons.**

11.4   Volumes

The three **dimensions in space** are measured along three mutually perpendicular lines, each perpendicular to the other two. On a flat plane of two dimensions the three dimensions in space are shown by a perspective drawing of the corner of a box (Fig. 65). Rays $\overrightarrow{OY}$ and $\overrightarrow{OZ}$ are in the plane of the paper and $\overrightarrow{OX}$ is to be viewed as extending outward from the plane. Any of the three rays may be extended in the opposite direction through O.

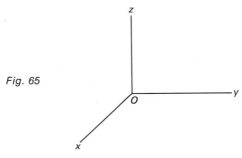

Fig. 65

Volumes are computed from linear measures in three dimensions. The three dimensions in space may be called length, width, and altitude.

When we discuss a figure in three dimensions, sometimes we are considering the union of the planes which make up its surface, and the figure has a hollow interior. At other times we are concentrating on the solid figure whose interior is full of material. The formulas relating the lengths, areas, and volumes are the same for both conditions, and in general we will not be concerned with which meaning is being considered.

Postulate 18   **The volume of a rectangular solid whose mutually perpendicular edges are length, width, and altitude is the product of the length, width, and altitude. The volume is measured in cubic units.**

Corollary   **The volume of a solid of uniform cross section is the product of the area of the right section and the altitude.**

Solid figures can be similar as plane figures are.

Postulate 19   **All corresponding lengths of similar solid figures are proportional and all corresponding angles are congruent.**

Postulate 20   **All corresponding areas of figures are proportional to squares of corresponding lengths. All corresponding volumes are proportional to cubes of corresponding lengths.**

11.5   Derivation of Formulas

The many measures of objects and their parts are all based on linear measures. All areas are squares, or the second power of linear measures. All volumes are cubes, or the third power of the linear. The units of measure (inches, centimeters, or any distance between two marks on a stick) are built into a system of relationships. A large number of these relationships are expressed in formulas. Each formula shows a symbol for each measure and the arithmetic process by which these symbols are related. The resulting measure is a logical consequence.

These formulas were discovered, and can be tested, empirically— by experience. They can also be proved from postulates of measure which lay the foundation for the system. Some of the proofs are rather long and involved. A few formulas of areas have already been given as theorems. A few of the others will be postulated—given without proof. The rest will be **derived**. Derivation is very important in the work of science and should be practiced by all students of mathematics and science. A derivation is a proof that the fundamental measures are accurately related in terms of mathematical principles to produce the declared results.

In the formulas we shall use the following system of letter symbols; all the lowercase letters are linear measures.

A = area of a plane figure

B = area of the base of a solid

S = area of sides of a solid

T = total area of a solid

V = volume of a solid

a = altitude, apothem

b = base of a plane figure

c = circumference of a circle

d = diameter of a circle; diagonal

e = edge of a solid

h = lateral height of a solid

l = length

p = perimeter of a base

r = radius of a circle

s = side of polygon

w = width

Rectangle:
$$A = lw \quad \text{or} \quad A = ba$$

Square:
$$A = s^2$$

Parallelogram:
$$A = ba$$

Triangle:
$$A = \frac{ba}{2}$$

Trapezoid:
$$A = a\,\frac{b_1 + b_2}{2}$$

Rectangular solid:
$$V = lwa$$

Cube:
$$V = e^3$$

Prism:
$$V = Ba \quad \text{or} \quad V = Bl$$

Pyramid:
$$V = \frac{Ba}{3}$$

Solid of uniform cross section:
$$V = Bl$$

The following formulas we derive:

Diagonal of a square:
$$d^2 = s^2 + s^2$$
$$d = s\sqrt{2}$$

(a)

Equilateral triangle:
$$a^2 = s^2 - \frac{s^2}{4} = \frac{3s^2}{4}$$
$$a = \frac{s}{2}\sqrt{3}$$
$$A = \frac{1}{2}\left(s \times \frac{s}{2}\sqrt{3}\right) = \frac{s^2}{4}\sqrt{3}$$

(b)

Fig. 66

When a derivation produces a square root in a denominator, algebraic practice dictates that the numerator and the denominator shall be multiplied by the square root, so as to leave a radical in the numerator only.

EXERCISE 11.5

1. Derive a formula for the diagonal of a cube of edge e.

2. Given a square-based right pyramid whose sides are equilateral triangles, with each edge e, derive:

(a) Lateral height   **(b)** Altitude   **(c)** Volume
(d) Lateral surface area

3. Given a square with sides of length s, derive:

(a) The radius and area of the inscribed circle
(b) The radius and area of the circumscribed circle
(c) The ratio of the areas of the circumscribed to the inscribed circle

4. Given a regular hexagon with sides of length g, derive:

(a) The radius and area of the inscribed circle
(b) The radius and area of the circumscribed circle
(c) The ratio of the areas of the circumscribed to the inscribed circle

5. GIVEN: Square $ABCD$ with sides of length s; $\overline{AC}$ is a diagonal; E is the midpoint of $\overline{BC}$; F is the midpoint of $\overline{CD}$. Derive:

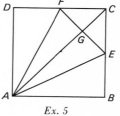

(a) AE **(b)** EF **(c)** AG
(d) The area of $\triangle AEF$
(e) The radius of the circle inscribed in $\triangle ABC$

Ex. 5

6. The total area of a cube is 384 square inches. Find its volume.

7. The areas of two similar triangles are 90 square inches and 40 square inches. Find the side of the smaller which corresponds to a 15-inch side of the larger.

8. The volume of an irregular stone is found by immersing it in a tank of water. The base of the tank is 2 feet by 4 feet. If the stone raises the level of water 9 inches, find its volume.

9. A prism has a rectangular base 6 feet by 8 feet. Its volume is 432 cubic feet. Find its total surface area.

10. The base of a prism is an isosceles right triangle. Each of the congruent legs is 4 centimeters long. If the volume is 72 cubic centimeters, find the altitude.

11. Two prisms are similar. The length of one is 3 inches, of the other is 4 inches. Find:

  (a) The ratio of their surface areas
  (b) The ratio of their volumes

12. A right pyramid has an equilateral triangular base with sides of 6 inches. Each lateral edge is 5 inches long. Find the total surface area.

13. A right pyramid has a square base with sides of 10 centimeters. Each lateral edge is 13 centimeters long. Using the symbols of this section, find to the nearest whole number:

  (a) h (b) a (c) B (d) S (e) T (f) V

14. A pyramid has a volume of 450 cubic feet. Its altitude is 15 feet. Find the area of its base.

11.6   Circular Figures

Wheels and other circles have held a strategic place in the development of man since very early times. The constant ratio of the circumference to the diameter was discovered early and was found to be also the ratio of the area of the circle to the square of the radius. The **area** is that of a circular region which is the union of the circle and its interior. The same ratio is used in finding the volume of a sphere.

> DEFINITIONS   The locus of points in space a given distance from a given point is a **sphere** with the given point as **center** and the given distance as **radius**. A segment passing through the center whose endpoints are points of the sphere is a **diameter**. A plane which passes through the center intersects the sphere in a **great circle**. A great circle bisects the sphere into two **hemispheres**.

All other circles made by intersecting planes are smaller than the great circle. The radius of the great circle is the same as the radius of the sphere.

A sphere has the least surface area per given volume of any solid. A rubber balloon because of its elasticity contracts to its smallest possible area as it is expanded. Therefore it is a sphere.

> DEFINITIONS   A segment in the interior of a sphere whose endpoints are points of the sphere is a **chord of the sphere**. The **interior of a sphere** is the set of all points whose distance from the center is less than the radius.

All points of the **exterior** are at a greater distance from the center than the radius. A line or plane which intersects the sphere at exactly one point is **tangent to the sphere**. A **secant plane** intersects the sphere in a circle.

DEFINITIONS   A solid whose bases are circles and whose lateral side is a curved surface is a **circular cylinder**. Between corresponding points of the bases are parallel segments. If the parallel segments are perpendicular to the bases, the cylinder is a **right cylinder**.

DEFINITIONS   A **circular cone** has a circle as a base and lateral segments extending from the edge of the base to a point, the **vertex**. The altitude extends from the vertex perpendicular to the plane of the base. If the altitude intersects a circular base at its center, the cone is a **right circular cone**. The length of the segment from the edge of the base to the vertex is the **lateral height**. The surface of the cone above the base is the **lateral surface**.

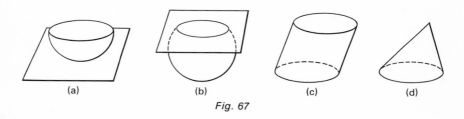

(a)   (b)   (c)   (d)

Fig. 67

Fig. 67(a) is a hemisphere tangent to the plane on which it is lying. Its top is a great circle of the sphere. Fig. 67(b) is a sphere intercepted by a secant plane whose intersection is a circle smaller than a great circle. Fig. 67(c) is a cylinder, and Fig. 67(d) is a cone. These last two are not "right."

The formulas for circular figures are given without proof:

Circle:

$$A = \pi r^2 \qquad \text{or} \qquad A = \frac{cr}{2}$$

Sphere:

$$T = 4\pi r^2 \qquad V = \frac{4}{3}\pi r^3$$

Right circular cone:

$$S = \frac{ch}{2} \qquad V = \frac{\pi r^2 a}{3}$$

A sphere is a very strong physical structure. The United States Pavilion at Expo 67 in Montreal is a sphere 250 feet in diameter. Each plastic bubble is contained in a steel hexagonal pyramid frame. The bases of the pyramids have sides in common, welded together and to lateral bars at common endpoints. The vertices of the pyramids are welded to a network of steel tubing forming equilateral triangles. The whole is a structure very light in weight compared to conventional forms. Photo by Edith Reichmann.

THEOREM 77   The volumes of two spheres are proportional to the cubes of their radii.

$V_1 = \frac{4}{3}\pi r_1^3$; $V_2 = \frac{4}{3}\pi r_2^3$. Divide the members of one equation by those of the other, and

$$\frac{V_1}{V_2} = \frac{r_1^3}{r_2^3}$$

When a plane intersects a cone or a pyramid in a section parallel to the base, the section is similar to the base and is called another **base**. The part of the figure between and including the two bases is a **frustum**. The volume of the frustum is the volume of the original figure minus the volume of the subtracted part.

THEOREM 78   In a cone or a pyramid the areas of the two parallel bases are proportional to the squares of their distances from the vertex.

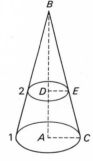

GIVEN: Cone with $\odot A$ as base 1, $\odot D$ as section 2, B as vertex; section 2 $\parallel$ base 1.

PROVE: $\dfrac{\text{Area}_2}{\text{Area}_1} = \dfrac{DB^2}{AB^2}$.

Draw radii $\overline{AC}$ and $\overline{DE}$. $\angle DEB \cong \angle ACB$; $\angle BDE \cong \angle BAC$; trans $\parallel$, corresp $\angle\!\!\!\!\angle \cong$. $\triangle DEB \sim \triangle ACB$; AA $\sim$ AA. Then $\dfrac{DE}{AC} = \dfrac{DB}{AB}$; corresp sides $\sim \angle\!\!\!\!\angle$ prop. Area$_2 = \pi DE^2$; area$_1 = \pi AC^2$. Then, dividing, $\dfrac{\text{area}_2}{\text{area}_1} = \dfrac{DE^2}{AC^2} = \dfrac{DB^2}{AB^2}$; first = second = third.

EXERCISE 11.6

1. GIVEN: Right circular cylinder with radius of base r and altitude a, find:

    (a) Lateral area   **(b)** Total area   **(c)** Volume

2. GIVEN: Two spheres of radius q and r, respectively. Describe the intersection of the spheres if the distance between their centers is:

   (a) Greater than either q or r and less than $q + r$
   (b) Equal to $q + r$
   (c) Greater than $q + r$

3. A circle of 20-inch diameter is cut from a square of metal with sides of 20 inches. How much metal is wasted outside the circle?

4. Find the area of one surface of a flat washer whose inside diameter is 1 inch and whose outside diameter is 2 inches.

5. A plane intersects a sphere of 25-inch radius. The center of the circle of intersection is 20 inches from the center of the sphere. Find the radius of the circle.

6. The great circle of a hemisphere has radius r. Find the ratio of the area of the spherical surface of the hemisphere to the area of the circle.

7. Oranges of 2-inch diameter cost 56¢ a dozen. Neglecting skin thickness, what should one pay for oranges of 3-inch diameter.

8. A lawn roller 2 feet long has a diameter of 20 inches. How many square feet of area does it cover in 200 revolutions?

9. A concrete pipe 10 feet long has an inside diameter of 2 feet. The thickness of the concrete is 2 inches. Find the volume of concrete in cubic inches.

10. Find the number of gallons of liquid in a cylinder whose base has a diameter of 3 feet and is filled to a depth of 49 inches. There are 231 cubic inches per gallon. (NOTE: Use $\pi = 22/7$.)

11. The altitude of a right circular cylinder is decreased by 25%. The radius of its base is increased by $33\frac{1}{3}\%$. Find the ratio of:

    (a) The second lateral surface to the first
    (b) The second volume to the first

12. The frustum of a right pyramid has square bases whose sides are 10 and 8 inches, respectively. The bases are 5 inches apart. Find the altitude of the original pyramid.

13. An ice cream cone is a frustum whose bases have diameters of 2 inches and 1 inch, respectively, and whose altitude is 4 inches. Two spheres of ice cream of 2-inch diameter are put on. If the ice cream is left to melt, will it overflow the cone?

11.7 Summary Test

On answer sheet write the word(s) or symbol(s) which are necessary to fill in each blank.

1. A polygon which has 10 sides has __(a)__ vertices. A regular polygon has all sides __(b)__ and all angles __(c)__. Similar polygons have corresponding sides __(d)__ and corresponding angles __(e)__.

2. A convex polygon is fully contained in each __(a)__ formed by a side of the polygon extended. A segment joining any two points of the interior of a convex polygon intersects the polygon at __(b)__. Each interior angle of a convex polygon has a measure __(c)__.

3. A segment joining the center of a regular polygon and __(a)__ is the radius of the circumscribed circle. A segment joining the center and __(b)__ is the radius of the inscribed circle. Each side of the polygon forms a(n) __(c)__ triangle with two radii of the __(d)__ circle. A radius of the __(e)__ circle is the altitude of each triangle. The area of each triangle is __(f)__ the length of a side of the polygon times __(g)__. The area of the polygonal region is __(h)__ the areas of the triangles.

4. A __(a)__ of a convex polygon joins two nonconsecutive vertices. In a convex polygon of n sides there are __(b)__ of these with endpoints at one vertex. They divide the polygon into __(c)__ (number) triangles.

5. In a regular polygon, the larger the number of sides, the __(a)__ the number of degrees in each interior angle. The number of degrees in an interior angle of a regular octagon is __(b)__; the measure of an adjacent exterior angle is __(c)__.

6. An area is the __(a)__ of two lengths measured __(b)__ to each other. The area of a parallelogram is the area of the rectangle with the same __(c)__. Two triangles which have the same base have areas __(d)__ their __(e)__. The areas of similar polygons are proportional to __(f)__ __(g)__.

7. Polygons are geometric figures of __(a)__ dimensions. Polyhedrons are geometric figures of __(b)__ dimensions.

8. All cubes are a subset of __(a)__ which are a subset of __(b)__ which are a subset of __(c)__ which are a subset of __(d)__.

9. A piece of material of uniform cross section has all lateral edges __(a)__. If its ends are parallel sections, it has the shape of a __(b)__. If its lateral planes are two pairs of parallel faces, it is a __(c)__. If two sides of a base of a prism are congruent, the two faces of which each of these is a side are __(d)__. All faces of regular polyhedrons are __(e)__. The lateral faces of a regular pyramid are all __(f)__.

10. Areas are measured in __(a)__ dimensions; volumes are measured in __(b)__ dimensions. The volumes of two similar polyhedrons are proportional to the __(c)__ __(d)__. To determine the volume of any prism, the area of a __(e)__ is calculated; this measure multiplied by __(f)__ gives the volume. If a cone and a cylinder have the same base and the same altitude, the volume of the cone is __(g)__ the volume of the cylinder.

11. If the radius of a circle is increased by 1 foot, the circumference is increased by _____.

12. If a plane intersects a sphere, the intersection is either __(a)__ or __(b)__.

13. The diameter of a sphere is also the diameter of a _____ circle of the sphere.

14. A frustum has two bases; in shape they are __(a)__; the lengths of their sides are __(b)__; their planes are __(c)__.

chapter **12**

Coordinate Geometry

12.1 The Coordinate System

Euclidean geometry had until recently a rather clumsy way of proving two figures congruent or of relating geometric figures. While it was being passed down through the centuries, other concepts were being developed which would come to the aid of geometry. Algebra was perfected by the Arabs and began to flourish in Europe with the Renaissance. Then came Descartes, a seventeenth-century French philosopher, who invented the system of coordinates with which we draw graphs. This system is now recognized to be ideal for relating geometric figures by means of numerical expressions.

The system of Descartes, called Cartesian coordinates, is based on two mutually perpendicular lines in a plane. Each one is an **axis** (plural axes) and is marked off with a scale, usually a uniform scale. In the plane of these axes any point can be located by recording two numbers. The lines x and y are the axes. The point of their intersection is the **origin**.

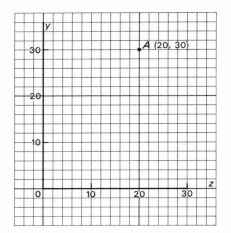

Fig. 68

The scale used in Fig. 68 gives five spaces the value of ten units. The origin is zero for each axis. The point *A* is at a distance of 20 units in a positive direction from the origin on the *x*-axis and 30 units in a positive direction from the origin on the *y*-axis. These two coordinates, called an **ordered pair**, are recorded in parentheses with the *x*-value first and the *y*-value after a comma. Coordinates are equally valid in the negative direction. The *x*-coordinate is called the **abscissa** and the *y*-coordinate is called the **ordinate**.

The coordinate system of Chapter 2 was taken from this Cartesian system using one axis and one coordinate for a point. The concept of one-to-one correspondence between a point and a number is due to the fact that each point has exactly one coordinate on each axis. There the number of axes was one; here the number is two. There the point could be located along a line; here it can be located on a plane. And each point of the plane has exactly one ordered pair of numbers which denote its location on the plane for each position of the axes and each set of scales used for the axes. If either the location of the axes or the scale of either axis is changed, the same point of the plane has a new ordered pair of coordinates. The scales for the two coordinates are not necessarily the same.

The scale was 20 units per inch on the coordinates in Fig. 68 and is 10 units per inch in Fig. 69. Thus the coordinates of *B* are (6, 9) and of *C* are (−8, 12). Between the lines the points and their corresponding numbers are estimated. Point *D* has the ordered pair (7.5, −3.4). What are coordinates of point *E*?

The two axes separate the plane into four **quadrants**. It will be observed that distances from axes are located in the same manner in all quadrants; the only difference is the sign(s) of the number(s). The quadrants are commonly numbered I to IV. The customary number and the

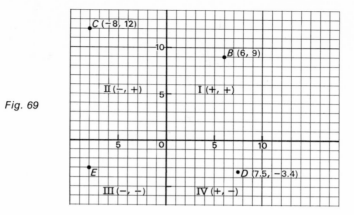

Fig. 69

signs of coordinates in each are shown in Fig. 69. In a graph which can have only positive values, three quadrants can be omitted.

   A line perpendicular to and intersecting the x-axis at 6 has the coordinate $x = 6$. Every point of the line has a different y-coordinate, positive or negative, but it has only an x-coordinate of 6. Therefore, the locus of this line can be fully expressed by the equation $x = 6$. A line perpendicular to and intersecting the y-axis at 9 has the equation $y = 9$. Each point of the line has a different coordinate of x. The point where these two lines intersect is the one point of the plane where $x = 6$ and $y = 9$, and the ordered pair of coordinates for the point B above is $(6, 9)$. It is apparent that there is a one-to-one correspondence between the set of all points of the xy-plane and the set of all ordered pairs of real numbers.

12.2   Properties of a Line

Chapter 2 includes the definition: "The absolute value of the difference of the coordinates of two points is the measure of the distance between the points." In a two-dimensional system the distance is apparent when the two points are on the x-axis or on the y-axis or on a line parallel to either axis. But for all other pairs of points some further calculation must be done. Drop perpendiculars from point A to the x-axis and to the y-axis ($\overline{AR}$ and $\overline{AT}$ in Fig. 70). Do the same for point B ($\overline{BS}$ and $\overline{BU}$). The segment of the x-axis intercepted by the two perpendiculars is $\overline{RS}$, which is the **projection** of $\overline{AB}$ on the x-axis. Each point of the segment of the axis is the projection of a point of the given segment. The projection on the y-axis, $\overline{TU}$, is of the same nature. The coordinates of each projection are the coordinates on one axis of the given segment, such as $3 \leq x \leq 8$ and $4 \leq y \leq 10$.

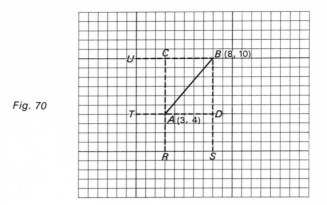

Fig. 70

Extend the two perpendiculars through A until they intersect the perpendiculars from B (at C and D). Then $\overline{AB}$ and perpendicular segments form two right triangles. A leg of each of these triangles is congruent to the projection on each axis. The difference of the coordinates of the endpoints equals the length of the leg which is projected onto the axis. Now the *length* of the segment $\overline{AB}$ is found by means of the Pythagorean Theorem.

If the coordinates of A are (3, 4) and the coordinates of B are (8, 10), then the projection on the x-axis is 5 units long and the projection on the y-axis is 6 units long. By the Pythagorean Theorem the length AB is $\sqrt{61}$ units. Since a distance between points is always a positive number, the abslute value of all these differences is taken. In general terms, let (x_1, y_1) be the coordinates of one end of a segment and (x_2, y_2) be the coordinates of the other end. Then by the Pythagorean Theorem the length of the segment is

$$\sqrt{(x_2 - x_1)^2 + (y_2 - y_1)^2}$$

Every segment in a coordinate system is either parallel to one of the axes or oblique to both of them. As the x-coordinate of each oblique segment increases, the y-coordinate either increases or decreases. This relationship is shown numerically in Fig. 71. Consider the point $P\ (x_1, y_1)$ and the point $Q\ (x_2, y_2)$. The ratio of the lengths of the y-projection to the x-projection of the segment is the **slope** of the segment. If we take the difference $x_2 - x_1$ with $x_2 > x_1$, the difference is a positive number. The difference of the y-coordinates must be also $y_2 - y_1$. The slope of the segment is then

$$\frac{y_2 - y_1}{x_2 - x_1} = m \quad \text{(the symbol for slope is } m\text{)}$$

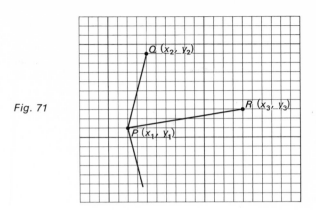

Fig. 71

Thus, when the segment inclines upward from left to right, as x increases, y increases and the slope is positive. A segment which inclines downward, so that as x increases y decreases, has a negative slope. The slope is independent of the order of the points, since $\dfrac{y_1 - y_2}{x_1 - x_2}$ will give m of the same number and sign as will the ratio above. A segment parallel to the y-axis has no change of x and, since a number cannot be divided by zero, this one is not included in slope considerations. The slope of a line is the same as the slope of any segment of it, and all the segments or rays of each line have the same slope.

With the coordinates of points given in Fig. 72, the slope of $\overline{PQ}$ is

$$m = \frac{9 - 1}{4 - 2} = 4$$

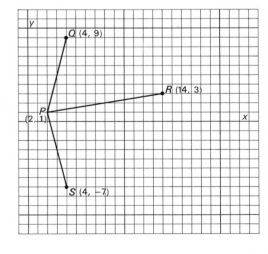

Fig. 72

The slope of $\overline{PR}$ is

$$m = \frac{3-1}{14-2} = \frac{1}{6}$$

a very small number. The slope of $\overline{PS}$ is

$$m = \frac{-7-1}{4-2} = -4$$

a negative slope.

EXERCISE 12.2

1. Graph the locus of the points (x, y) in a plane which satisfy each of the following:

    (a) $x = 6$ **(b)** $y = 4$ **(c)** $(6, 4)$ **(d)** $(0, -7)$
    (e) $(-9, -1)$
    (f) One point is $(0, 0)$ and the slope is -3
    (g) $x = -5$ and $0 \leq y \leq 8$
    (h) $3 \leq x \leq 10$ and $-2 \leq y \leq 10$

2. Find the distance between two points with the coordinates:

    (a) $(0, 0)$ and $(5, 12)$ **(b)** $(3, 0)$ and $(-6, -12)$
    (c) $(-8, 10)$ and $(16, -22)$

3. Find the slope of each segment in Ex. 2.

12.3 Equations of a Line

An algebraic equation can be written which is the numerical representation of exactly one line. The equation takes the form of terms containing x and y as variables and constant numerical terms.

    Taking advantage of the slope concept, the first form of equation of a line to be developed is the **point-slope** form. If a line contains one known point, whose coordinates are (x_1, y_1), the equation contains the ordered pair (x, y) of variables which are coordinates of any other possible point of the line. From an expression for the slope,

$$m = \frac{y - y_1}{x - x_1}$$

the equation can be written

$$y - y_1 = m(x - x_1)$$

This is the point-slope form. For instance, a line containing the point $(-5, -4)$ with a slope of 2 has the equation: $y + 4 = 2(x + 5)$. For every other value of x there is exactly one value of y which satisfies the equation, and the ordered pair are the coordinates of a second point of the line. For the point whose x-coordinate is $+1$, substitute 1 for x in the equation and the y-coordinate is 8, and the line contains the point $(1, 8)$.

Since a second point of the line is readily found from the point-slope form of the equation, the **two-point** form is written. Taking the first point (x_1, y_1) and the second point (x_2, y_2),

$$m = \frac{y_2 - y_1}{x_2 - x_1}$$

In the point-slope form:

$$y - y_1 = \frac{y_2 - y_1}{x_2 - x_1}(x - x_1)$$

Then

$$\frac{y - y_1}{x - x_1} = \frac{y_2 - y_1}{x_2 - x_1}$$

When the two points are $(-5, -4)$ and $(1, 8)$, the equation becomes

$$\frac{y + 4}{x + 5} = \frac{8 + 4}{1 + 5}$$

Then

$$6(y + 4) = 12(x + 5)$$

which reduces to

$$y + 4 = 2(x + 5)$$

Another common form of the equation is

$$\frac{x - x_1}{x_2 - x_1} = \frac{y - y_1}{y_2 - y_1}$$

The **slope-intercept** form of the equation of the same line defines the **intercept** of the y-axis, the point of the y-axis which the line intersects. This is given the symbol b, and the equation is in the form

$$y = mx + b$$

We recognize that b is the coordinate of y when $x = 0$. Taking the point-slope form of the above equation,

$$y + 4 = 2x + 10$$

solve for y when $x = 0$ and $y = 6$. Thus the line intersects the y-axis at 6, and the equation $y = 2x + 6$ shows that $m = 2$ and $b = 6$.

Another form of the equation, the **intercept** form, names the intercepts of both axes. It is given in the form

$$\frac{x}{a} + \frac{y}{b} = 1$$

where a is the point of the x-axis which the line intersects. From the equation

$$y - 2x = 6$$

when $y = 0$, $x = -3$ and the line intercepts the point -3 of the x-axis. The intercept form of the equation of the line becomes

$$\frac{x}{-3} + \frac{y}{6} = 1$$

To convert this equation into the other forms is an exercise left to the student.

Fig. 73

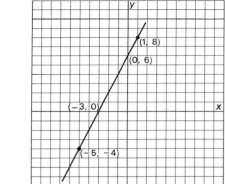

The graph of the line whose equation has all four of the above forms is shown in Fig. 73. We notice that the line contains the point $(-5, -4)$, that $(y_2 - y_1)(x_2 - x_1) = 2$, that the y-intercept is 6 and the x-intercept is -3. This line is the locus of all the points which satisfy the equation in any of its forms.

The equation of a line also has a **general form**:

$$ax + by + c = 0$$

in which a, b, and c are constant numbers, but not the same as the a and b of the intercept form. a and b cannot both be zero in the same equation.

The variables x and y are the ordered pair of coordinates of any point of the line. The equation of this section in general form is

$$2x - y + 6 = 0$$

In summary, (1) if data about a line are known, its equation can be written, and (2) if the equation is known, the other values can be found. In this section it has been shown:

1. (a) The coordinates of one point are $(-5, -4)$ while the slope of the line is 2. Hence:

$$y + 4 = 2(x + 5)$$

(b) The coordinates of two points are $(-5, -4)$ and $(1, 8)$. Hence:

$$y + 4 = \frac{8 + 4}{1 + 5}(x + 5)$$

or

$$y - 8 = \frac{8 + 4}{1 + 5}(x - 1)$$

(c) The slope is 2 and the y-intercept is 6. Hence:

$$y = 2x + 6$$

(d) The x-intercept is -3 and the y-intercept is 6. Hence:

$$\frac{x}{-3} + \frac{y}{6} = 1$$

(e) All of these can be converted into $2x - y + 6 = 0$.

2. (a) Solve $2x - y + 6 = 0$ for y:

$$y = 2x + 6$$

the slope is 2 and the y-intercept is 6.

(b) Choose either an x-coordinate or a y-coordinate and find the other half of the ordered pair. Substitute -5 for x and

$$y = -10 + 6 = -4$$

and a point of the line has coordinates $(-5, -4)$. Substitute 8 for y and

$$2x = 8 - 6 = 2$$

therefore $x = 1$, and the coordinates of the point are $(1, 8)$.

(c) To find both intercepts of $2x - y = -6$, when the right member of the equation is 1,

$$\frac{2x - y}{6} = -1 \qquad \text{and} \qquad \frac{x}{-3} + \frac{y}{6} = 1$$

The intercepts are −3 and 6. Each intercept can also be found by finding the value of one coordinate when the other is zero. Here, when $x = 0$, $y = 6$; when $y = 0$, $x = -3$.

EXERCISE 12.3

Draw the locus of points of each equation in Exs. 1–4.

1. $2y = 5x$ **2.** $x = 4y + 12$ **3.** $2x + y = 0$ **4.** $y = x - 6$

Determine whether the points with the pairs of coordinates given in Exs. 5–8 are collinear. **(a)** *Use algebraic methods.* **(b)** *Then draw the graph of each.*

5. $(-6, 11)$ $(0, 3)$ $(3, -1)$

> *Solution:* **(a)** The slope of the segment joining the first two points is
>
> $$m = \frac{11 - 3}{0 - (-6)} = -\frac{4}{3}$$

Joining the second and third points,

$$m = \frac{-1 - 3}{3 - 0} = -\frac{4}{3}$$

At least the slopes of two possible segments are the same. We now solve the point-slope form of the equation for each of the three points in succession:

$$\frac{y - 11}{x + 6} = -\frac{4}{3} \qquad \frac{y - 3}{x - 0} = -\frac{4}{3} \qquad \frac{y + 1}{x - 3} = -\frac{4}{3}$$
$$3y - 33 = -4x - 24 \qquad 3y - 9 = -4x \qquad 3y + 3 = -4x + 12$$
$$4x + 3y - 9 = 0 \qquad 4x + 3y - 9 = 0 \qquad 4x + 3y - 9 = 0$$

(b)

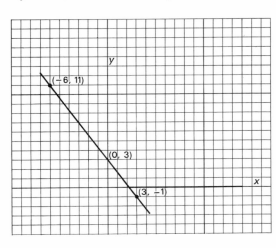

6. $(0, -6)$ $(4, -4)$ $(10, -1)$ **7.** $(5, -3)$ $(1, -2)$ $(-7, 2)$
8. $(5, 7)$ $(5, -9)$ $(8, 1)$

In Exs. 9–18 data are given which apply to a linear equation. Complete the table. Then graph each equation.

two points of the line	slope m	x-inter-cept, a	y-inter-cept, b	general form of the equation
9. $(3, 5)$ $(4, 10)$				

> *Solution:* Slope
>
>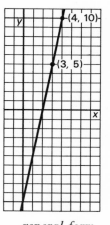
>
> $$m = \frac{10 - 5}{4 - 3} = 5$$
>
> Point-slope equation:
>
> $$y - 5 = 5(x - 3)$$
>
> General form of the equation:
>
> $$y - 5x + 10 = 0$$
> $$\text{or} \quad 5x - y - 10 = 0$$
>
> When $y = 0$, $x = 2$. When $x = 0$, $y = -10$.

two points of the line	slope m	x-inter-cept, a	y-inter-cept, b	general form of the equation
10. $(0, \quad)$ $(2, \quad)$		-1	4	
11. $(2, 15)$ $(\quad, 0)$	3			
12. $(4, 8)$ $(-3, -6)$				
13. $(5, \quad)$ $(-5, \quad)$	$\frac{1}{2}$	-5		
14. $(\quad, 1)$ $(\quad, -5)$				$3y - x + 6 = 0$
15. $(12, \quad)$ $(-2, \quad)$		4	2	
16. $(1, 2)$ $(-6, \quad)$	-1			
17. $(3, \quad)$ $(\quad, 4)$				$2x + y + 8 = 0$
18. $(\quad, -8)$ $(2, \quad)$	-4		8	

12.4 Vectors

A **vector** is a directed segment: it has magnitude and direction. The direction is shown by placing an arrowhead on one end. When a scale is taken the length of the segment represents exactly one magnitude. The arrowhead is the **terminal point** of the vector and the opposite end is the **initial point**. Vectors with the same magnitude and direction are **equivalent vectors**.

Vectors are used to represent several physical phenomena. One is **displacement**, a change of location. If a cyclist travels 2 miles east, then 4 miles north, then 1 mile northwest, where is he with respect to his starting place? Choosing a scale of 1 inch to represent 2 miles, draw a map of the route (Fig. 74). Each straight line of the trip is represented by a vector. The initial point of each is the terminal point of the preceding one. Then a single vector from the initial point of the first to the terminal point of the third represents the trip the cyclist would have taken if he had gone directly. His displacement from the starting point is a single vector, the **vector sum** of the three separate vectors. Laying a ruler on it we find that it is 4.4 inches long. A protractor gives the direction as 15° east of north or 75° north of east. This is an example of **vector addition**. In **vector subtraction** the negative of a vector is the vector of the same magnitude in the opposite direction.

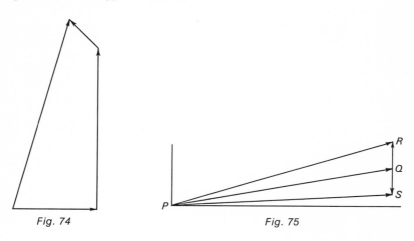

Fig. 74   Fig. 75

Displacement in a unit time is **velocity**. It includes direction as well as speed. When two forces in different directions apply to one motion, the two separate velocity vectors can be added (Fig. 75). An airplane is traveling in a direction of 80° east of north. Then a wind, blowing from due south, carries it off course. If the speed of the plane with respect to the air is 300 mph, its vector is PQ; if the speed of the wind is 40 mph, its vector is QR. The result of the combined velocities is the vector PR with a velocity of 303 mph and in a direction of 73° east of north. The sum of the vectors in both magnitude and direction is the **resultant**.

In aviation terminology the three directions, all measured in degrees clockwise from north, are:

Heading: The direction a plane's nose is pointing: $PQ = 80°$.

Course: The direction over the ground in which the plane is actually moving: $PR = 73°$.

Wind: The direction from which the wind is blowing: 180°.

The vector is drawn in the direction to which the wind is blowing: $QR = 0°$.

The magnitude of a vector is proportional to a speed and to the distance covered in a time interval. Two of the speeds are:

Air speed: The speed of the plane with respect to the air.

Ground speed: Its speed with respect to the ground.

The magnitude of the heading vector is air speed, of the course vector is ground speed, and of the wind vector is wind speed.

Knowing the course in which a plane must fly and the wind vector, a navigator subtracts the wind vector from the course vector to find the heading in which the pilot must direct the plane. In Fig. 75, if the plane is on course from P to Q, the body during the flight will actually be oriented in the direction PS.

For example, in Fig. 76, a course is at 210°, and the wind is from 290° at 30 mph. From an origin construct a line in the direction of the course. We do not yet know its magnitude. To subtract the wind vector from it, construct the wind vector AC from the initial point of the course vector, in the direction 110°. With C as a center construct an arc with radius = 190 mph, the air speed of the plane, intersecting the course vector at B. The course vector is AB. Draw CB which is the heading vector. Since the addition of AC and CB would produce the resultant AB, then AC subtracted

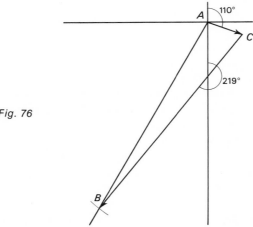

Fig. 76

from *AB* gives *CB*. When point *B* is determined, we have the direction of the heading, 219°, and also the magnitude of the ground speed, which is by scale 186 mph.

An important use of vectors is in the study of force. Different forces acting upon a body are charted graphically. If the body is stationary or moving at constant velocity, the resultant of the forces is zero, and the body is in **equilibrium**. If the resultant is not zero, the body is experiencing a change of velocity, an acceleration.

Now, the body to which three forces are applied will be in equilibrium if a fourth force is applied equal and opposite to the resultant of the three. The fourth is the **equilibrant** of the others. Any three of these can be added and the fourth will be found to be the equilibrant of the three. The vector sum of the four is zero.

Consider the three known forces whose vectors can be drawn. One way to find the resultant is to plot the vectors in any order one after another, as in the cycle example (Fig. 74). Another way is to make the resultant the diagonal of a parallelogram. In Fig. 77, *PA*, *PB*, and *PC* are the given vectors. *PA* and *PB* are sides of a parallelogram of which *PD*, their sum, is a diagonal, all three vectors having the same initial point. The resultant added to the third vector, *PC*, gives the sum *PR*, which is the resultant of the three forces. *PE* is the equilibrant, equal and opposite to *PR*.

Sometimes a given force is the resultant of two others and they need to be found. A lawnmower moves along the ground horizontally, but a man does not push it horizontally. He is willing to exert more force than is required to move it in order to travel in a walking position. The requirement is to determine the force necessary to push the mower in the direction of travel and the force perpendicular to that. These two perpendicular forces are two **components** of the applied force.

A man pushes on a lawnmower at an angle of 40° to the ground. What is the force which is moving the mower forward and the force which is pushing it into the ground? In Fig. 78, a 5-centimeter vector represents 1 pound of force at an angle of 40° to the horizontal. Draw a rectangle with this vector *PQ* as a diagonal. The scale gives the horizontal force *PH* as 0.77 pound and the vertical force *PV* as 0.64 pound for every pound pushing along the handle. In terms of trigonometry the force *PH* is *PQ* cos 40° and the vertical force *PV* is *PQ* sin 40°.

If the handle of the mower were being pushed vertically downward, the force would have no component along the ground. A vector has a zero component perpendicular to its direction, and a component parallel to it is equal to it in magnitude. If a man could push the mower directly forward, he would need only 77% of the required force.

The components of a vector on axes of coordinates are the **projec-**

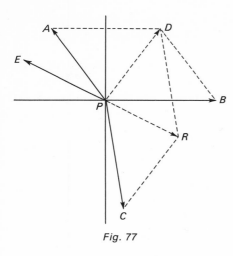

Fig. 77

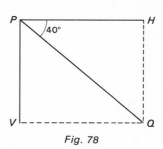

Fig. 78

tions of the vector. Let the origin be the point at which forces are applied. The coordinates of the terminal ends will measure the components. The algebraic sum of the lengths of the coordinates on one axis is the coordinate of the resultant of the forces. The coordinates of these two summations are the ordered pair of coordinates of the resultant. If the forces are in equilibrium, the sum of the x-coordinates and the sum of the y-coordinates are both zero.

The sum of the lengths of the three x-components of PA, PB, and PC is the length of the x-component of PR. The same is true for the y-components. In Fig. 79, the x-components are, respectively,

$$-3 + 10 + 1 = 8$$

The y-components are

$$3 + 0 - 6 = -3$$

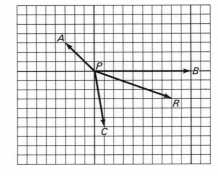

Fig. 79

EXERCISE 12.4

Solve Exs. 2–11 by drawing vectors.

1. Two forces acting at a point have the magnitides of 15 and 20 pounds, respectively. State the magnitude of the resultant when the forces act: **(a)** In the same direction. **(b)** Perpendicular to each other. **(c)** In opposite directions.

2. A plane's heading is 40° with an air speed of 180 mph. The wind is blowing at 25 mph from 280°. Find the course and the ground speed of the plane.

3. A plane has a heading of 210° at a speed of 200 mph. The wind is from 260° at 50 mph. Find the course and the ground speed.

4. A pilot must fly on a course at 80°. When his air speed is 240 mph and the wind is at 40 mph from 300°, find his heading and ground speed.

5. A plane has a course at 120°. The wind from 50° is blowing at 30 mph. The air speed of the plane is 300 mph. Find the heading and the ground speed.

6. Wind on a kite produces a force perpendicular to the kite's surface. The angle between the wind vector and the string is 160°. Find the component of force on the string for 10 pounds of force on the kite by the wind.

7. A box is dragged along a horizontal floor by a rope at an angle of 36° to the floor. If the force on the rope is 80 pounds, find the force which moves the box and the force which lightens its weight.

8. A cart is on a ramp which makes an angle of 30° with the horizontal. If the cart and its contents weigh 300 pounds, find the component which keeps it from rolling and the force perpendicular to the ramp.

9. A cable is suspended from two points whose coordinates are (0, 10) and (10, 10). A weight of 1000 pounds hangs from its center at (5, 8). Find the force on each half of the cable.

10. A cable is suspended from two points with coordinates (0, 10) and (10, 8). A weight of 1000 pounds is suspended at (7, 5). Find the force on each part of the cable.

11. A child is swinging, suspended from point (0, 10). His father pulls him back with a horizontal force to point (3, 2).
    (a) If the force exerted by the father is 20 pounds, what is the weight of the child?
    (b) What force must the father exert to pull the child back to (5, 3)?

12. With an inclined plane man can raise a body against gravity with a force less than the body weight. If BW is the vector of the weight, then BR is the component in the direction of the inclined plane. Since m$\angle PBW$ = m$\angle RWB$ = m$\angle A$, the ratio of BR to BW equals the ratio of two measures on the structure of the ramp. If CD = 3 feet, DA = 4 feet, and BW = 100 pounds, write the proportion and find BR. Neglecting friction, BC = BR = the force necessary to roll the body up the ramp.

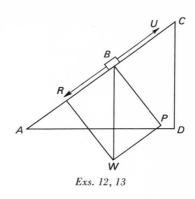

Exs. 12, 13

13. The coefficient of friction is the ratio of the force which moves a body along a surface to the force perpendicular to the surface, $BR : BP$. Raise one end of the inclined plane until the block begins to move. If a block begins to slide just as one end of a 5-foot board reaches a height of 3 feet, write the proportion and find the coefficient of friction.

12.5   Geometric Figures on the Coordinate Plane

When plane geometric figures are related to systems of two coordinates, their vertices are ordered so that the procedures are as simple as possible. For instance, a parallelogram may be so located with respect to the axes that no side is parallel to an axis. But this would unnecessarily complicate the problem. In general we locate it so that one side coincides with the x-axis, all the coordinates are positive, and one vertex is at the origin. If one end of a segment is at the origin — with coordinates $(0, 0)$ — the coordinates of the other end give the lengths of the components.

THEOREM 79   Two lines with equal slopes are parallel.

GIVEN: Lines k and l with equal slopes.

PROVE: $k \parallel l$.

If k and l are not $\parallel$, they intersect at a point, such as $P(x_1, y_1)$. Let $Q(x_2, y_2)$ be a second point of l. If k and l are not vertical, there is a vertical line through Q whose x-coordinate is x_2 which intersects k at $R(x_2, y_3)$. The slope of k through points R and P is $m = \dfrac{y_1 - y_3}{x_1 - x_2}$ and the slope of l through Q and P is $m = \dfrac{y_1 - y_2}{x_1 - x_2}$. Then $\dfrac{y_1 - y_3}{x_1 - x_2} = \dfrac{y_1 - y_2}{x_1 - x_2}$. Multiply both sides of the equation by the denominator and $y_1 - y_3 = y_1 - y_2$ and $y_3 = y_2$. Then point R would become point Q and the two lines would coincide, for two points determine exactly one line. Therefore, the two lines do not intersect and are parallel.

THEOREM 80   Parallel lines have equal slopes.

GIVEN: Line $k \parallel$ line l.

PROVE: Slope of $l =$ slope of k.

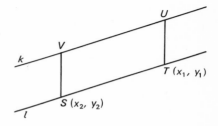

Let $S(x_2, y_2)$ and $T(x_1, y_1)$ be two points of l. Through them draw vertical lines $\parallel$ the y-axis intersecting k at V and U, respectively. Then $SV = TU$; segments of $\parallel$ intercepted by $\parallel \cong$. Let the lengths SV and $TU = a$. The coordinates of V are $(x_2, y_2 + a)$; and of U are $(x_1, y_1 + a)$. The slope of l is $m = \dfrac{y_1 - y_2}{x_1 - x_2}$. The slope of k is $m = \dfrac{(y_1 + a) - (y_2 + a)}{x_1 - x_2} = \dfrac{y_1 - y_2}{x_1 - x_2}$. The slope of $l =$ slope of k; first = second = third.

THEOREM 81   A point separates a segment into parts, the lengths of whose x-components and y-components are proportional to the lengths of their corresponding parts.

GIVEN: Segment $\overline{PQ}$; R separates it into parts a and b; $\overline{PS} \parallel \overline{RT} \parallel x$-axis; $\overline{RS} \parallel \overline{QT} \parallel y$-axis.

PROVE: $\dfrac{PS}{RT} = \dfrac{a}{b} = \dfrac{RS}{QT}$.

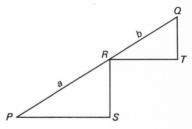

$\overline{PS} \parallel \overline{RT}$; $\overline{RS} \parallel \overline{QT}$. $\angle SPR \cong \angle TRQ$; $\angle SRP \cong \angle TQR$; trans $\parallel$, corresp $\angle \cong$.

$\triangle SPR \sim \triangle TRQ$; $AA \sim AA$. $\dfrac{PS}{RT} = \dfrac{a}{b} = \dfrac{RS}{QT}$. Corresp sides $\sim$ $\triangle$ prop.

COROLLARY 81.1   A point separates a segment into parts, the lengths of whose x-components and y-components are proportional.

COROLLARY 81.2   A midpoint separates a segment into parts whose x-components and y-components are congruent.

COROLLARY 81.3   The coordinates of the midpoint of a segment are midway between the coordinates of the endpoints.

THEOREM 82   The slopes of two perpendicular lines are such that their product is negative one.

GIVEN: $\overline{RP} \perp \overline{RQ}$; slope of $\overline{RP} = m_1$; slope of $\overline{RQ} = m_2$.

PROVE: $m_1 m_2 = -1$.

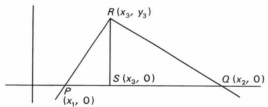

$m_1 = \dfrac{y_3 - 0}{x_3 - x_1}$; $m_2 = \dfrac{0 - y_3}{x_2 - x_3}$. Then $m_1 m_2 = \dfrac{y_3}{x_3 - x_1} \times \dfrac{-y_3}{x_2 - x_3}$. Draw $\overline{RS} \perp \overline{PQ}$; through a point 1 line $\perp$ given line. $\triangle PRS \sim \triangle RQS$; altitude on hypotenuse separates rt $\triangle$ into 2 $\sim$ $\triangle$. Corresp sides prop: $\dfrac{y_3 - 0}{x_3 - x_1} = \dfrac{x_2 - x_3}{y_3 - 0}$. Then $m_1 = -\dfrac{1}{m_2}$ or $m_1 m_2 = -1$.

COROLLARY 82.1   The slope of a line is the negative reciprocal of the slope of its perpendicular.

NOTE: The intersection of two lines is the unique point at which the variable x-coordinates of the two lines are the same number and the variable y-coordinates are the same. In algebra one variable is eliminated from the two equations long enough to solve for the second, and then the corresponding coordinate of the first variable is found.

Many theorems and problems of previous chapters can be proved by the use of coordinates. Two examples follow.

1. Diagonals of a parallelogram bisect each other.

GIVEN: $\square\, RSTU$.

PROVE: $\overline{RT}$ and $\overline{SU}$ bisect each other at W.

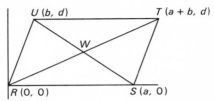

Let the coordinates of the vertices be as shown. One equation of $\overline{RT}$ is $\dfrac{x-0}{a+b-0}=\dfrac{y-0}{d-0}$; then $\dfrac{x}{a+b}=\dfrac{y}{d}$. An equation of $\overline{US}$ is $\dfrac{x-a}{b-a}=\dfrac{y-0}{d-0}$, and $\dfrac{x-a}{b-a}=\dfrac{y}{d}$. Solve for the point of intersection: $by+ay=dx$ and $by-ay=dx-ad$. Then $y=\dfrac{d}{2}$, the y-coordinate of the point of intersection, and $x=\dfrac{a+b}{2}$, the x-coordinate of the point of intersection. The x-coordinate of W is midway between 0 and $a+b$ or a and b. The y-coordinate of W is midway between 0 and d.

2. The segment joining the midpoints of two sides of a triangle is parallel to the third side and its length is half the length of the third side.

GIVEN: $\triangle QRS$; T is the midpoint of $\overline{QS}$; U is the midpoint of $\overline{RS}$.

PROVE: $\overline{TU}\parallel \overline{QR}$; $TU=\tfrac{1}{2}QR$.

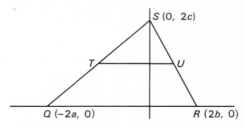

Arrange the triangle so that the coordinates give the most convenient relationship. The coordinates are as shown. The coordinates of T are $(-a,\, c)$ and of U are $(b,\, c)$; midway between the coordinates of the ends. The length $TU=b-(-a)=b+a$. The length $QR=2b-(-2a)=2b+2a$.

Then $TU = \frac{1}{2}QR$. The y-coordinate of $T = c$ and of $U = c$; the slope of $\overline{TU} = 0$. The slope of $\overline{QR} = 0$, and $\overline{TU} \parallel \overline{QR}$.

EXERCISE 12.5

1. Determine the relationships between the slopes and lengths of segments, and state the kind of figure whose vertices are:

(a) $(0, 0)$ $(3, 5)$ $(-4, 10)$ $(-7, 5)$

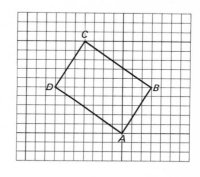

Solution: Show opposite sides $\parallel$: $m_1 = \dfrac{5 - 0}{3 - 0} = \dfrac{5}{3}$; $m_2 = \dfrac{10 - 5}{-4 + 7} = \dfrac{5}{3}$. Then $\overline{AB} \parallel \overline{CD}$. Show opposite sides $\cong$: $AB = \sqrt{25 + 9}$; $CD = \sqrt{25 + 9}$, and $\overline{AB} \cong \overline{CD}$. Show $\overline{BC} \perp \overline{AB}$: slope of $\overline{BC}$ is $\dfrac{10 - 5}{-4 - 3} = -\dfrac{5}{7}$, which is

not the negative reciprocal of $\dfrac{5}{3}$, and $\overline{BC}$ is not $\perp \overline{AB}$. Therefore, the figure is a parallelogram.

(b) $(2, 1)$ $(4, 6)$ $(9, 4)$ $(7, -1)$
(c) $(0, 2)$ $(8, 0)$ $(7, -4)$ $(-1, -2)$
(d) $(-1, -1)$ $(-1, 3)$ $(5, 2)$ $(5, -2)$
(e) $(0, 0)$ $(5, 0)$ $(2, 4)$ $(-3, 4)$

2. The midpoint of a segment has coordinates $(8, 2)$; one end is at $(0, 4)$. Find the coordinates of the other end.

3. A parallelogram has vertices at $(-2, -2)$, $(4, -1)$, and $(6, 4)$. Find the coordinate of the fourth vertex.

4. The coordinates of vertices of a triangle are: $(-5, -2)$, $(-3, 6)$, and $(3, 0)$. Show that it is an isosceles triangle.

5. The vertices of a right triangle are at $(-4, 2)$, $(-4, 14)$, and $(12, 2)$. Show that the midpoint of the hypotenuse is equidistant from the three vertices.

6. Find the lengths of the diagonals of the parallelogram with vertices at $(0, 0)$, $(7, 0)$, $(8, 6)$, and $(1, 6)$, leaving one length as a radical.

7. The coordinates of the vertices of a triangle are: $(-3, -3)$, $(3, 5)$, and $(15, -4)$. Show that it is a right triangle.

8. A rhombus has vertices at (0, 0), (4, 3), (4, 8), and (0, 5). Show that the diagonals are perpendicular.

9. Given a quadrilateral with vertices at: (2, 0), (8, 6), (4, 18), and (0, 12). Show that segments joining the midpoints of the sides of the quadrilateral form a parallelogram.

10. Given the coordinates of the vertices of a triangle: (1, 1), (7, 9), and (15, 1). Show that the segment joining the midpoints of two sides is parallel to the third side, and its length equals half the length of the third side.

11. The equation of line n is $3x - 8y = 24$. Find the equation of the line through (5, 8) which is: **(a)** $\parallel n$. **(b)** $\perp n$.

12. Give the equation for the locus of all points equidistant from the points (0, 0) and (8, 6).

12.6   Summary Test

On answer sheet write the word(s) or symbol(s) which fill in each blank.

1. An ordered pair of numbers gives the ___(a)___ of a point on a two-coordinate plane with the ___(b)___ always written first. On a given coordinate system with a definite scale, the ordered pair locates ___(c)___ point. The ordered pair of coordinates at the origin of the coordinates is ___(d)___. To the left of the origin each ___(e)___ is ___(f)___. A line perpendicular to and intersecting the y-axis at -5 has the equation ___(g)___.

2. The length of a segment of the line $x = 2$ from the x-axis to $y = 10$ is ___(a)___; the coordinates of the points of the segment are ___(b)___ $\leq$ ___(c)___ $\leq$ ___(d)___. When a segment is not parallel to an axis, the length of its projection on the axis is always ___(e)___ the length of the segment.

3. If e and f are lengths of legs of a right triangle and g is the length of the hypotenuse, the Pythagorean Theorem states that ___(a)___. If the coordinates of A are (8, 3) and the coordinates of B are (24, 15), then $AB =$ ___(b)___, and the slope of $\overline{AB}$ is ___(c)___. The point-slope form of this equation is ___(d)___; the y-intercept is ___(e)___ and the x-intercept is ___(f)___. If the x-intercept of a line is 5 and the y-intercept is 2, the line has the slope, ___(g)___; the general form of the equation of this line is ___(h)___.

4. Each vector has a definite __(a)__ and a definite __(b)__. In vector addition the __(c)__ of the second vector is placed at the __(d)__ of the first; the sum is the vector extending from the __(e)__ of the first vector to the __(f)__ of the second. The vector which represents the sum is called the __(g)__. In vector subtraction the negative of a vector is the positive vector with this change: __(h)__.

5. In air navigation the __(a)__ is the direction in which the plane's body is pointing, and the __(b)__ is the direction in which the plane is proceeding over the ground. The __(c)__ vector minus the __(d)__ vector is the __(e)__ vector which the navigator must calculate; the magnitude of this result is called the __(f)__.

6. Forces pulling on a point can be graphed with vectors; if the vector sum of the forces is __(a)__, they apply no resulting force on the point, and the point is in the state of __(b)__. If there is a resulting force exerted, the point will undergo a change of motion unless a(n) __(c)__ is applied, which has __(d)__ magnitude and __(e)__ direction of the resultant.

7. When we need to know the effect of a force in a direction different from its applied direction, we find two __(a)__ of the force, one in the desired direction and the other __(b)__. A force applied in a certain direction exerts __(c)__ force in a direction perpendicular to it.

8. The __(a)__ of the x-components of several forces is the x-component of __(b)__.

9. The slope of the x-axis is __(a)__. The slope of a certain line is 2/5; the slope of a line parallel to it is __(b)__; the slope of a line perpendicular to it is __(c)__.

10. Three collinear points have coordinates $(2, 9)$, $(6, 15)$, and $(x, 27)$; $x = $ __(a)__. The coordinates of A are $(3, -8)$ and the coordinates of B are $(-13, 12)$; the coordinates of the midpoint of $\overline{AB}$ are (__(b)__, __(c)__); the coordinates of the point 3/4 of the way from A to B are (__(d)__, __(e)__). The quadrilateral with vertices at $(0, 0)$, $(0, 6)$, $(6, 6)$, and $(6, 0)$ is a __(f)__.

appendix

NOTE: The symbol ≅ can be read: "congruent," "is congruent to," "are congruent." The same applies to the symbols =, ∼, ∥, ⊥. The word *equals* is the condensation for "equal numbers." The numbers in parentheses are page references.

A. Postulates Condensed

1. 2 points, 1 line.   (10)
2. Every line, 2 points.   (10)
3. 3 noncollinear points, 1 plane.   (10, 211)
4. 1 plane, 3 noncollinear points.   (10, 211)
5. Plane contains 2 points of line, contains line.   (10, 211)
6. Space contains 4 noncoplanar points.   (10, 213)
7. To each point corresp 1 coord; to each coord corresp 1 point.   (14)
8. To each ray corresp 1 coord; to each coord corresp 1 ray.   (22)
   Cor.   To each point of ⊙ corresp 1 coord; to each coord corresp 1 point. (146)
9. With given center and radius, 1 ⊙.   (68, 200)
10. SAS ≅ SAS.   (71)

11. Line separates plane into sets, segment joining point of one to point of other intersects line at 1 point.   (95, 214)

12. Figure separates plane into regions, segment joining point of one to point of other intersects figure at 1 point.   (95, 214)

13. Through point 1 line ∥ given line.   (110)

14. Corresp segments of trans intercepted by ∥ prop.   (181)

15. Plane separates space into sets, segment joining point of one to point of other intersects plane at 1 point.   (214)

16. 2 planes, intersection is 1 line.   (216)

17. Area rect $=$ length $\times$ width.   (230)

18. Volume of rect solid $=$ length $\times$ width $\times$ altitude.   (238)

Cor.   Volume of solid of uniform cross section $=$ area rt section $\times aH$.   (238)

19. Corresp lengths of similar figures prop and corresp $\angle$s $\cong$.   (238)

20. Corresp areas prop to lengths^2; corresp volumes prop to lengths^3.   (238)

B. Theorems Condensed and Grouped

Theorem numbers are given in boldface, followed by page references.

REFLEXIVE, SYMMETRIC, AND TRANSITIVE PROPERTIES

First ≅ second ≅ third.   First ≅ second ≅ first.   Segment (∠, △, arc, ⊙) ≅ itself.
   (**4**, 56; **40**, 147)
Name sub for name of ≅.   (**4**, 56)
Lines ∥ same line ∥.   First ∥ second ∥ first.   First ∥ second ∥ third.   (**21**, 111;
   69, 215)
First △ ~ second ~ third.   △ ~ itself.   First △ ~ second ~ first.   (**58**, 178)
Line ⊥ plane, plane ⊥ line.   (**71**, 217)

SEPARATION

Points separate segment (arc) into parts, sum lengths (m) = length (m) of whole.
   (**1**, 41; **41**, 148)
Rays separate ∠ into parts, sum m = m whole.   (**2**, 42)
Part = whole − part.   (**1**, 41; **2**, 42; **41**, 148)
Sum of numbers > any one.   Whole > any part.   (**16**, 91)
2 lines, intersection is 1 point.   (**3**, 43)
1 point, length of segment is constant.   1 point, segment ≅ segment.   1 point,
   dist is multiple.   (**9**, 69)
1 ray, m∠ is constant.   1 ray, ∠ ≅ ∠.   1 ray, m∠ is multiple.   (**10**, 70)
1 point, m arc is constant.   1 point, arc ≅ arc.   1 point, m arc is multiple.   (**40**,
   147)
Doubles (halves) of ≅ segments (∡, arcs) ≅.   (**4**, 56; **40**, 147)

ANGLE RELATIONS

Supp ≅ ∡ ≅.   Supp same ∠ ≅.   (**5**, 61)
Comp ≅ ∡ ≅.   Comp same ∠ ≅.   (**6**, 61)
Vertical ∡ ≅.   (**7**, 62)
∡ ≅ and supp are rt ∡.   m st ∠ = 2 m rt ∠.   m rt ∠ = $\frac{1}{2}$ m st ∠.   2 lines forming
   1 rt ∠ form 4 rt ∡.   (**8**, 62)
Alt int (corresp, alt ext) ∡ ≅, lines ∥.   (**22**, 112)
Trans ∥, alt int (corresp, alt ext) ∡ ≅.   (**23**, 113)
Sides ∥ and in same directions, ∡ ≅.   (**24**, 116)
Consecutive ∡ of ▱ supp.   Trans ∥, int ∡ on same side of trans supp.   (**31**, 124)

TRIANGLE RELATIONS

ASA ≅ ASA.   Leg, acute ∠ ≅ leg, acute ∠.   (**11**, 72)
SSS ≅ SSS.   (**14**, 79)
AA ≅ AA, A ≅ A.   (**26**, 117)

Hyp, leg ≅ hyp, leg.   (**28**, 118)
Hyp, acute ∠ ≅ hyp, acute ∠.   (**29**, 120)
AA ~ AA.   Acute ∠, rt △ ~ acute ∠, rt △.   (**61**, 182)
SSS ~ SSS.   SAS ~ SAS.   (**62**, 183)
Altitude to hyp of rt △ forms ~ △.   (**63**, 189)

PARTS OF TRIANGLES

Sides of △ ≅, ∠ opp ≅.   Equilateral △ is equiangular.   Base ∠ of isosceles △ ≅.
   (**12**, 78)
∠ of △ ≅, sides opp ≅.   Equiangular △ is equilateral.   (**13**, 79)
Sides of △ ≠, ∠ opp ≠ in same order.   ∠ opp longer side is > ∠.   (**18**, 98)
∠ of △ ≠, sides opp ≠ in same order.   Side opp > ∠ is longer side.   (**19**, 99)
m ext ∠ > m nonadjacent int ∠.   (**17**, 98)
m ext ∠ = sum m nonadjacent int ∠.   (**27**, 118)
Sum of lengths of 2 sides > length of third side.   Length of segment joining 2
   points is shortest dist.   (**20**, 101)
Sum m ∠ of △ = m 1 st ∠ (180°). Only 1 ∠ of △ is rt or obtuse. Acute ∠ of rt △
   comp.   (**25**, 116)
Hyp² = leg² + leg².   Leg² = hyp² − leg².   (**64**, 189)

BISECTORS

Segment 1 midpoint.   (**9**, 69)
Every point equidist from ends of segment is point of ⊥ bisector.   Every point of
   ⊥ bisector is equidist from ends of segment.   (**37**, 133)
Arc 1 bisector.   (**40**, 147)
Line through center of ⊙ ⊥ chord bisects chord and arc.   (**44**, 149)
Locus of points equidist from 2 points is ⊥ bisector.   (**37**, 200)
Locus of points equidist from 2 intersecting lines is bisectors of ∠.   (**67**, 201)

PARALLELOGRAMS

Opp sides and opp ∠ of ▱ ≅.   Diag separates ▱ into ≅ △.   (**30**, 124)
Two sides ≅ and ∥, quad is ▱.   (**32**, 125)
Opp sides ≅, quad is ▱.   (**33**, 125)

PERPENDICULARS

2 lines forming ≅ adjacent (supp) ∠ ⊥.   (**8**, 62)
Through a point 1 line ⊥ given line.   (**35**, 130; **36**, 132)
Lines ⊥ same line ∥.   (**38**, 134)
Line ⊥ 1 of 2 ∥ lines ⊥ other.   (**39**, 134)
Line through center of ⊙ bisects chord, ⊥ chord.   (**45**, 149)
Prod of slopes of 2 ⊥ lines is −1.   Slope of line is negative reciprocal of slope of ⊥.
   (**82**, 267)

CIRCLES

In $\odot$ ($\cong$ $\circledS$) $\cong$ central (inscribed) $\measuredangle$ intercept $\cong$ arcs. In $\odot$ ($\cong$ $\circledS$) central (inscribed) $\measuredangle$ which intercept $\cong$ arcs $\cong$. (**40**, 147; **51**, 160)

Chords (arcs) $\cong$, arcs (chords) with same endpoints $\cong$. (**42**, 148; **43**, 149)

Chords equidist from center $\cong$. (**46**, 150)

$\cong$ chords equidist from center. (**47**, 150)

Tan $\perp$ radius. (**48**, 154)

Line $\perp$ radius on $\odot$ is tan. (**49**, 154)

Tan segments from point $\cong$, make $\cong$ $\measuredangle$ with line to center. (**50**, 155)

MEASURES OF ANGLES AND ARCS

m inscribed $\angle = \frac{1}{2}$ m arc. $\angle$ inscribed in semicircle is a rt $\angle$. (**51**, 160)

m $\angle$ formed by chords $= \frac{1}{2}$ sum m arcs. (**52**, 161)

m $\angle$ formed by tan and chord $= \frac{1}{2}$ m arc. (**53**, 161)

m $\angle$ formed by tan and sec (2 tan, 2 sec) $= \frac{1}{2}$ diff m arcs. (**54**, 162)

PROPORTIONS

Prod means = prod extremes. Any arrangement of factors which makes prod means = prod extremes. (**55**, 173)

Perimeters $\sim$ $\triangle$ prop corresp sides. (**62**, 183)

Sum (diff) : one = sum (diff) corresp one. (**56**, 175; **57**, 176)

Altitude to hyp of rt $\triangle$ is mean prop between segments of hyp. (**63**, 189)

Point separates segment, components prop (to parts). Midpoint separates segment, components $\cong$. Midpoint separates segment, coord midway between coord of endpoints. (**81**, 266)

PARALLEL LINES AND PROPORTIONS

Segments of $\|$ intercepted by $\|$ $\cong$. (**30**, 124)

$\|$ lines intercept $\cong$ segments of 1 trans, of every trans. Line bisects 1 side of $\triangle$, $\|$ second side, bisects third side. (**34**, 126)

Line $\|$ 1 side of $\triangle$ divides 2 sides prop. Line $\|$ 1 side of $\triangle$ divides 2 sides, side : segment = side : segment. (**59**, 181)

Line divides prop (bisects) 2 sides of $\triangle$, $\|$ third side. (**60**, 181)

Line $\|$ 1 side of $\triangle$ forms $\sim$ $\triangle$. Segment joins midpoints of 2 sides of $\triangle$, length $= \frac{1}{2}$ length of third side. (**61**, 182)

PARALLEL LINES

Locus of points given dist from line is pair of lines $\|$. (**65**, 200)

Locus of points equidist from $\|$ lines is line $\|$ and midway. (**66**, 201)

2 lines with = slopes $\|$. (**79**, 265)

$\|$ lines have = slopes. (**80**, 266)

PLANES

1 line and 1 point, 1 plane contains them.   2 lines intersect, 1 plane contains them.   (**68**, 213)

2 ∥ lines contained in 1 plane.   (**69**, 215)

Intersections of ∥ planes with third plane are ∥ lines.   (**70**, 216)

Line ⊥ intersecting lines ⊥ plane containing them.   1 plane ⊥ line at point of line.   (**71**, 217)

∥ planes intersect dihedral ∠ in ≅ ∡.   (**72**, 220)

AREAS

Area $\square$ = base × altitude.   Area square = side^2.   Area trap = altitude × $\frac{1}{2}$ sum of bases.   ▱ (▲) with = bases and altitudes have = areas.   ▱ (▲) with = bases have areas prop altitudes.   ▱ (▲) with = altitudes have areas prop bases.   (**73**, 231; **74**, 231)

Area △ = $\frac{1}{2}$ base × altitude.   Area rt △ = $\frac{1}{2}$ leg × leg.   Areas ≅ polygons =.   (**74**, 231)

Areas ~ ▲ (polygons) prop squares of corresp sides.   (**75**, 232)

SOLIDS

Bases of prism are ≅ polygons.   Lateral faces of prism are ▱.   Opp faces of parallelepiped are ▱.   ∥ sections of prism are ≅ polygons.   (**76**, 237)

Volumes of spheres prop radii^3.   (**77**, 244)

Cone or pyramid, areas of ∥ bases prop squares of distances from vertex.   (**78**, 244)

C. Properties of Real Numbers

The numbers in the real number system have precise relations, and the operations performed upon them are due to their specific properties. The first properties are postulates; the others, derived from the first, are theorems. The properties important for algebra are listed below. The letters used are given as elements of the set of real numbers. When an element may be positive, zero, or negative, no limitation is mentioned. When a restriction is required, a positive number is indicated by >0, a negative number by <0, and both of these by $\neq 0$.

EQUALITY AND INEQUALITY

Reflexive: $a = a$.
Symmetric: If $a = b$, then $b = a$.
Transitive: If $a = b$ and $b = c$, then $a = c$.
Trichotomy: Either $a < b$ or $a = b$ or $a > b$.
Transitive: If $a < b$ and $b < c$, then $a < c$.
Substitution: If $a < b$ and $b = c$, then $a < c$.

ADDITION

Closure: $a + b = n$ (n is a unique real number).
Equality: If $a = b$, then $a + c = b + c$ and $a - c = b - c$.
Order: If $a < b$, then $a + c < b + c$.
Association: $(a + b) + c = a + (b + c)$.
Commutation: $a + b = b + a$.
Identity: Zero is a unique real number such that $a + 0 = a$.
Inverse (negative): For every number a there is the number $-a$ such that $a + (-a) = 0$ and $a + (-a) = a - a$.
Cancellation: If $a + c = b + c$, then $a = b$.

MULTIPLICATION

Closure: $a \times b = n$ (n is a unique real number).
Equality: If $a = b$ and $c > 0$, then $ac = bc$ and $a/c = b/c$.
Order: If $a < b$ and $c > 0$, then $ac < bc$.
Association: $(ab)c = a(bc)$.
Commutation: $ab = ba$.
Identity: One is a real number such that $1 \times a = a$.
Inverse (reciprocal): If $a \neq 0$, there is the number $1/a$ such that $a(1/a) = 1$ and $a(1/a) = a/a$.
Cancellation: If $ac = bc$, then $a = b$.

ADDITION AND MULTIPLICATION

Distribution: $a(b + c) = ab + bc$; $(b + c)/a = b/a + c/a$ $(a \neq 0)$.

D. The Logic of Implications

Every proposition contains a hypothesis and a conclusion. In this discussion the concept in the hypothesis is p, and the concept in the conclusion is q. And then the proposition is $p \rightarrow q$, meaning "p implies q." Every theorem in this text accepts p as given and proves that q is the logical result. Therefore $p \rightarrow q$ is true. The other implications related to a proposition are: converse, $q \rightarrow p$; inverse, not-$p \rightarrow$ not-q; contrapositive, not-$q \rightarrow$ not-p.

When a proposition cannot be proved directly, one indirect alternative is to prove the contrapositive. When "exactly one" or "every one" is required, this is completed by proving the proposition and either its inverse or its converse.

It is instructive to see how the parts of a logical statement fit together to succeed or not succeed in completing a deductive proof. If they succeed, the proof is true. A compilation of the possible cases is a "truth table." In these relationships p can be true or false, q can be true or false, as can the implication. From this it follows that the other three implications are established as true or false.

Truth Table

Case	p	q	Proposition $p \rightarrow q$	Converse $q \rightarrow p$	not-p	not-q	Inverse not-$p \rightarrow$ not-q	Contrapositive not-$q \rightarrow$ not-p
1	T	T	T	T	F	F	T	T
2	T	F	F	T	F	T	T	F
3	F	T	T	F	T	F	F	T
4	F	F	T	T	T	T	T	T

For p or q, the notation "T" means that it satisfies all the conditions of our postulated system, and "F" means that under these conditions it is false. For the implication, "T" means that it is valid; "F" means that it is not valid.

Case 1 is the usual geometric proposition. Taking the proposition, "Two consecutive angles of a parallelogram are supplementary," the hypothesis, p, is "Two angles are consecutive angles of a parallelogram," while the conclusion, q, is "Two angles are supplementary." In Case 2, if there can be found two consecutive angles of a parallelogram which are not supplementary, then the proposition is not valid. In Case 3, if two angles which are not consecutive angles of a parallelogram are still supplementary, the proposition is still valid. Two angles not found in a parallelogram and not supplementary still allow Case 4 to be valid.

The converse of a proposition has q given and implies p. With q as its hypothesis and p as its conclusion, the converse statements are true or false as shown in the table.

In the next place, when p or q is true, its negation is false. If q is true, not-q is false, while if p is false, not-p is true. The inverse and the contrapositive follow the same logical sequences as the proposition. Furthermore, the table shows that in all cases when a proposition is valid its contrapositive is valid, and the converse and the inverse are alike.

We can compare the truth table with Venn diagrams (Fig. 80) to see whether they both indicate the same facts. The implication $p \to q$ means that the set of p's is a subset of the set of q's. In (a) p is a proper subset of q. The implication is also true when every element of one is an element of the other and the two are equal sets as in (b). The other possible relation is that q is a subset of p. Then all q's are p's and $q \to p$, as in (c).

The exteriors of the Venn diagrams are related in the same way. All elements not included in p are not-p, and in the exterior of q are all the elements which are not-q.

Now relate the diagrams to the truth table. We found that "Two consecutive angles of a parallelogram are supplementary" is a theorem whose converse is not valid. We cannot say that "All the sets of two supplementary angles are consecutive angles of a parallelogram," and so p is a subset of q, and Fig. 80(a) is an illustration of Case 3. Furthermore, not-q is a subset of not-p, and so the inverse is false and the contrapositive is true.

With the same reasoning, when all q's are p's, Fig. 80(c) is an illustration of Case 2.

Definitions in geometry all fit Fig. 80(b). All figures which satisfy a certain condition have a certain name. All triangles which have two sides congruent are isosceles triangles. Here set $p =$ set q, and (b) applies. The interior of the figure is the proposition and the converse. The exterior of the figure is the inverse and the contrapositive.

Both the truth table and the Venn diagrams verify other terminology of logical implications. Cases 1, 3, and 4 of (a) and (b) show: "If p, then q; only if q, then p." Cases 1, 2, and 4 of (b) and (c) show: "If q, then p; only if p, then q." Then, where $p = q$ in (b), the expressions are consolidated to read: "If and only if p, then q," or "If and only if q, then p." Furthermore, the first of these groupings shows: "q is necessary for p; p is sufficient for q." The second group shows: "p is necessary for q; q is sufficient for p." In Cases 1 and 4 the two combine in: "p is necessary and sufficient for q," and "q is necessary and sufficient for p."

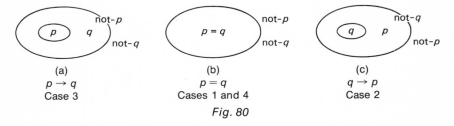

(a)
$p \to q$
Case 3

(b)
$p = q$
Cases 1 and 4

(c)
$q \to p$
Case 2

Fig. 80

E. A Geometric Interpretation of Limits

The Greek philosopher Archimedes calculated the perimeter of a regular polygon of 96 sides circumscribed about a circle and the perimeter of a regular polygon of 96 sides inscribed in the circle. He knew that the circumference of the circle was a measure between these two perimeters.

As the numbers of sides is further increased, the two perimeters come closer to being equal. Increasing the number of sides to a very high number decreases the length of each side to a very short distance. This causes the length of either perimeter to approach the length of the circumference of the accompanying circle. The circumference is the largest possible length of the inscribed polygon and the smallest possible length of the circumscribed polygon. The circumference is the length to which each perimeter continually approaches as the number of sides is increased, but never quite reaches. It is the *limit* of each perimeter. It is possible to define the circumference of a circle as the limit of the perimeters of the inscribed or the circumscribed polygons.

The area of a circle may be defined as the limit of the areas of the inscribed polygons. Let a side of the polygon be the base of a triangle whose third vertex is the center of the polygon. Then the altitude of the triangle is the apothem of the polygon. The area of all the triangles of the polygon is one half the sum of the lengths of the bases multiplied by the apothem. The sum of the lengths of the bases is the perimeter, whose limit is the circumference of the circle. The limit of the apothem is the radius of the circle. The limit of the total area of the triangles is $\frac{1}{2}Cr$. Since $C = 2\pi r$, the area of the circle is πr^2.

The concept of limits is the foundation of the calculus. Raise the number of sides of the polygons to an infinite and the length of each side is an infinitesimal. The difference between the perimeter of an inscribed polygon and the circumference of the circle is less than any real number and approaches zero as a limit.

selected answers

Ex. 3.4, p. 38

2. H: A plane contains two points of a line.
    C: The plane contains the entire line.
    If a plane contains two points of a line, then it contains the entire line.
14. The intersection of two figures is common to the figures.

Ex. 3.7, p. 44

5. (S) In the figure there are two points, G and H.
16. (C) They put their knowledge of the 3–4–5 triangle to practical use.

Ex. 4.2, p. 54

1. (a) $\angle DEF$; (h) $\overline{EU}$
3. (a) Vertical; (e) nonadjacent
4. (a) 105°; (e) 155°
7. (a) 56° 10′; (e) 125° 43′ 40″

Ex. 4.4, p. 59

1. c
9. Congruent angles have the same measure.
19. The name of a figure may be substituted for the name of another to which it is congruent.

Ex. 4.7, p. 74

1. (a) $\overline{UT}$
5. SAS
10. Neither
18. (a) $\overline{EG} \cong \overline{EH}$
19. (a) $\overline{FG}$ and $\overline{GH}$

Ex. 4.8, p. 81

1. (a) 180°
2. (a) 120°

Ex. 5.2, p. 92

1. (b) $10 > 8$, reverse; (e) $18 < 24$, same
2. (b) $22 < 28$, same; (e) $18 < 24$, same
3. (a) $>$

Ex. 5.3, p. 96

1. (c) $12 \leq x \leq 20$
2. (b) X is the set of points of a ray whose endpoint is 20, extending in a positive direction.
3. $AB < AC$

13. (a) $=$; (f) blank
14. (a) A number $=$ itself
15. (a) $40°$
16. (a) $u = 0°$ and $25°$

Ex. 5.4, p. 101

1. $\angle A$, $\angle C$, $\angle B$

Ex. 6.1, p.113

1. (a) $\angle w$
2. (a) $\angle FBC$
3. (a) Adjacent
4. (a) If a transversal intersects two parallel lines, the bisectors of a pair of alternate interior angles are parallel.

Ex. 6.2, p. 120

7. (a) $60°$
11. $23°$

Ex. 6.3, p. 127

1. The set of all parallelograms is a subset of the set of all polygons.

Ex. 6.5, p. 135

5. $74°$

Ex. 7.1, p. 146

1. $\overline{FB}$ and $\overline{AD}$

Ex. 7.2, p. 150

1. (a) A diameter of a circle and a chord parallel to the diameter intercept congruent segments of the circle.
2. (a) Radii of a circle are congruent.
3. (a) $RS > TU$

Ex. 7.3, p. 155

1. 38

Ex. 7.4, p. 163

1. (a) $90°$
2. $108°$
3. (a) $48°$
4. (a) $48°$
5. (a) $40°$

6. (a) 42°
7. (a) $\angle SCA$
8. m arc $< 180°$
23. m$\widehat{a} = 122°$; m$\angle x = 87°$

Ex. 8.1, p. 176

1. (a) $\dfrac{5}{9}$
2. (a) $\dfrac{14}{3}$
3. (a) 7
4. 45°, 135°

Ex. 8.2, p. 180

4. (a) 12 : 1
5. (a) 2.54
6. (a) 2 mm
7. (a) 25 ft
8. (a) 8 in.

Ex. 8.4, p. 185

1. (a) f
2. (a) $\dfrac{UV}{VR} = \dfrac{UX}{XS} = \dfrac{TW}{WS}$
4. (a) 27
5. (a) 27
6. (a) 50
24. 125 ft

Ex. 8.5, p. 190

1. (a) $\angle DBE$, $\angle BHC$
6. (a) 15
17. 35 ft
24. (a) 50; (d) 12
25. (a) 21; (f) 12
26. (a) 24; (c) 7
27. (a) 27
28. (a) 12

Ex. 9.1, p. 202

2. A diameter perpendicular to the given diameter
9. A region in the interior of a circle of radius 7 in. and in the exterior of a circle of radius 3 in., both with the same center as the given circle

Ex. 9.3, p. 206

1. The median to the given side
8. (a) The locus of points equidistant from two parallel lines is the line parallel to the given lines and midway between them.
    (b) The locus of points a given distance from a point of one line is a circle with the point as center and the distance as radius.
    (c) The points which satisfy both conditions are the intersections (lettered on the drawing).
16. (a) The locus of points equidistant from the sides is the bisector of $\angle C$.
    (b) The altitude from B is perpendicular to $\overline{AC}$.
    (c) The point which satisfies both conditions is the intersection of the bisector and the altitude.
24. (a) The intersection is the empty set.
    (d) The two circles are tangent, H in the interior of G.

Ex. 10.3, p. 216

1. (a) The empty set
2. (a) Six half-planes, pairs of which are coplanar, with one common edge
7. (a) Yes, as in Ex. 2(a) above

Ex. 10.4, p. 218

1. 1
5. Sometimes
14. A circle

Ex. 10.5, p. 221

1. (a) Yes
13. The interior of a sphere with the given point as center and radius of 10 in.
21. A line perpendicular to the plane of the triangle intersecting it at the concurrent point of the perpendicular bisectors of the sides of the triangle
24. Two planes intersecting the plane of the given lines at the bisectors of the angles and perpendicular to the plane of the lines

Ex. 11.1, p. 227

1. (c) The sum of the measures of the angles of an n-gon is $n-2$ straight angles.
3. 4, 90°, 90°, 25

Ex. 11.2, p. 233

1. (a) 360, 180
4. (a) 60
8. (a) $\dfrac{3}{2}$
13. (b) One half the product of the apothem and the perimeter of the polygon

Ex. 11.5, p. 240

1. $d = e\sqrt{3}$

2. (a) $h = \dfrac{e\sqrt{3}}{2}$

3. (a) $r = \dfrac{s}{2}$, $A = \dfrac{\pi s^2}{4}$

5. (a) $AE = \dfrac{s\sqrt{5}}{2}$

13. (a) $h = 12$

Ex. 11.6, p. 244

1. (a) $S = 2\pi ra$
2. (a) A circle whose center is a point of the line joining the centers of the spheres
3. 86 in.^{2}
9. 376.8 in.^{3}
13. $\dfrac{8\pi}{3} - \dfrac{7\pi}{3}$

Ex. 12.2, p. 254

2. (a) 13

Ex. 12.3, p. 258

6. Collinear
10. (0, 4) (2, 12)   4   −1   4 $y - 4x - 4 = 0$

Ex. 12.4, p. 265

12. $\dfrac{BR}{BW} = \dfrac{CD}{AC}$

Ex. 12.5, p. 269

1. (b) A square
2. (16, 0)
4. $AB = AC$
12. $3x + 4y - 24 = 0$

index